Church, Capitalism, and Democracy in Post-Ecological Societies

Church, Capitalism, and Democracy in Post-Ecological Societies

A Chinese Christian Perspective

Cheng-tian Kuo

WIPF & STOCK · Eugene, Oregon

CHURCH, CAPITALISM, AND DEMOCRACY IN POST-ECOLOGICAL SOCIETIES
A Chinese Christian Perspective

Copyright © 2018 Cheng-tian Kuo. All rights reserved. Except for brief quotations in critical publications or reviews, no part of this book may be reproduced in any manner without prior written permission from the publisher. Write: Permissions, Wipf and Stock Publishers, 199 W. 8th Ave., Suite 3, Eugene, OR 97401.

Wipf & Stock
An Imprint of Wipf and Stock Publishers
199 W. 8th Ave., Suite 3
Eugene, OR 97401

www.wipfandstock.com

PAPERBACK ISBN: 978-1-5326-5817-4
HARDCOVER ISBN: 978-1-5326-5818-1
EBOOK ISBN: 978-1-5326-5819-8

Manufactured in the U.S.A.   10/04/18

This book cites English Biblical verses from the New Revised Standard Version, Hebrew and Greek verses from the BibleWorks, and meets the standards of fair use.

Contents

Preface	vii
Abbreviations of Scripture	x
1. Introduction: Scientific and Christian Post-Ecology	1
Convergence of Scientific and Christian Post-Ecology	1
Lynn White's Challenge to Christianity	5
Methodological Assumptions	7
A Chinese Christian Perspective	9
Chapter Outlines	13
2. Neuro-Institutional Human	14
Neuroscientific Human	15
Neuro-Institutional Human	33
Rational Human, Posthumanism and Ecology	40
Summary	42
3. Neurotheological Human	44
Neurotheological Origin of Human	46
God Brain in the Bible	54
Emotional Brain in the Bible	61
Rational Brain in the Bible	75
Balanced Brain in the Bible	83
Summary	87
4. Church and Post-Ecotheology	89
Re-discovered Chinese Ecotheories	90
Vanity of Ecotheologies	94
Biblical Verses of Ecology and Post-Ecology	109
Church and Post-Ecotheology	112
Summary	125

5. Capitalism and Post-Ecotheology   127
    Vanity of Rightist and Leftist Ecological Solutions   128
    Vanity of Sustainable Ecotheology   139
    Capitalism and Post-Ecotheology   147
    Summary   155

6. Democracy and Post-Ecotheology   157
    Vanity of Green/Red Authoritarianism   158
    Vanity of Deliberative Democracy   163
    Vanity of Global Ecological Institutions   168
    Vanity of the Kingdom of God on Earth   172
    Democracy and Post-Ecotheology   182
    Summary   191

7. Conclusion: Too Little to Save and Too Many to Save   194

Appendix 3.1: Neurotheology in the Bible   199
Appendix 4.1: Ecology and Post-Ecology in the Bible   204

Bibliography   217

Preface

"Vanity of vanities! All is vanity" (Eccl 1:2)

TWENTY YEARS AGO, WHEN I first started to teach courses related to ecological politics, I used to laugh at my students: "According to the scientific evidence available today, there is a 90 percent chance that your generation will actually witness Parousia when you are about to retire; congratulations!" With a grin on my face, I would also add: "And I will be long gone to heaven by then." Never more will I laugh at my students. Annually revised scientific evidence reveals that the global ecology consistently degenerates faster than previous expectations and that there is a good chance that I myself (and you) will witness Parousia, too.

My adventure to ecotheology is filled with nothing but theological and empirical puzzles like those updated ecological news. I was born and raised in a family of Chinese religions and was converted to Christianity at the age of thirty-seven, when I was teaching international relations and Asian politics at the University of Wisconsin - Milwaukee. Many of the current ecotheologies seem to try to distance themselves from "anthropocentric" Christianity while embracing "nature-centric" Chinese religions, such as Zen Buddhism (for its meditation method) and Daoism (for its emphasis on harmony with nature). "Was I converted to a wrong religion?" This was my theological puzzle. Trained as a political economist at the University of Chicago and turned into a political theologian afterwards, I was also amazed by the considerable distance between current ecotheologies on the one hand and theories and empirical findings in political science, economics, and sociology, on the other. Most of their ecological prescriptions simply cannot work in the real world of cognitive dissonance, bounded rationality, organizational inertia, mass media's framing effects, competitive economy, bureaucratic turf, democratic deficit, judicial passivism, and anarchic international power politics.[1] Yet, eco-

---

1. For introduction to these works, see Nobel Laureate in Economics, Kahneman,

theologies of this genre continue to bombard the global book market without mercy as if these human natures and behaviors do not exist.

Furthermore, while writing this book, I was involved in the negotiation between conservative religious groups and homosexual groups with regard to same-sex marriage bill in Taiwan from 2013 to 2017. Christian groups were leading other religious groups in this "Holy War" against LGBT groups. To my surprise, these Taiwanese Christian groups copied the same theological and political tactics that American fundamentalist Christians used, without screening for theological accuracy and political adaptability. The consequences were disastrous for Taiwanese Christianity: The Constitutional Court declared civil laws prohibiting same-sex marriage to be unconstitutional, and many churches and Christian charity organizations lost a lot of young believers and God-fearing young people. I figured out later that the problems of theological accuracy and political adaptability might also occur in Western ecotheology when applied to the Chinese context.

The only source of comfort and inspiration in my theological adventure came from the Holy Spirit through the spirits of my beloved wife, son, and daughter. Like most Christians in the world, they were very committed to the noble ideas of ecological protection indeed. However, they were equally committed, in action, to new dresses, shoes, accessories, hair-dos, overseas tourism, and cell phones with ever-expanding selfie functions, memory spaces, and powerful batteries. Whenever I pushed too far my ecological programs at home, they would always roll their eyes at me. Besides, did I have a right to complain about them? Probably not. I managed my academic works on one desktop computer, three laptops, four 64-GB USBs, and a "new" cell phone retired by my wife and daughter every other year. Oh! Did I mention that our cabinets were full of eco-friendly shopping bags and water bottles (souvenirs from overseas tourism and academic conferences), some of which we have never used? Finally, I gave up on the advice from existing ecotheologies and developed a moderate version of ecotheology, not to save the ecology but to save the serenity of my family life.

I would like to thank the Ministry of Science and Technology of the Taiwan government (NSC 102-2410-H-004-135-MY3) and the Research Center for Chinese Cultural Subjectivity at the National Chengchi University for providing generous funding to this book project. Parts of this book were written while I was the Taiwanese Chair of Chinese Studies, International Institute for Asian Studies (IIAS) at Leiden University, the Netherlands, in the

---

Thinking; Huddy et al., *Political Psychology*.

first half of 2016. The IIAS provided the friendliest academic environment. Credits of excellent logistic works should be directed to my research assistants Kuenlong Hsieh and Li Chen. Leon van Jaarsveldt meticulously proofread the first draft of this book.

As a growing common but awkward practice in academic publishing, especially in light of the abuses of corporation-sponsored "ecological" studies, I need to declare that I have no financial or personal relationships (except for those mentioned above) which may have inappropriately influenced me in writing this book. However, I must declare also that my financial and personal relationships with the Holy Spirit and my beloved wife have definitely influenced me in writing this book.

Abbreviations of Scripture

Hebrew Bible / Old Testament:

Gen	Exod	Lev	Num	Deut	Josh
Judg	Ruth	1-2 Sam	1-2 Kgs	1-2 Chr	Ezra
Neh	Esth	Job	Ps (*pl.* Pss)	Prov	Eccl
Song	Isa	Jer	Lam	Ezek	Dan
Hos	Joel	Amos	Obad	Jonah	Mic
Hab	Nah	Zeph	Hag	Zech	Mal

New Testament:

Matt	Mark	Luke	John	Acts	Rom
1-2 Cor	Gal	Eph	Phil	1-2 Thess	1-2 Tim
Titus	Phlm	Heb	Jas	1-2 Pet	1-3 John
Jude	Rev				

1.

Introduction: Scientific and Christian Post-Ecology

Is it too late? For myself the answer is Yes.[1]

Convergence of Scientific and Christian Post-Ecology

EVERY MONTH WE ARE bombarded by updated ominous ecological news like the following: "2016 Climate Trends Continue to Break Records";[2] "Sea Ice Extent Sinks to Record Lows at Both Poles on March 7, 2017";[3] "Between 1981 and 2003, 24 per cent of global land was degraded";[4] "Due to vast overfishing, nearly 90 percent of global fish stocks are either fully fished or overfished" in 2016;[5] "Some 46–58 thousand square miles of forest are lost each year—equivalent to 48 football fields every minute";[6] "From 1996 to 2017, the numbers of threatened vertebrates increase from 3,314 to 8,170, threatened invertebrates increase from 1,891 to 4,553, and threatened plants increase from 5,328 to 11,674";[7] and "superbugs to kill more than cancer by 2050."[8]

---

1. Cobb, *Is It Too Late*, 81.
2. NASA, "2016 Climate."
3. NASA, "Sea."
4. United Nations Convention to Combat Desertification, "Desertification," 12.
5. EcoWatch, "Global."
6. World Wild Life Foundation, "Overview."
7. International Union for Conservation of Nature, "Table 1."
8. BBC, "Superbugs."

It is not just what "breaks the record" that catches our eyes, but also the petrifying speed of ecological deterioration that leaves us conjecturing whether we will actually meet ecological doomsday face to face in the next thirty years or so. According to the estimates by the Intergovernmental Panel on Climate Change (IPCC) in 2000, the global population will reach 8.4 to 11.3 billion by 2050, and 7.0 to 15.1 billion by 2100; global temperature change, relative to 1990, will be 0.8 to 2.6 °C hotter in 2050, and 1.4 to 5.8 °C hotter in 2100; global sea-level rise will be 5 to 32 cm in 2050, and 9 to 88 cm in 2010.[9] The IPCC is the largest community of ecological scientists. Because of its "intergovernmental" nature, it tries to publish analytical results that are acceptable to most scientists and the majority of governments which might weigh economic development more highly than ecological concerns. So, their reports are regarded by the global scientific community as most reliable but on the conservative side.

Since the year 2000, when these estimates were conducted, new data seem to hurry away from the lower ends of these estimates. "Global warming set to pass 2°C threshold in 2050," seven of the world's top climate scientists warned in September 2016.[10] "Global temperature rise could hit 2°C threshold by 2050," the IPCC updated its reports in September 2016.[11] The United Nations reported in 2017 that global population growth is expected to reach 9.8 billion in 2050 and 11.2 billion in 2100.[12] Since 1987, the Earth Overshoot Day has calculated illustrative calendar dates on which human beings' annual consumption for the year exceeds Earth's capacity to regenerate those resources that year. In 1987, it was by December 19 that we had already consumed Earth's annual regeneration capacity. Afterwards, the dates continuously moved earlier. In 2017, it was August 2.[13] "It is not a question of "if," but "when" the ecology will collapse," many ecologists warned decades ago. We are living in the age of post-ecology in the sense that the primary goal of ecological programs is no longer to save the un-savable ecology but to prepare for the continuing and inevitably total collapse of the ecology.

Never before are scientific analyses and projections about ecological collapse so close to the doomsday prophecies of the Bible in terms of their content, scale and immanence. Their contents consist of a variety of natural

9. Intergovernmental Panel on Climate Change (IPCC), "Working."
10. PHYS, "Global."
11. International Institute for Applied Systems Analysis, "Global."
12. United Nations, "World."
13. Earth Overshoot Day.

and human disasters; the scale is global; and the immanency likely falls within this new-born generation.

The scientific analyses and projections are best represented by the book series of *Limits to Growth*, which have generally been regarded by the ecological community as the most reliable and moderate perspectives on ecological crises. To their political right are those "ecologists" who simply dismiss ecological crises as "crying wolf" or "hoaxes." Many of their 'scientific" findings are clandestinely funded by big oil, coal and steel companies.[14] To their political left are those "eco-nuts" who seemed to cry wolf about ecological crises as if they would occur in the next decade or so. However, as more scientific evidence and hypotheses are updated, the projections of the *Limits to Growth* are merging with those of the "eco-nuts." That is, the collapse of the global ecological environment is likely to occur around 2050, plus or minus 30 years.

The book series of the *Limits to Growth* (LTG) started in 1972 by the System Dynamics Group of the Sloan School of Management at the Massachusetts Institute of Technology. In 1992, they published the revised edition, *Beyond the Limits*, with newer data and improved computer models, and warned the global community that humanity had already overshot the limits of the earth's support capacity at that time, as stated by the title of the book. In 2004, they published yet another edition, *Limits to Growth: The 30-Year Update*, to issue the final call to the global community to take comprehensive actions before ecological crises become irreversible ("passing the point of no return"). Indeed, by the time the final call was issued (2004), the earth had already passed their predicted point of no return (2002), which would have happened even if all their recommended actions were adopted then. In 2012, a related book to the LTG was published, *A Global Forecast for the Next Forty Years*, which recommended the global community to prepare for the inevitable consequences of ecological collapse.[15]

The methodology and collection of empirical data of the LTG series were not without challenges, particularly from some scientists, journalists, capitalists, and politicians, who identity with the camp of Climate Skeptics. In the late 1980s and the early 1990s, the criticisms were so overwhelming that it was regarded as politically incorrect to even mention the LTG, unless for its criticism. Skeptics picked on minor technical problems of the LTG models and imposed various political conspiracies on LTG authors. However, few,

14. Hoggan, *Climate*.

15. Meadows et al., *Limits*; Meadows et al., *Beyond*; Meadows et al. *30-Year*; Randers, *Global*.

if any, built their criticisms on the actual use of the methodology, empirical data, and computer programs which the LTG authors have provided without charge. It took another decade for the LTG followers to successfully rebut all these criticisms one by one.[16] Today, the LTG models and warnings remain valid in the eyes of most ecotheorists.

By the end of 2017 the only global "achievement" in ecological cooperation was a non-binding, non-enforceable, non-regressive Paris Climate Accord which aimed to start ecological actions only in 2020, twenty years after the LTG's predicted point of no return. Even worse, American President Donald Trump reneged on the Accord in June 2017 and replaced it with an aggressive anti-climate development strategy, including re-opening coal mines, de-regulating environmental protection policies, and exploring the Alaskan oil field.

The LTG series of books are based on a constantly-improved computer model which test-runs thousands of hypotheses with regard to a set of most significant variables related to ecological crises, including resources, industrial outputs, services, population, pollution, land and food. The more devastating political variables to ecological crises, such as war, terrorism, and corruption, are intentionally excluded from the model because it will immediately extinguish the last hope of sustainable development in this computer model.[17] The authors constructed nine of the most reasonable scenarios concerning different hypotheses about the above variables and found out that only two scenarios would lead to sustainable development and only IF the global community would immediately adopt all the ecological actions they recommend. The other seven scenarios take only part of their recommendations into consideration and are simply too weak to save the world; all result in ecological collapse around 2050. Among these seven scenarios, Scenario 1 assumes that the global community takes no coordinated policy to prevent ecological crises, as it seems to have been the case exemplified by the Paris Agreement, the result is ecological collapse around 2020.[18] Although the authors specifically avoided making precise predictions about when the ecological collapse would occur, their prediction charts reveal the collapse time around the year 2050 plus or minus 30 years. This book takes this imminent time-frame as the assumption of the arrival of the post-ecology era. It is consistent with the imminent assumption of Parousia in the Bible. However, it does not and dares not set

---

16. Bardi, *Limits*, 85–93.
17. Meadows et al., *30-Year*, 150.
18. Meadows et al., *30-Year*, 169.

a precise date for Parousia because "of that day and hour no one knows, not even the angels of heaven, nor the Son, but the Father alone,"[19] and in Christian history we have seen so many false prophesies made only to be broken.

These "limits to growth" will likely lead to "limits to peace" around the world. As "nation will rise against nation, and kingdom against kingdom,"[20] these wars will speed up the arrival of ecological crises. How should Christians think about themselves and the ecology in post-ecology? What should Christians do in their daily life in post-ecology? Should Christians look for answers in the Bible? Is not Christianity itself to be blamed for ecological crises?

Lynn White's Challenge to Christianity

Who is to blame for global ecological crises? Positively or negatively, most eco-theologians start their arguments in response to Lynn White's path-breaking thesis that it is Christianity to blame; in his words, "Christianity bears a huge burden of guilt." White traces the origin of Christianity's responsibility for ecological crises to the Medieval Christian theology about the relationship between humans and the ecology. At that time, "Christianity inherited from Judaism not only a concept of time as non-repetitive and linear but also a striking story of creation." God created humans in God's image. "Man named all the animals, thus establishing his dominance over them." Derived from the creation story, "it is God's will that man exploit nature for his proper ends," and thus making Christianity "the most anthropocentric religion the world has seen." When modern science emerged in the thirteenth century, scientists began to use this Christian theology to justify their use of science and technology to exploit nature exponentially. "From the thirteenth century onward, up to and including Leibnitz and Newton, every major scientist, in effect, explained his motivations in religious terms." Since religion is the source of ecological crises, White suggests that the solution is either to promote Eastern religions, such as Zen Buddhism, which have a similar creation story but without the human domination theology of Christianity, or to "ponder the greatest radical in Christian history since Christ: Saint Francis of Assis" who proposed "the virtue of humility – not merely for the individual but for man as a species" and "tried to depose man from his monarchy over creation and

---

19. Matt 24:36.
20. Matt 24:7; Mark 13:8; Luke 21:10.

set up a democracy of all God's creatures." White calls Francis as "a patron saint for ecologists."[21]

There are undoubtedly logical flaws in White's arguments. For instance, before he addressed the religious origin of ecological crises, he argued that

> Science was traditionally aristocratic, speculative, intellectual in intent; technology was lower-class, empirical, action-oriented. The quite sudden fusion of these two, towards the middle of the nineteenth century, is surely related to the slightly prior and contemporary democratic revolutions which, by reducing social barriers, tended to assert a functional unity of brain and hand. Our ecological crisis is the product of an emerging entirely novel, democratic culture. The issue is whether a democratized world can survive its own implications.[22]

Instead of blaming the merger of science and technology as well as the merger of science and democracy in the nineteenth century, White shifted the blame to the Christian theology of the thirteenth century. Would Christianity have caused ecological crises today had the two mergers not happened in the nineteenth century? Did the Industrial Revolution of science and technology in the nineteenth century contribute to contemporary ecological crises? Was not there a Christian hostility toward science in the Middle Ages? Did not the "anthropocentric" Christianity contribute to the expansion of science and technology through promoting capitalism and democracy only in the nineteenth century?

Furthermore, by the beginning of the twenty-first century, Christianity had worked with other religions to become "a leading voice telling us to respect the earth, love our nonhuman as well as our human neighbors, and think deeply about our social policies and economic priorities. Religions now offer Earth Day prayers, critical comments on the environmental effects of World Bank loans, cautions about the dangers of genetic engineering, and Sunday School lessons about how Christians should respond to environmentally induced asthma."[23]

Finally, if (Protestant and Catholic) Christianity is responsible for ecological problems, is it also responsible for ecological problems in India (mainly Hinduism) and China (mainly atheism)? In terms of their share of global CO_2 emissions in 2016, China is ranked number one for its 28.21 percent of

---

21. White, "Historical," 1203–07.
22. White, "Historical," 1204.
23. Gottlieb, *Greener*, 9.

global CO_2 emissions; the United States is in the second place, 15.99 percent; India is ranked number three, 6.24 percent; the Eastern Orthodox Russia is ranked number four, 4.53 percent; and Japan, a country of Shinto belief, is ranked number five, 3.67 percent. In fact, seven of the top ten countries (China, India, Russia, Japan, Korea, Iran, and Saudi Arabia) having the largest shares of global CO_2 emissions are not Christian countries.[24] Besides, in terms of population, China (1.4 billion) and India (1.3 billion) have the largest populations in the world, constituting about one-quarter of the world's population. While India's population is expected to surpass China's population in 2020 due to India's lack of mandatory birth control program, China relaxed her compulsory birth control program from one-child (implemented from 1979 to 2015) to two-child in 2015. Is Christianity, or any religion, truly responsible for ecological problems?

Despite Lynn White's logical flaws, his analysis inspired the holistic approach most ecologists endorse, i.e., to cope with global ecological crisis requires solutions at economic, political and religious levels to reform both individuals and institutions.

Methodological Assumptions

This book is unique among its counterparts in its balanced interdisciplinary composition, combining theories of cognitive science, Christian theology, economics and political science. It starts with an integration of cognitive science and theology, called neurotheology. As cognitive scientist James B. Ashbrook first coined the term, neurotheology is the study of relationships between the human brain and religious phenomena.[25] Many disciplines and sub-disciplines have contributed to this new research subject, such as neuroscience, neuropsychology, cognitive psychology, social psychology, education, sociology, economics, political science, philosophy and theology. Therefore, this book takes an interdisciplinary approach to study spiritual, economic and political solutions to ecological crises.

Regarding theological methodology, I call myself a neo-evangelical social scientist in the sense that I combine different methodologies to uphold the major doctrines of evangelical theology, including the Trinity, the inerrancy of the Bible, and literal interpretation of the Bible. These methodologies include

24. Statista, "Largest producers."
25. Ashbrook, "Neurotheology," 331–50.

those of exegesis, hermeneutics, literary criticism, natural science, and social sciences.

The adoption of natural science and social sciences methodologies is based on the evangelical assumption that God created nature and natural law. Nature includes both physical materials and human being, and natural law covers both physical materials and human beings. Natural science and social sciences are nothing but the sciences to study nature and natural law which God created. Theology also starts with the assumption that God created nature and natural law. It goes on to elaborate, not so much on nature, but much more on the "natural law" between God and human being. Therefore, I assume that science and theology are and must always be compatible and harmonious because God cannot contradict Himself. Theologian of evolutionary ethics, Stephen J. Pope, says it well: "If one accepts the axiom that, ultimately, "truth cannot conflict with truth," then one can argue that the knowledge provided by the natural sciences . . . is consistent with, and can help to shed light on, the truth affirmed in Christian faith."[26]

However, the history of the relationship between modern science and conservative theology has been one without compatibility and harmony, starting from Nicolaus Copernicus' teaching of the "heretic" science of cosmology in the sixteenth century to the current debate about creationism versus evolutionism. The acrimonious conflict between science and theology is derived from either one of two sources, or both: (1) when one discipline insists on the past erroneous arguments, (2) when one discipline makes more claims than its methodology warrants.

Holding science and theology as compatible is not a new idea. As early as in the seventeenth century, when modern science was on the rise, many Puritan scientists of the Royal Society of London promoted science "as an ally of true religion."[27] Later, when modern psychology made its debut by atheist Sigmund Freud and B F Skinner, the credibility of theology was under another wave of attack.[28] But other leading psychologists, like Freud's collaborator Carl Jung, continued to support the compatibility between psychology and theology.[29]

---

26. Pope, *Human*, 2.

27. Jeeves and Brown, *Neuroscience*, 164. For ecological reasons, this book uses the digital version of a book, if available. Most of Amazon digital books are numbered by Locations, not pages. So, I use, for example, "L12-24", to cite their location numbers.

28. Freud, *Totem*; Skinner, *Beyond Freedom*.

29. Jung and Franz, *Man*; Jeeves and Brown, *Neuroscience*, 237–84; Rollings, *Soul*.

Theologian John Haught found God in the post-Big Bang sciences: "In order for our universe to become alive and, at least in human beings, conscious of itself, the physical characteristics of this universe had to be remarkably right from the beginning. The mathematical values associated with the physical constants and initial conditions that would allow for the eventual emergence of life and mind billions of years after the Big Bang seem to have been fine-tuned very precisely at the very start. Even the slightest variation in mathematical values, and life and mind could never have appeared."[30]

Neuroscientist Justin L Barrett finds complementarity between science and theology: 'science and Theology talk to each other. Science tells Theology what its latest and greatest accomplishments are and then Theology scurries to figure out how to accommodate those findings ... Theology points out the dependence of Science on certain prescientific assumptions and commitments that are often supplied by Theology, and insists that without Theology to inform discussions concerning values (what we ought and should think or do), the findings of Science are just as likely to be harmful as beneficial."[31]

A Chinese Christian Perspective

The subtitle of this book "A Chinese Christian Perspective" is adopted for four methodological reasons. First, there are significant similarities in social and political conditions between that of Chinese churches and that of ante-Nicene churches.[32] Chinese Christians constitute about 3 percent in mainland China, 4 percent in Taiwan, and 7 percent in Hong Kong; they are the numerical minority religion. They are also the political minorities; the communist China has been ruled by Marxists; Taiwan was ruled by three Christian presidents from 1945 to 2000 and by presidents of traditional Chinese religions afterward; Hong Kong was returned to communist China in 1997 and the Chief Executives have been believers of traditional Chinese religions. By contrast, ante-Nicene churches constituted about 10 percent of the Roman population by the end of the third century.[33] Most the polytheist Roman emperors were hostile to Christians before 314 AD. When the percentages of Christians in most European countries now fall to an average of 40 percent or below, a

30. Haught, "Science," 269–70.

31. Barrett, *Cognitive Science*, 68, 70.

32. On the subject of ante-Nicene churches, see Schaff, *Nicene*; McManners, *Oxford Illustrated*.

33. Stark, *Discovering*, 313.

Chinese Christian perspective may help bring back Western theologians to their common origin – the ante-Nicene churches.

Secondly, these similarities in social and political conditions produce similar political theologies between Chinese churches and ante-Nicene churches. There is a high degree of religious tolerance among the churches and between the churches and non-Christian religions. Their political theologies emphasize religious freedom and separation of the church and state. They have little motivation to build a religious state of Christianity. Instead, they eagerly engage in evangelism in anticipation of the annihilation of this world, followed by the fast arrival of the kingdom of and from heaven. This book argues that any ecotheology should take these ante-Nicene theological assumptions seriously.

Thirdly, some Western ecotheologians, disillusioned with Christianity like Lynne White was, have become attracted to Chinese religions (especially Daoism and Buddhism) as a religious alternative to save the ecology. As a Chinese Christian political theologian who has published several works on religious politics in Chinese societies,[34] I would like to say that Chinese religions are no friendlier than Christianity to ecology as they thought, and that the Chinese communist government has produced little long-term tangible ecological record to become their "green Messiah."

Robert P Weller, a sociologist of Chinese religions, points out that "Both 'nature' and 'environment' entered the Chinese vocabulary in their modern forms only in the early twentieth century, but both terms also resonated broadly with earlier ways of thinking about how humanity relates to the physical world around it." They did not "discover" nature until the mid-to-late 1980s. What are the earlier and new mixed ways of "ecological" thinking? It is an "anthropocosmic" view of the universe of *qi* (ether) energy. Through manipulating the *fengshui* (wind and water; referring to the mystical order of nature), the universe of *qi* will enhance personal health and wealth as well as bring blessings to one's offspring. The methods of manipulation include deforestation, consumption of exotic (endangered) species, and tourism to spirited mountains and rivers where few humans ever visited.[35] In 2016, Taiwanese temples and shrines burned 240,000 tons of ghost money used in worship rituals, equivalent to the carbon emission of 20,000 cars.[36]

---

34. My major works on Chinese religious politics include: Kuo, *Global*; *Religion and Democracy*; *Religion and Nationalism*; "Sacred," 249–67.

35. Weller, *Discovering*, 2, 4, 39-41.

36. *United Daily News*, "Why do."

Introduction: Scientific and Christian Post-Ecology

If Chinese Daoism or Chinese Buddhism does not help as much with ecological protection, how about Tibetan Buddhism? Ecological activist Andrés R. Edwards builds his theory of "Thriving beyond Sustainability" primarily on Tibetan Buddhism and other primitive religions to replace Chinese religions and socialist ideology. He develops a framework for successful initiatives nicknamed SPIRALS (scalable, place-making, intergenerational, resilient, accessible, life-affirming, and involve self-care). His SPIRALS project promotes collaboration and abundance. "Rather than seeking to limit our impact by being "less bad," thriveability supports actions that regenerate natural systems and our quality of life." Among his proposals is to "develop a green economy with jobs in manufacturing hybrid cars, installing solar panels and wind turbines, retrofitting buildings, upgrading the energy grid and transportation infrastructure and retorting habitats."[37] Leftist ecologists, as will be discussed in chapter 5 of this book, will be very much alarmed by this dubious green capitalist project which only serve to increase production efficiency but does little to halt global warming in absolute terms.

I am not saying that we should not give credits to Daoist ecotheology, Chinese Buddhist ecotheology, and the Chinese government for what they said or what they did. It is always good to have more people jump on the ecological wagon, both in theory and practice. Nevertheless, we need to differentiate between what they said and what they did on the one hand, and what they actually did and their overall impact on ecology, on the other. The evidence so far does not show a narrowing gap between the two. The first section of chapter 4 will discuss the brief history and content of Chinese ecotheologies. Chapter 6 will provide more analysis on Chinese performance in ecological programs.

If there is something to be learned from the Chinese case, it is the ecological programs of the Buddhist Compassion Relief Tzu Chi Foundation, whose chairwoman Venerable Chengyen was chosen as one of the one hundred most influential persons in the world by Time magazine in 2011. In addition to its 432 disaster relief branch offices in more than 50 countries (including China), the Foundation establishes about 6,450 ecological units for about 87,750 volunteers in 14 countries.[38] How can it be so successful and welcome across countries? For one thing, Venerable Chengyen has consistently held the principle of "non-interference in politics" everywhere.

---

37. Edwards, *Thriving Beyond*, 4–5, 9–12, 94, 135–7.

38. Buddhist Compassion Relief Tzu Chi Foundation, *From the Years*, 286–317, 318, 354–55. About the political attitude of Tzu Chi, see Kuo, *Religion and Democracy*.

For another, its ecological programs focus exclusively on recycling, including the production of disaster-relief blankets and Tzu Chi uniforms made from recycled plastic bottles. Never did the Foundation endorse or participate in any ecological protest movement, nor did it participate in the government's ecological policymaking process, except for recycling. It simply ignores the criticism from ecologists that "excessive reliance on recycling will shift the onus away from the recognition that more profound changes are required. The emphasis should be on reducing consumption rather than recycling that which has already been consumed."[39] Its attitude toward politics bears a striking similarity to that of the ante-Nicene church. In sum, contemporary Christians in the world should and can find the correct ecological answers in ante-Nicene Christianity, but probably not much in Chinese religions and Chinese ecological policies.

Finally, this book takes a balanced interdisciplinary approach to study ecology. How is this approach particularly Chinese? No, it is not. Yet, recent transcultural neuroscientific studies demonstrate that Westerners tend to think analytically, while East Asians favor holistic thinking.[40] Each chapter of this book is conducted analytically but integrated with the themes of other chapters to provide a holistic answer to ecological problems.

Two final notes on ecological terminology used in this book. I do not make a clear distinction between environmentalism and ecologism as ecological philosopher Andrew Dobson does. To highlight differences in scopes of ecological reforms, Dobson defines environmentalism as "a managerial approach to environmental problems . . . without fundamental changes in present values or patterns of production and consumption." By contrast, ecologism insists that "a sustainable and fulfilling existence presuppose radical changes in our relationships with the non-human natural world, and in our mode of social and political life."[41] The distinction between environmentalism and ecologism seems to imply that ecologism is superior to environmentalism in addressing ecological crises. It is not. This book does not make a distinction between the two terms because, on the one hand, most current ecotheories, be they rightists or leftists (as discussed in chapter 5 of this book), have gradually converged toward ecologism, although in different degrees and scopes. On the other hand, "radical changes in our model of social and political life" may cause chaos in our social and political life and precipitate ecological crises.

39. Dobson, *Green*, 79.
40. Han and Northoff, "Culture-Sensitive," 647.
41. Dobson, *Green*, 2–3.

Ecologism cannot work without a practical environmentalist "managerial approach." Therefore, the two words of ecology and environment, and their derivatives (e.g., ecological theory or environmental theory) are used interchangeably in this book unless the context deserves their distinction.

Another note on ecological terminology used in this book is that I do not make further distinctions among sub-fields of ecological studies, such as soil degradation, water pollution, air pollution, climate change, monoculture agriculture and crop pests, contagion of new human diseases, ocean level rise, ocean acidification, and overpopulation; to name just a few.[42] Granted that there are substantial differences among them in terms of idiosyncratic technological, social, economic, political, and religious complexities, all of them share the same structural dilemma of public goods or collective actions, which will be discussed in detail in chapter 5 of this book. Furthermore, it is just impossible to engage in substantive studies on all these sub-fields in a book. And finally, the complexities of these ecological issues can only strengthen the paradoxical conclusion of this book: Too Little to Save and Too Many to Save.

Chapter Outlines

The next chapter of this book discusses the neurotheology of human nature, institutional influences on human behaviors, and how human nature and institutions influence the success and failures of ecological programs. Chapter 3 matches the human natures of rationality, emotion and spirituality to Biblical chapters, demonstrating that Biblical teachings are consistent with these human natures. Chapters 2 and 3 thus complete the construction of the microfoundation of ecotheologies. Chapters 4, 5 and 6 then put human nature in the institutional context of the church, capitalism and democracy to evaluate current ecological theories and ecotheologies as well as to construct a neuro-institutional post-ecotheology. Chapter 7 concludes the analyses of this book.

---

42. I would like to thank Jeffrey Nicolaisen for his comments on the complexity of ecological issues.

2.

Neuro-Institutional Human

A CHRISTIAN SOLUTION TO the ecological crisis cannot but simultaneously address human factors at three levels: church, capitalism, and the state. While the individual human is the primary agent to damage the ecosystem, individual behaviors alone can rarely reverse ecological crises. In fact, current ecological crises are mostly the direct result of individual rationality leading to collective irrationality at all three levels of collectivities. If human rationality is the leading cause of ecological crises, a solution relying solely on human rationality or super-rational Transhumanism is not likely to work but only to exacerbate the crises. Fortunately, recent findings in neuroscience about the human natures of rationality, emotion and spirituality may help us to find practical ecological solutions based on the combination of these human natures.

This chapter and the next chapter aim to construct a micro foundation of ecotheology. This chapter discusses the human natures of rationality, emotion and spirituality, how these human natures interact with social, economic and political institutions, and how they shed light on the implementation of ecological programs. Chapter 3 matches Biblical verses with the human nature of rationality, emotion and spirituality. Taking stock of new breakthroughs in neuroscience, the first section of this chapter elaborates the scientific findings of the human brain with regard to emotion, rationality and spirituality, and their implications for ecological behaviors. Moreover, ecological behaviors are influenced not only by what is inside the brain but also what is outside the brain, i.e., social, economic and political institutions. Thus, the second section explores the relationships between human nature and institutions of ecology to point out the strengths and weaknesses of ecological institutions.

The third section briefly evaluates the rationality-based Transhumanism as a possible solution to ecological crises.

Neuroscientific Human

> If you contemplate God long enough, something surprising happens in the brain. Neural functioning begins to change. Different circuits become activated, while others become deactivated. New dendrites are formed, new synaptic connections are made, and the brain becomes more sensitive to subtle realms of experience. Perceptions alter, beliefs begin to change, and if God has meaning for you, then God becomes neurologically real.[1]

Since the late 1980s, the invention of brain-scan technologies such as magnetic resonance imaging (MRI), functional magnetic resonance imaging (fMRI), magnetoencephalography (MEG) and other fancy phrenology technologies has significantly challenged how we think about human nature in the past three thousand years. Two significant findings probably wreak havoc on those philosophical arguments that are based on human rationality alone. First, the human is not as rational as we think. Even worse, rationality is basically a slave to emotion. Secondly, spiritual/religious thinking is somewhat autonomous from emotion and rationality, and sometimes prevails upon emotion and rationality. Let us start with what neuroscientists have discovered about the locations of emotion, rationality and religion in the human brain.

The basic unit of the human brain is called "neuron."[2] An adult human brain consists of about 86 billion neurons.[3] A neuron has four major parts: soma, dendrite, axon, and terminal button. The soma is like the central processing unit of a computer, responsible for the reproduction of neurons, the coordination of different parts of neurons, and the communication with other neurons. The soma contains a nucleus which stores DNA. A dendrite is like the input device of a computer, receiving information from other neurons and forwarding information to soma for processing. These activities may stimulate further growth of dendrites in both number and complexity to cope with information flows. Functioning like a computer output device, the axon is a thin tube extended from the soma to send information to other neurons. An axon

---

1. Newberg and Waldman, *How God Changes*, 71.

2. The following basic and updated knowledge of neuroscience is from Sternberg, *Cognitive*.

3. Herculano-Houzel, "Human Brain," 1–11.

does so through the knots at the tip of the axon, called "terminal buttons," which release electrical signals (e.g., alpha particles) or chemical signals (e.g., endorphin and dopamine) to the terminal buttons of other neurons. Each neuron can grow about 1000 connections (dendrites and axons) with other neurons. Electrical signals travel through these connections much faster than sound; for instance, the human brain can catch an image in 100 milliseconds.

We do not need to allocate too many of our neurons to memorize these neuroscientific jargons, the functions of different groups of neurons, or the fancy technologies spying on them. Nevertheless, it is essential for later discussion to remember three simple behavioral rules of neurons, which determine human behavior: (1) Each neuron has autonomy to function normally or abnormally due to genetic or environmental reasons. (2) Neurons interact with one another. The interaction can be in harmony, conflict, or one-sided domination. (3) Neurons may grow in complexity and capacity when regularly stimulated, but may also decline in complexity and capacity when left alone for too long.[4] In a nutshell, neurons behave just like individuals in a tightly knitted society in which individuals compete, cooperate, dominate, obey, and, sometimes, go nuts.

The next step of dissecting human brain is to divide it into different functional areas. Neuroscientists have developed complicate categories and subcategories of brain functions for various research purposes. For our purpose, we select seven functional areas as starting points for constructing a neurotheological human: thalamus, amygdala, septum, hippocampus, anterior cingulate, frontal lobe, and parietal lobe. The first four parts constitute a "limbic system" located deep inside the "temporal lobe" which is near our ears.[5]

Located at the center of the brain is the thalamus, which functions like a telephone operator in the brain. It receives incoming signals from sensory organs (eyes, ears, nose, mouth and skin) and forwards these signals to different parts of the brain to respond. Below the thalamus is the amygdala, which generates emotional responses of anger, aggression, fear and sexual desire. In front of the thalamus is the septum, which regulates anger, fear and pleasure. When magnetic stimulation was applied here, some subjects felt "like a thousand orgasms rolled into one."[6] (Don't try this at home.) The hippocampus

---

4. Newberg and Waldman, *How God*, 276.

5. Some neuroscientists consider parietal lobe and anterior cingulate also as parts of the limbic system.

6. Ramachandran and Blakeslee, *Phantoms*, 175.

curves around the thalamus with a shape like a . . . hippocampus. It is responsible for memory and learning. Located above the thalamus is the anterior cingulate. Its primary function seems to be that of a thermostat to regulate an under- or over-reactive amygdala. It gives us a sense of peace, loving, and compassion. The frontal lobe is in the front of the brain and is the favorite part of philosophers; it conducts rational thinking. The parietal lobe, located in the upper-rear of the brain, gives us the ability to comprehend space and time as well as anything transcendental like gods, aliens, ideology, nationalism, or other mystical powers. These complete the description of where emotion (the limbic system), rationality (the frontal lobe) and spirituality (the parietal lobe) are physically located in the brain.

Without modern technology, neuroscientists were not able to pinpoint religious thinking in the brain until the mid-1980s when a Canadian psychologist Michael Persinger stimulated his temporal lobe with a primitive magnetic stimulator. He reported that he experienced God for the first time in his life. This little experiment caught the attention of a world-famous neuroscientist, V S Ramachandran. He began to conduct series of experiments on the brain and published the seminal book on neurotheology, *Phantoms in the Brain*.[7]

Ramachandran and his research team probed the limbic system, but not the frontal lobe or the parietal lobe. They found that patients with minor seizures in the limbic system reported intense emotions about God, which included: "finally I have insight into the true nature of the cosmos," or 'suddenly it all makes sense." Ramachandran and Blakeslee were surprised to find out that "this sense of enlightenment, this absolute conviction that Truth is revealed at last, should derive from limbic structures concerned with emotions rather than from the thinking, rational parts of the brain that take so much pride in their ability to discern truth and falsehood." They also found out that once formed, these beliefs sometimes "permanently alter the patient's personality" even without seizures. These patients tended to be "obsessively preoccupied with philosophical and theological issues."[8] Does this mean that many of our pastors, priests, rabbi, monks or ulama might have this 'seizure personality" when they deliver a sermon?

Employing the technologies of fMRI and quantitative electroencephalography which measures electrical patterns of brain activities at the surface of the scalp, Mario Beauregard and Denyse O'Leary conducted experiments on Carmelite nuns in Canada. Their findings refute the "God spot" argument

---

7. Ramachandran and Blakeslee, *Phantoms*.
8. Ramachandran and Blakeslee, *Phantoms*, 179–80.

proposed by materialist/atheist neuroscientists, but reveal that religious, spiritual, and mystical experiences "are complex and multidimensional and mediated by a number of brain regions normally implicated in perception, cognition, emotion, body representation, and self-consciousness." Different regions of the brain worked together to generate mystical experiences of these nuns, including the inferior and superior parietal lobule, visual cortex, caudate nucleus, left brain stem, and others.[9]

Newberg and Waldman describe how different parts of the brain work together as "circuits" to generate full-fledged religious experiences.[10] The parietal lobe, which processes information about time and space, collaborates with the occipital lobe to enable humans to identify "God as an object that exists in the world." It is probably the source of sanctification, i.e., to sanctify any real or imagined person, object, feeling, and ethical codes to induce full compliance of the believers to the religion. For instance, the founder of every great religion is often sanctified as a god or a unique semi-god, who is above all humans. Their main scriptures are sanctified by attributing it to god's words and would contain magical power. Moreover, certain religious ethical and ritual codes are regarded by the believers as lexicographically higher codes than those of secular laws such that they would rather take severe punishment from the secular government by violating secular laws than violating these religious codes.

The parietal lobe also coordinates with the frontal lobe to build a rational relationship between human and God in both time and space. The frontal lobe, which is the rationalist's favorite, "creates and integrates all of your ideas about God—positive or negative—including the logic you use to evaluate your religious and spiritual beliefs." The telephone operator of the brain, the thalamus, helps human to form "a holistic sense of the world and appears to be the key organ that makes God feel objectively real." The amygdala, which generates fear, aggression and sexual desires, also generates "emotional impression of a frightening, authoritative, and punitive God." Sometimes, though, it also 'suppresses the frontal lobe's ability to logically think about God." Both the striatum and the anterior cingulate, functioning like a thermostat to suppress the runaway amygdala, give humans the feeling of safety, love, and compassion from God, and thereby, reducing anxiety, guilt and anger.

Malcolm Jeeves, an active Christian, is probably the most prolific neuroscientist promoting the application of neurotheology to other disciplines,

---

9. Beauregard and O'Leary, *Spiritual Brain*, 267–76.
10. Newman and Waldman, *How God*, 756.

such as legal study, philosophy, theology and social sciences.[11] He conducted more sophisticated studies on the brain than his predecessors such as Persinger, Ramachandran, Albright and Ashbrook, and concluded that the temporal lobe could be considered as the "God spot" or "God module."[12] However, Jeeves argues that, based on new findings, religious behaviors are not restricted to the limbic system. Instead, most of the brain parts are involved in religious experiences.[13]

The initial findings of religious thinking as reported by neuroscientists generated heated debate between Christian believers and atheists. Enthusiastic believers rushed to the conclusion that these neuroscientific findings proved that God exists, while atheists argued the contrary, stating that these neuroscientific findings proved that God does not exist outside the brain, but only appear as human-made "phantoms" or "delusion" in the brain.[14] Even worse, several neuroscience studies found that some people developed intense religious experiences while they had head injuries, epilepsy, schizophrenia, bipolar disorder, and obsessive-compulsive disorder, thus implying that devoted religious people have personality disorders.[15] This debate between Christian believers and atheists will never cease, because they have different definitions of what constitutes "proof." To the Christian believers, the proof is mainly subjective and inter-subjective; while to the atheists, the proof has to be scientifically verifiable. To the former, these neuroscientific findings "prove" the subjective and inter-subjective "existence" of God; while to the atheists, these neuroscientific findings only show brain waves but not God Himself. It is similar to the debate between literati and un-romantic neuroscientists about the existence of love. While romance literature abounds with poetic love, un-romantic neuroscientists find only effects of pheromone generated by the amygdala and the stratum.

Currently, most neuroscientists, atheists or Christian believers, agree that there is no evidence so far to "prove" the existence of a single "God spot" or "God gene." Neither is there any scientific evidence to "disprove" the existence of God. Regardless, "circuits," "modules" or "loops" of religious thinking can

11. Jeeves and Brown, *Neuroscience*; Jeeves, *Minds*; and other Jeeves' works.

12. Persinger, *Neuropsychological*; Albright and Ashbrook, *Were God Lives* probably coined the term "God spot;" Britton and Bootzin, "Experiences," spoke first about "God module".

13. Jeeves, *Minds*, 2434.

14. Dawkins, *God Delusion*; Alper, *"God,"* 1294, 1431, 1498.

15. Persinger, *Neuropsychological*; Simon et al. *Conquering*. See Fingelkurts and Fingelkurts, "Is Our," 297 for a list of these researches.

be observed by neuroscientific technologies.[16] Newberg and Waldman even provide a list of concrete DIY steps to train oneself on how to feel intimate relations with God, enlightenment, or transcendent beings.[17] Whether the existence of God can be "proved" by these "circuits," "modules" or "loops" of religious thinking depends on how we define "proof." When Christian neuroscientist Malcolm Jeeves argued that neurotheology "proves" the existence of God, he probably said it more from a believer's perspective than a scientist's perspective.[18] "If God exists and has created humans so that they may enjoy a relationship with him, it is not surprising that there is a physical mechanism that makes possible development of that relationship."[19] After reviewing more than two hundred neuroscientific reports on religious thinking, Fingelkurts and Fingelkurts conclude that "neuroscience cannot provide a reliable explanation for religious experience . . . However, already today cognitive neuroscience in a broad sense may contribute to an overall description of religious experience with regards to biological and psychological dimensions." They also recommend that 'spirit and soul are not at all scientific concepts, their origins lie in a theological point of view."[20] This position is shared by this book: Humans are genetically wired to think about God, just like humans are genetically wired to speak, hear, see, eat, feel, sing, think and have sex. However, the analysis of relationships between God and humans need to be done theologically with the help from neuroscientific findings, as elaborated later in this chapter. In sum, neuroscience is mainly about what's going on within the brain, but not outside the brain. God exists both inside and outside the brain but also leaves footprints ("God circuits") for neuroscientists to observe and analyze.

Once we identify those parts of the brain that are related to religious thinking, the next step in constructing a neurotheology is to generate hypotheses about the relationships among these parts of the brain. Since contemporary brain-scan technologies have not been able to track the complexity of information flow among neurons, these hypotheses derive from the behavioral rules of neurons as described before. Different parts of the brain have their primary functions (emotion, rationality and spirituality), but also coordinate these functions with other parts of the brain via electronic and chemical agents

16. Jeeves and Brown, *Neuroscience*, 41–43; Jeeves, *Minds*, 881; Haidt, *Happiness*, 3387.
17. Newberg and Waldman, *How Enlightenment*.
18. Jeeves, *Minds*, 2349.
19. Jeeves, *Minds*, 2411.
20. Fingelkurts and Fingelkurts, "Is Our," 315–316.

sent out by neurons. As they interact with one another, their physical connections (dendrites, axons and terminal buttons) multiply in both number and complexity. Depending on variations in internal and external stimuli in a person's life experience, relationships among these parts of brain vary across individuals in terms of harmony, conflict or domination. When certain parts of the brain "go nuts" because of gene defections or excessive stimuli, other parts of the brain may also suffer and generate abnormal behaviors.

Theologically speaking, the most fascinating part of the brain is the parietal lobe, which enables humans to generate temporal and spatial concepts. As theologian John Haught argued, "from a Christian point of view the purpose of the universe is to give expression in space and time to the infinite love that is the ground and source of all being."[21] When the parietal lobe is working properly, we are able to perform deeper and wider rational thinking; we are also able to control our emotional response to external stimuli. For instance, a diligent high school student with a strong parietal lobe can perform better on subjects related to time and space. More importantly, he needs to resist the daily temptation from his peers to join wild parties after school. His parietal lobe tells him that working hard now will enable him to receive a better salary and joy than his peers in the future. Alternatively, the god in his mind tells him that going to wild parties is a temptation by the devil. Most religions start their theologies with supernatural deities or forces, which are framed in unlimited time and space. These deities or forces, then, guide human rationality and emotion in their daily lives.

From a Christian perspective, the transcendental God, or the Holy Spirit, is more likely staying in the parietal lobe than the amygdala or other parts. In particular, the parietal lobe of the right brain has the most potent reaction to transcendental presentations of God.[22] Newberg and Waldman concluded from their research experiences that "If you decrease activity in your parietal lobe through meditation or intense prayer, the boundaries between you and God dissolve. You feel a sense of unity with the object of contemplation and your spiritual beliefs."[23] A word of caution is in need here: as a spiritual force, demons may also find it comfortable staying in the parietal lobe.

---

21. Haught, "Science," 6395.

22. Left brain and right brain are connected by corpus callosum. Major functional parts of left brain and right brain are identical, but the right brain tends to be more active in dealing with emotional feeling, while the left brain is stronger in dealing with reasoning. Some research suggests that the balance between left and right brain may cause one to be religious or atheist. Newberg and Waldman, *How God,* 959.

23. Newberg and Waldman, *How God,* 759.

Neuroscientists Newberg and Waldman warned, "If a belief in God provides you with a sense of comfort and security, then God will enhance your life. But if you see God as a vindictive deity who gives you justification for inflicting harm on others, such a belief can actually damage your brain as it motivates you to act in socially destructive ways."[24]

Now, how do these different parts of our brain cooperate to react to an incoming signal, process it, and send out behavioral instructions to different parts of our body? Psychologist and Nobel Laureate in Economics, Daniel Kahneman, developed a heuristic typology to describe the mental process: fast thinking and slow thinking.[25] In order to save energy, our brain utilizes mental routines, called "fast thinking," to minimize the use of reasoning in dealing with our daily work routines, such as morning wash-ups, eating, walking or driving to work, routine work assignments, grocery shopping on the way home, and performing evening rituals at home before bedtime. Occasionally, our brain receives strong, complex or new signals that our fast thinking cannot handle by itself. These trigger other parts of the brain to do further analysis of these signals and send out more complicated behavioral instructions to our body. This 'slow thinking" requires much more energy for the brain to do its job. Therefore, it is not as active as fast thinking in our daily behaviors, unless some professionals, like scientists and academics, are required to engage in slow-thinking works every day. In fact, Daniel Kahneman received his Nobel Prize in Economics for discovering that most of New York stock brokers, who are supposed to engage in sophisticated number-crunching works, rely instead on fasting thinking (guts feeling and rules of thumbs) to sell and buy stocks by millions of dollars.

From where do these "fast thinking" and 'slow thinking" routines come? They come from our learning experiences at home, schools, works, and other social institutions. When we learn and follow the behavioral norms or laws of these social institutions, we receive encouragement, praise or material reward. If we do not conform to these norms or laws, reprimand and punishment will fall upon us. Conceptually, we can think of our neurons, encouraged by a positive feedback from the environment, making direct and indirect connections to other neurons by growing and strengthening their dendrites and axons, thus forming routines of fast and slow thinking. If the feedback from the environment is negative, these dendrites, axons, or even neurons wither

---

24. Newberg and Waldman, *How God*, 93.
25. Kahneman, *Thinking*.

or die and will be replaced by new routines, thus transforming routines of fast and slow thinking.

How "fast and slow thinking" are linked back to our previous discussion of brain functions, especially to the theological foundation of this book? For the sake of theoretical simplicity, we can merge Newberg and Waldman's six "circuits" of our brain functions and roughly divide them into three parts: emotional brain (EB), rational brain (RB) and God brain (GB). The emotional brain consists of the thalamus, amygdala, septum, hippocampus and anterior cingulate; the frontal lobe is the rational brain; while the parietal lobe is the God brain.

We need to bear in mind again that religious experiences involve all three types of brain in different degrees, and these three types of brain continuously interact with one another, resulting in "loops" or "circuits" of thinking. Therefore, some neuroscientists prefer to call EB, RB and GB as emotional circuits, rational circuits and God circuits.[26] The term "circuit" is not without controversy either, due to its analogy borrowed from the computer science. The human brain is significantly more complex and flexible than fixed computer circuits. Besides, the "circuit" itself is probably a loaded term in favor of rationality at the expense of emotion and religiosity.

Thus, we can speak of various ideal types of individuals according to the relative strength of their brain routines. Religious prophets are likely to be GB-dominant persons because they do not get along with other people (weak EB) and they are not interested in sophisticated theological studies (weak RB). Newberg and Waldman found that when Pentecostals speak in tongues, the activity in their parietal lobe increases.[27] Atheist scientists or philosophers are likely to be RB-dominant persons because they restrict their temporal and spatial thinking to things that are scientifically verifiable (weak GB), and they usually work with machines in long hours and have little time to deal with emotional issues of themselves or others (weak EB). Among the several hundred scientific Nobel Laureates and those scientists elected to the National Academy of Sciences, only a handful can be categorized as Christians.[28] Actors and actresses are likely to be EB-dominant persons who do not need to spend much time analyzing the literary values of a script (weak RB) or acting according to those cues or rules beyond what are provided by their directors (weak GB).

26. Newberg and Waldman, *How God*, 71.
27. Newberg and Waldman, *How God*, 891.
28. Dawkins, *God Delusion*, 1617–21.

There can be types of persons that have more balanced brain routines. Theologians in theological seminaries are trained to balance GB and RB, but probably not good at shepherding a church (weak EB). A talented pastor is likely to be a balanced person of GB and EB, but not having much time to do theological studies (weak RB). A charismatic atheist leader is likely to be well-equipped with both EB and RB, but has no respect for gods (weak GB). The ideal type of a religious person or a church is to have balanced development with all GB, RB and EB.

What are the major implications of these different types of Christians for ecological actions? First, some EB Christians take ecological actions because they love trees and animals. Other RB Christians take ecological actions because they do so only after a prudent calculation of their benefits and costs. Still, other GB Christians take ecological actions probably because God tells them to do so in a dream. Most Christians take ecological actions probably because they have mixed motives derived from all EB, RB and GB. Secondly, because Christians are different in terms of their motives and goals, their ecological actions are likely to be different; so are among the churches in the choice of ecological programs. Thirdly, it probably takes years to change a Christian's 'slow thinking" toward the ecology and takes generations to change a church's collective 'slow thinking" toward the ecology, if the slow thinking is ever changeable. Therefore, ecological programs in a church should be implemented only incrementally, and the goals of these programs probably should shift from saving the earth (which is impossible) to saving more souls. Finally, if the above neuroscientific arguments are correct, those ecological programs which are based on human rationality alone are based on only one-seventh of the human brain. They ignore EB, GB, RB-EB interaction, RB-GB interaction, EB-GB interaction, and RB-EB-GB interaction. No wonder they hardly work.

Why are there different types of personalities mentioned above? The consensus among cognitive psychologists seems to be: "It is a combination of both nature and nurture."[29] Some people, through inherited or mutated DNA, are born with a large and active part of the brain that is EB, RB or GB. With complementary education and environmental stimuli, this part of the brain grows even larger and more active. Then, *voila*! There comes the people renown in natural sciences (RB), arts (EB) and religions (GB). Nevertheless, their pathological development may also lead to the most destructive socio-paths in our societies. Most of us are average people in DNA composition and

---

29. Barrett, *Cognitive Science*, 475–486.

education, but probably enjoy a happier and more balanced life of rationality, emotion and religiosity.

However, if we accept biological and anthropological findings about the human brain, there seem to be asymmetrical relationships among EB, RB and GB. Human EB probably developed first and remains most influential among all three types of the brain. Just like other kinds of animal, EB stands on the front line of everyday survival needs, including eating, drinking, walking, reacting to threats, and procreation activities. With the emergence of Homo sapiens around 200,000 years ago,[30] human RB began to develop faster and more sophisticated than other animals in the survival game. When external stimuli did not call for instantaneous responses but allow time to react, human RB came to help EB to adopt the most rational methods to maximize or justify their survival needs, thus maximizing the long-term emotional needs of humans.[31] This maximization of emotional needs is why some cognitive psychologists conclude that "rationality is the slave of emotion," or the phenomenon of "confabulation" which means that it is our nature to fabricate reasons to explain our emotional behavior.[32] Although this is probably an exaggeration due to the fact that sometimes rationality helps to regulate or redirect emotional responses, it is probably the result of a split EB that allows rationality to serve two EB masters.

What about the power of GB versus EB and RB? To answer this question, we need to refresh our high-school biology class about human evolution. Most biologists would put the origin of the genus homo, "Lucy" the "first" human being, around 3.2 million years ago, for their ability (*habillis*) to use human-made tools.[33] Anthropologists discovered that Homo sapiens living in the Herto Village by the Awash River of Ethiopia probably practiced mortuary rituals around 160,000 years ago. This could be evidence that Homo sapiens began to develop their GB. About 40,000 years ago, the Neanderthals and Homo sapiens of the Middle Paleolithic and Upper Paleolithic developed sophisticated religious artifacts, along with language, drawing and ritual skills.[34] By 12,000 years ago, among all species of the genus homo, only Homo sapiens survived the viciously competitive world.

30. Cook, *Brief History*, 8.
31. Haidt, *Happiness*, 354–60.
32. Haidt, *Happiness*, 318.
33. Ghosh, "First human."
34. Trinkaus and Shipman, *Neanderthals*; Joseph, "Limbic System"; Logan, "Extended Mind."

The development of GB seemed to have enhanced Homo sapiens' competitiveness, but there is no way to tell how GB interacted with EB and RB then. So far, neuroscientists have only preliminary and still controversial speculations about their relationships due to the lack of large-quantity and high-quality experimental evidence. However, looking at religious practices of believers over the past 5,000 years across civilizations, it seems that GB and EB can be friends or enemies of different types, including equal footing, one-sided dominance, or unstable relations, pending on a human's nature and nurture. For instance, religious fanatics (e.g., suicide bombers) are willing to sacrifice their survival needs for a sacred cause. Regardless, most lay believers are willing to bend or ignore religious ethics when their survival needs (lust, violence, greed) are substantial. Pastors and priests face similar temptations every day: adultery with female believers or sexual assault on altar boys. With the invention of internet pornography, prostitution, and one-button shopping, the EB is getting a higher ground than GB. Bad news for personal finance!

Can RB come to help with GB to tame the reckless EB? Yes, they certainly can. Christian neuroscientist Justin L. Barrett called them "reflective beliefs" or "explicit beliefs."[35] Jeeves and Brown called them "higher-level loops," which distinguished Homo sapiens from chimpanzees.[36] However, as explained above, RB is usually the obedient slave of EB. Unless EB splits into two or more masters, the chances are not good for GB to overpower EB. This is not to say that GB always loses the war against EB. On the one hand, by nature or nurture, GB can grow in both size and power to hold EB at bay. This is the reason why religious leaders always encourage their believers to pray, read scripture, and perform religious rituals regularly. On the other hand, GB has an exclusive advantage over EB in its ability to develop concepts and values that are transcendental in time and space. This transcendence, holiness or sacredness provides abundant and powerful ammunition (endorphin, dopamine, or alpha-particles) to fight against the short-term, compulsive whims of EB.

Working together, GB and RB can regulate EB, particularly when EB has an internal split. But how does EB split? The split may come from the conflict between the selfish amygdala and other parts of the EB (the septum, hippocampus, and anterior cingulate). Amygdala puts personal survival and happiness first and above other people's survival and happiness; this is what

35. Barrett, *Cognitive Science*, 818.
36. Jeeves and Brown, *Neuroscience*, 654–76.

Richard Dawkins calls it the 'selfish gene."[37] However, other parts of the EB work to strengthen or regulate amygdala to provide an appropriate response to environmental stimuli. In particular, the anterior cingulate is the "white angel" in the brain, telling individual humans to love others and to perform altruistic behaviors. This neuroscientific finding may help to strengthen the thesis advanced by theorists of evolutionary morality like cultural anthropologist Christopher Boehm who hypothesized that through genetic and social evolution over 50,000 to 100,000 years, Homo sapiens probably by around 150,000 BC "were on the verge of cultural modernity . . . to becoming moral beings and to becoming significantly more altruistic than our more distant ancestors had been . . ." as well as more than other animals. By around 45,000 BC, the moral evolution of Homo sapiens "is likely to have become more genetically stabilized . . . an equilibrium would have been reached with respect to an optimized conscience and an optimized "altruism quotient."[38]

Evolution of humans at the collective level probably explains the existence of altruistic behaviors. Dawkins tried to explain these altruistic behaviors as results of selfish, rational calculation. Someone is an altruist only if altruism helps him to maximize his long-term selfish goals. So, parents love and care for their children only because they expect their children to take care of them when they get old. However, other biologists find this 'selfish gene" thesis difficult to explain most altruist behaviors which are instantaneous and even pose immediate threats to the altruist's life. For instance, some parents who do not know how to swim would immediately jump into a river to save their drowning children. Alternatively, most parents of permanently disabled children would tenaciously care for their children. Therefore, the alternative explanation is that there are "altruist genes" built into human brain as well so that the collective survival of human communities is maximized. Moreover, all human societies are equipped with educational institutions to encourage the growth of these altruist brain parts (especially the anterior cingulate) by promoting family values, tribal loyalty, social ethics, and nationalism.

This is not to say that altruist genes always trump selfish genes. They do not. In effect, it is more likely that selfish genes trump altruist genes in our daily life that make altruist behaviors so few and praise-worthy. But no human society can survive without a minimum level of instantaneous altruist behaviors. In addition to selfish incentives (salary, power and prestige), ethical codes and ethical institutions are critical for collective survival to guard against

37. Dawkins, *God Delusion*.
38. Boehm, *Moral Origins*, 321–22, 328–33, 336.

both threats from outside and within. The fact that in all major civilizations, religions have provided or sanctified long-lasting ethical codes suggests a close coalition between GB and RB at the collective level.[39] Social psychologist Jonathan Haidt argues that "respect for rules is enhanced when rules have an element of sacredness, and when they are backed up by supernatural sanction and the gossip or ostracism of one's peers."[40]

Why do humans need GB, RB and EB? What motivations that trigger us to use different parts of the brain in response to environmental stimuli? I propose three biological motivations of human behaviors: survival, happiness, and greed. The relationships among these motivations are depicted in Figure 2.1. These three motivations can work at both individual and collective levels.

Figure 2.1: Survival, Happiness, and Greed

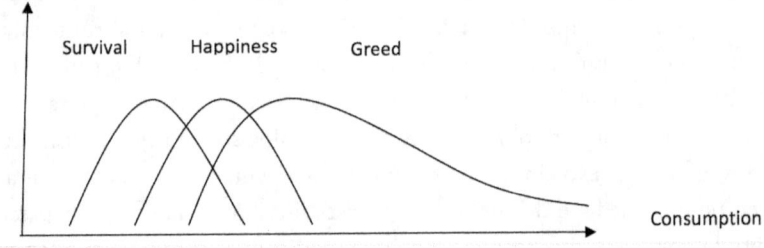

Evolutionary biology has built its theory on the assumption of "the survival of the fittest." At the individual level, or even at the cellular level, each human being needs to acquire a daily minimum of water, air and food to reproduce oneself (including procreation). Each person furthermore faces a constant threat from other people or animals who compete for these nutrients, or lives to satisfy their own survival needs. Therefore, the EB generates initial commands to body parts to acquire nutrients and to fight back threats. With the evolution of the rational brain, Homo sapiens continually invent sophisticated tools and human institutions to acquire nutrients in large and stable quantities to protect their survival. At the same time, Homo sapiens produce religions to strengthen the collective will and capacity of survival.

---

39. Alper, *"God,"* 3241–52.
40. Haidt, *Happiness*, 4284.

How much consumption, then, is needed to satisfy survival needs? The amount is both objective and subjective; it also varies among individuals. With the development of nutrition science, the objective amount of consumption can be defined by the World Health Organization. Although there is variation among individuals, the human body can only absorb so much food and water, beyond which apex they become wasteful or harmful to the body. Economists describe this consumption behavior as "decreasing marginal utility" of material consumption, as the parabola curves in Figure 2.1 show.

The survival need of security is also both objective and subjective and varies among individuals. Furthermore, it is a relative concept; the stronger the enemy, the less secure one feels. In theory of international relations, it creates spirals of arms races.[41] In Figure 2.1, this relative effect may move the survival curve to the right. That is, more consumption of goods and services is needed for people to compensate for their loss of sense of security.

Even before the need for survival is entirely satisfied, Homo sapiens have a strong motivation to seek happiness.[42] Happiness is built in our brain. The Darwinian law of evolution is not only "the survival of the fittest" but also "the survival of the happiest."[43] When we do something that conforms to our happy circuits, the brain releases large amounts of dopamine or the hormone oxytocin to keep us doing that. Although other species of animal also share some of this characteristic, the amount of time and energy Homo sapiens spend on "the pursuit of happiness" (American Declaration of Independence) probably finds few equals in the animal world. Furthermore, Homo sapiens look for happiness not just directly related to their survival needs, such as food and sex. They also engage in activities that are not directly related to survival needs (arts, music, entertainment, helping strangers, religion, etc.), or even harmful to their survival needs (alcohol, drugs, anorexia, cults, etc.).

We might think of happiness as an absolute concept concerning one's own consumption of material and spiritual goods. If I think I am happy, I am happy regardless of what other people say. Unfortunately, recent findings from positive psychology demonstrate that happiness has a strong relative aspect, too.[44] I am happier when I know that other people are not as happy as I am.

---

41. Jervis, *Perception*.

42. The founder of modern positive psychology, Seligman, *Authentic*, classified three types of positive emotions (happiness) associated with the past (satisfaction, contentment, fulfilment, pride, serenity), the present (momentary pleasures, gratification), and the future (optimism, hope, confidence, faith, trust). These types are too complicated for this book.

43. McMahon, *Happiness*, 421.

44. Carr, *Positive Psychology*, 34–35.

Or, I feel less happy when I learn other people are doing better. Several psychological experiments have been conducted with this similar format: A boy went into an experiment room and was given a chocolate cake. He was asked to describe his happiness by a number from 1 to 10. He chose 8. As soon as he chose the number, a girl came in and was given two chocolate cakes plus an ice cream. The boy was asked again to describe his happiness by a number from 1 to 10. He immediately chose 4 and cried out madly: "It's not fair!"

Happiness is a relative concept not only in an interpersonal sense but also in an intrapersonal sense. I am not happy this year because my salary remains the same as the previous year's. Or, "I am very depressed this year, because I get a five-percent cut in my salary, even though my annual salary is five million dollars," a Wall-Street banker would say. Consistent with the above analysis, neuroscientist Peter Whybrow uses more theories and data from neuroscience to explain "American Mania" of rampant consumerism and overconsumption, which would severely undermine any radical ecological program.[45]

Given external constraints, how can one maintain or increase her levels of happiness? Ancient Greek philosophers recommended that we look inside for a change.[46] If you cannot change the world, change yourself. If our neighbors are richer than us, ignore them. If my salary is cut by ten percent, I should be happy that I keep the ninety percent.

Rational as it sounds, this philosophical advice for happiness resolves only half, if not the superficial part, of the problem. We need to find compensation for the damaged ego by looking for alternative ways of happiness. "Happiness comes from within, and happiness comes from without," concludes positive psychologist Jonathan Haidt after combining the philosophic wisdom of the East and West with the results of psychological findings.[47] Later, I will argue that an effective ecological institution must provide both sources of happiness to ensure compliance.

When humans pursue relative happiness, many theologians and ecologists call this motivation as "greed." It is greed that differentiates Homo sapiens from other animal species. Once the survival need of Homo sapiens is wholly satisfied, they immediately become greedy. Greed is not just the excess of objective standards of survival needs as defined by nutritionists, or the World

---

45. Whybrow, *American*.
46. McMahon, *Happiness*, 24–75.
47. Haidt, *Happiness*, 156.

Health Organization. It is also the excess (or loss) of one's subjective happiness before and after other people's level of happiness is compared.

Among survival, happiness and greed, it is greed that seems to have the strongest aspect of relativity. A suburban entrepreneur is complacent to have a house with two-car garage and a Toyota car until her neighbor moves in and builds a mansion with a four-car garage for her four Mercedes, plus a heated swimming pool. Is this new neighbor happier? Yes, she is, until she finds out that the entrepreneur is her high-school classmate who stole her first love. Similarly, a clergy has all the needs of survival, happiness and greed too. To feed his family of four, he started with a pastor job in a small church in a poor neighborhood upon graduation from a theological seminary. After a few years, he moved on to a mid-sized church, to a mega church, and eventually became the president of a national church association. He could not be happier now because he received adorations from both the religious community and the political community. However, for greed, the sky is the limit. He entered the American presidential race. He wanted to be the leader of both the church and the state in order to restore God's kingdom on earth. In his campaign trail, he developed extra-marital affairs with his beautiful and competent assistant. The scandal broke out, and he retired to anonymity. The grass is always greener on the other side of the fence until you live with it.

This typology of survival, happiness and greed might be criticized for being too simple or too complex. It might be too simple because psychologists have developed more complex typologies, for instance, variations of Abraham Maslow's hierarchy of needs (physiological, safety, love/belonging, esteem, self-actualization, and peak experiences).[48] It might be too complex, with regard to ecological studies, because many ecological scholars prefer to use the dichotomy of "need" versus "greed."

I take a position halfway between the Maslow typology and the dichotomy of need versus greed to build a practical ecotheology. On the one hand, the Maslow typology is too complex for institution-building. Furthermore, it seems to justify all kinds of consumption behaviors. On the other hand, the dichotomy of need versus greed risks the danger of treating humans as animals by unduly compressing the scope of happiness.

There are biological, ethical and political reasons why we need to insert happiness between survival and greed. Biologically speaking, the pursuit of happiness is human nature. Ethically speaking, a human life without happiness is not worth living. Moreover, politically speaking, some extremist

---

48. Maslow, *Religions*.

ecological propositions to return lifestyles to the Puritan era or primitive agricultural society, when most non-religious forms of happiness were regarded as sin, are simply impractical. By differentiating happiness from greed, ecological institutions could target greedy consumption and re-direct happy consumption to ecologically friendly activities.

Another tricky part of human behaviors that relate to survival, happiness and greed in post-ecology is that human consumption of these goods and services do not stop at the top of the curves, i.e., where marginal increases in satisfaction from consumption is zero, the favorite "equilibrium" point of economists. According to neoclassical economics, it is not "rational" to consume additional units of goods and services after the equilibrium point because it will only bring a smaller amount of satisfaction than the previous unit of consumption. However, cognitive psychology tells us that humans are not as rational as economists assume. Human satisfaction derived from consumption of goods and services is more influenced by the total quantity, instead of marginal utility, of goods and services consumed. Most humans continue to consume after the point of equilibrium, e.g., I manage my academic works on three laptops and four 64-GB USBs. To any limit? The sky is the limit. That is why the curve of greed in Figure 2.1 does not intersect with the x-axis. Moreover, that is the root problem of ecological crises.

An excellent example of the application of the above neuroscience to the ecological issue is the work by anthropologist Kay Milton. She correctly points out the foremost reason why most ecological theories based on rationality fail to produce concrete ecological actions is that they assume ecological rationality automatically produces ecological actions. It does not. Instead, she argues that emotional attachment to ecological values provides a much stronger motivation than rationality to ecological actions. Furthermore, she thinks that one's religious belief matters. Sacredness describes what matters most to people among their personal values and results in commitment and action. "An enspirited landscape will still be a sacred landscape as long as spirit is what makes things most meaningful to people, what induces their strongest emotional responses. Similarly, wholeness, beauty and mystery will form the basis of sacredness wherever these are the most valued, the most emotionally powerful qualities."[49]

Kay Milton's arguments sit well with the eighteenth-century philosopher David Hume (1711 – 1776), who cautioned long ago about the proper relationships between rationality and emotion before any social justice policy can

---

49. Milton, *Loving Nature*, 104-5.

be adopted and implemented. Consistent with the neuroscientific findings discussed above, Hume correctly argued that "reason alone can never be a motive to any action of the will; and . . . it can never oppose passion in the direction of the will." That is, "Reason is, and ought only to be, the slave of the passions, and can never pretend to any other office than to serve and obey them." Derived from Hume's argument, the key to a successful ecological program is not to appeal to human rationality only, but, more importantly, to stimulate the human nature of "love," "compassion," or 'sympathy" (the functional area of the anterior cingulate). Then from where does love, compassion or sympathy come? Hume points to education, custom, repetition, conventions, government, and, reluctantly, religion, because he is not a big fan of religion.[50]

Neuro-Institutional Human

Cognitive psychology has long confirmed that human behavior is affected by not only what is going on inside the head but also outside the head, as well as the interaction between the inside and the outside. It is both nature and nurture that together affect human behaviors. In the discipline of psychiatric counseling, the family therapy approach was developed to deal with those patients who recovered from a Freudian in-hospital treatment and released back home but returned soon to the doctor with the same mental illness, or even worse. If their family members do not change their behaviors toward the patient, the patients are likely to suffer the illness forever, even though the patients take all the "rational" advice from the psychiatrist. The family therapy approach is also applicable to those patients who derived their illness from school or work environment.[51]

Neuroscientists have expertise in what is going on inside the head. They do acknowledge the influence of what is outside the head on what is inside. However, the outside world is too convoluted to fit into an experimental room. Therefore, in most of their experiments, they need to simplify (control) the outside stimuli to a few variables, and squeeze them into an audio or video machine behind a sound-proof door to test their hypotheses. Based on these experiments, some neuroscientists make hasty generalizations or reductionisms about the real world from what they observe inside the brain in a controlled laboratory. For instance, the love between a couple is defined as

50. Hume, *Treatise*, 21, 111–12, 121–22, 133–35, 189–205, 235–39, 310–11.
51. Barker and Chang, *Basic*.

nothing but an increase or decrease of pheromones; or, for the purpose of this book, God does not exist because they cannot find His smiling face on fMRI pictures; or, one can use electrical and chemical stimulants to create various religious hallucinations and behaviors.

Therefore, in order to get a fuller understanding of human behavior, we need to consult other social sciences theories to amend the weaknesses of neuroscientific findings. In particular, I choose the theories of new institutionalism developed in sociology, economics and political science in the past three decades due to their relevance to ecological theology.[52] The literature on new institutionalism is too vast to cover here. Nevertheless, there is a core assumption shared in this literature: both formal and informal institutions affect human behaviors. Formal institutions include constitutions, laws, government structures, associations, companies, community organizations, and families, which observers can find in formal documents or physical buildings. Informal institutions include culture, conventions, norms, social values, and peer pressure within and among formal institutions, which observers can describe by interviewing members of these institutions.

Although there are many similarities in the human brain, human behaviors are notoriously diversified across different ages, genders, families, communities, organizations, religions and states. At the same time, to maintain a minimum level of cohesion for collective survival and happiness, formal and informal institutions are developed to encourage conforming behaviors and to punish disruptive behaviors. Therefore, we need to consider the history, function, structure, power and content of these institutions (particularly church, capitalism and the state) to fully understand their impact on human behavior.

A laboratory-controlled experiment may not fully or correctly explain human behaviors. Take the famous Milgram Experiment for example. Subjects are brought to a laboratory to decide on whether another person in another room receives graduated electrical shocks. Unknown to the subject is that the other person will not actually receive the shocks. Even though most subjects realize that the final decision is likely to electrocute the other person, they go ahead and push the deadly button, only because they are told to do so by an actor who pretends to be the professor directing this experiment. The general conclusion from the experiment is that humans tend to obey authority; it is built into the brain. But is it? In controlling the responses of fight or flight, the amygdala may tell someone to submit to the authority, but it may

---

52. March and Simon, *Organizations*; North, *Institutions*; Rhodes et al., *Oxford*; Williamson, *Economic*.

also tell someone to fight against the authority. Family and school education may influence how subjects react to the fake professor's fatal instruction. However, it is more likely that the experimental design leaves little room for the subjects to make a different decision. Later experiments, which allow the subjects to consult one another (to set up a countervailing institution), reveal that more subjects would rise to challenge the professor. From the perspective of new institutionalism, the similarity and difference in human behaviors are determined not by what is inside the brain but also by what is outside the brain, and, more often, jointly by both.

New institutionalism suggests that institutions affect human behaviors. When institutions change, human behaviors are likely to change as well. Then, why would institutions make changes? Just like individual people, institutions need to survive to bring happiness to their members or to pursue the goals dictated by greed. When demands initiated from within the institution (e.g., leadership change) or from outside the institution (e.g., competition or merger), institutions would have to change their formal and informal rules.

The literature on Social Darwinism describes institutional changes like what Darwin describes as animal evolution. However, Social Darwinism errs on the side of overextending Darwin's principle of "survival of the fittest" to the principle of "survival of the strongest." In fact, in both the animal and human history, the strongest do not necessarily last longer than the fittest. Dinosaurs used to be the strongest and roamed the earth. They could not survive the Ice Age as the feebler hominids could. Great, historical empires equipped with overwhelming military forces, such as the Chinese, the Maya, the Greeks, the Romans, the British, Napoleon's France and German empires, rose and fell despite their mighty powers. However, major religions, such as Daoism, Judaism, Christianity, Buddhism and Hinduism adapted and survived largely without keeping an army of their own. Science has made humans the strongest animals on earth but is also taking humans along with the ecology down to the path of extinction. Human institutions need rapid adaptation to endure the incoming ecological collapse.

What enables an institution or culture to remain adaptable and long lasting? Although there are numerous explanations offered by social scientists, a general consensus is "diversity." Those cultures and institutions that suppress diversity and promote a homogeneous set of values may be efficient in the short-term mobilization of their human resources. However, when faced with large-scale natural or human disasters, past cultures and institutions often collapsed suddenly. By contrast, those cultures and institutions which allow or encourage a sufficient level of diversity tend to last longer and weather natural or human disasters more easily.[53]

New institutionalism is a critical component in any ecotheology since ecological crises are usually a collective-action problem of public goods. Game theorists use the metaphors of the Prisoners' Dilemma (PD) and public/collective goods to describe the dilemma of how individual rationality leads to collective irrationality.[54] In a PD game, two paroled suspects are arrested for committing a serious crime together. A wise prosecutor puts them in separate interrogation rooms and offers each a deal. If Suspect A betrayed his partner and confessed the crime, and if Suspect B refused to talk, then, Suspect A would be released immediately, and Suspect B would get the maximum penalty of 30 years in jail. If both suspects betrayed each other and told the truth, both would get 10 years in jail. If both suspects cooperated with each other and denied their involvement in the serious crime, the prosecutor could only put them in jail for 2 years for violating parole conditions. The same deal is offered to both suspects. It turned out that both suspects would betray the other and tell the prosecutor the whole truth even though both would be better off collectively by cooperating with each other and not telling the truth. That is, individual rationality leads to collective irrationality.

Figure 2.2: Prisoner's Dilemma

Suspect B

		No Truth	Truth
Suspect A	No Truth	A2, B2	A30, B0
	Truth	A0, B30	A10, B10

Game theorists also offer some possible solutions to the dilemma. Both suspects might ask a third party (e.g., a gang boss) to enforce cooperation

---

53. Diamond, *Guns*; Cook, *Brief History*; Davis, *Human Story*.
54. Hardin, *Collective*.

commitment between them so that the one who betrays his partner would be immediately murdered upon release from court. Moreover, the "honest" thief would receive better treatment from other cell-mates while in prison.

Most ecological problems have a similar payoff structure like the Prisoners' Dilemma. If I live in an ecologically friendly lifestyle and spend time and money to protect the ecology while other people do not, we all suffer from ecological crises. However, I would feel significantly more miserable because all my efforts to protect the ecology had gone down the drain without any visible improvements in the ecology. Therefore, no rational person would make any effort to protect the ecology, even though we all know that it is better for us to do so collectively.

In addition to the Prisoners' Dilemma, ecological problems are exacerbated by the very nature of ecological "goods." Clean environments and an ecological balance are "public/collective goods" in the sense that they are "indivisible" and "non-excludable." Indivisibility means that once the public goods (e.g., clean air and a public park) is supplied, someone's consumption of the public goods does not significantly reduce the amount of another person's consumption of it. Non-exclusiveness means that it will be very costly to exclude anyone from enjoying the public goods once supplied. So, when the public goods are supplied, everyone can enjoy it, including those "free-riders" who do not make any contribution to its supply. Hence, any rational person prefers not to make any contribution to the provision of public goods. Consequently, no public goods are supplied. All rational persons suffer from ecological crises even though they all know that they would be better off if the public goods are supplied.

For institutionalists, the solution to the Prisoners' Dilemma and the public goods problems is to design an institution which would change the material payoffs of cooperation and cheating so that any rational person would then choose cooperation over cheating. Game theorists prefer not to deal with preference change that involves non-material payoffs (such as praises from politicians, religious leaders, and mass media), because it would look "irrational." Thus, most ecologists have worked on rational material solutions, e.g., green tax, carbon quota trade, and pollution penalties. However, I will argue later that these material incentives probably have reached their limits, if indeed they actually worked to reduce the total amount of pollution. It is time to think about another set of institutions which may inspire the "irrational" part of people and voluntarily change the material payoffs by mixing in spiritual rewards and penalties.

One metaphor helps illuminate the importance of ecological solution at both individual and collective level. Can drug addicts and alcoholics treat themselves? Most cannot. They need to seek professional help from medical institutions. How do these medical institutions treat them? Do they gradually reduce the patient's consumption of drugs and liquors, or replace the patient's use of cocaine with methamphetamine ("Ice") and Johnny Walker with vodka in the hope to cure the original illness in a more "cost-effective" way? Or, as practiced in most medical institutions, they cut off any drug and alcohol supply to the patient and force the patient to join group therapy, usually with the help of local church workers. Likewise, we humans are easily addicted to exotic consumer products. Our ecology cannot be saved simply by encouraging "rational" consumers to continue using massive amount of "green products." The problem with both these medical institutions and most ecological institutions is that they do not or cannot cover most of the people who need such treatments, neither are they particularly effective in "curing" all the voluntary participants, and therefore, they have a negligible impact on the whole of society. Old habits die hard!

It is for the above reason that the institution of religion is so critical a solution to ecological problems. It has been the common premise of many inter-religious projects on the ecology, including the Deep Ecology movement and the Encyclopedia of Religion and Nature. If Lynn White is right that religion (Protestantism) is the major cause of ecological crises, these projects propose that all faiths should also be a critical part of the solution. Religions can provide sacredness to nature and place it at the top of all other social and materialistic values, hold liturgical services in honor of plants and animals to connect human experiences with nature, motivate believers to take political actions as their sacred responsibility, and educate children with ecotheologies.[55]

Ecological philosopher Roger S. Gottlieb explains how religious environmentalism can contribute to the ecology more effectively than secular liberalism or scientific ecotheories. First, it helps us to "grapple with the reality of our enormous carelessness and destructiveness" toward the ecology. Secondly, it provides us with "the proper language with which to express what we think and feel about what we"ve attended to." Singularly, it appeals to our guilt and repentance, pain and loss for destroying the sacred world God created. Finally, it inspires and sustains our hope for reconstructing a better world and reassures us "that though we should face up to our moral failings, we need not be paralyzed by the scope of what lies before us. We will not be able to fix

55. Barhhill and Gottlieb, *Deep*, 2–6; Taylor, *Encyclopediae*.

everything, for the only one responsible for "everything" is God. Nevertheless, it is up to us to do our part." All in all, religion is "the single strongest alternative to government, corporations, and consumerism."[56]

But not all religions can significantly contribute to ecology; it depends on whether they develop an ecological theology and religious organization compatible with ecological actions. Ecologist John B. Cobb, Jr. does not think primitive religions or Asian religions like Daoism, which many other ecologists have eulogized as alternatives to Christianity, are qualified to do the job.[57]

In his lifetime, theologian Reinhold Niebuhr (1892-1971) raised series of challenges to evangelical theologians: why do moral Christians constitute immoral societies?[58] In Western societies where Catholics and Protestants constitute the majority, why there exists child labor, class conflict, income inequality, gender inequality, and wars of aggression?

Evangelical theologians often assume that when a society is composed of a Christian majority, social justice will follow. It is not necessarily so, Niebuhr argued. The difference is institutional. Moral persons working in good institutions produce moral outcomes, but when moral persons are placed in an evil institution, they have no choice but to produce immoral outcomes, e.g., the Holocaust. The solution to immoral society, therefore, is to get both individuals and institutions right. The mission of the church should not be limited to the cultivation of righteous Christians, but should include active participation in social, economic and political reforms, as most ecotheologians would argue. Specifically, democratic institutions need to be constructed and consolidated to protect the weak from the strong. This is the central message of the Christian movement called the Social Gospel. This book will build on the central message of the Social Gospel to argue not only that the church is an indispensable part of any institutional solution to cope with ecological crises, but that the church itself needs to be democratized to become a solution, instead of another problem, to ecological crises.

Combining the above neuroscientific arguments with new institutionalism, this book proposes that those human societies which encourage a balanced development of institutions associated with rationality, emotion and spirituality may last longer and better weather through natural or human disasters than those institutions which appeal only to rationality. In this book, democracy is treated largely as an institution of rationality; capitalism

---

56. Gottlieb, *Greener*, 9–12, 15, 17, 83.

57. Cobb, *Is It Too Late*, 26–30.

58. Niebuhr, *Moral Man*.

is principally an institution of emotion (greed); and religion is an institution of spirituality. These institutions of rationality, emotion and spirituality also need to encourage a sufficient level of diversity from within in order to compete with other institutions of the same category. After all, human societies cannot last long if built upon partial human nature or inhuman nature. Unfortunately, most current ecological solutions are built upon the millennium-long premises of human rationality.

Rational Human, Posthumanism and Ecology

Before the rise of modern neuroscience, philosophers in the East and West developed their philosophies based on what human behaviors they observed and concluded as human natures. Some (founders of religions or religious philosophies) studied religious behaviors and concluded that religiosity is human nature. Some (hedonists) regarded happiness as the most important goal of human life which is short. So, enjoy your life and indulge in your desires as much as possible whenever you can. Others (e.g., Aristotle and Confucius) abhorred excessive religious and emotional behaviors and upheld rationality as the highest norm of human behaviors. It is the rationality school that seems to have had the dominant influence on ecological theories and theologies.

A comprehensive survey of philosophical discussions on human nature is beyond the scope of this book. It suffices to briefly comment on a few leading philosophers of the rationality school whose works might have a significant impact on ecological theories and theologies. The Greek culture dominated the Mediterranean Sea from about 400 BC to about 300 AD and was renowned for its plethoric origins of philosophies, particularly the philosophies of Plato and Aristotle. Plato (428-348 BC) was not happy with the moral chaos derived from the polytheist Greek culture. Although he probably had read portions of the Old Testament and was impressed with its concept of a morally perfect God, Plato preferred a moral system derived from rational education, through which philosopher rulers were trained. "The philosopher is in love with truth, not with the changing world of sensation, which is the object of opinion, but with the unchanging reality which is the object of knowledge." Among good political regimes which promoted morality and justice, he preferred monarchy (run by philosopher rulers) over aristocracy and timarchy (similar to modern democracy). He thought that among the degenerated forms of the good political regimes (tyranny, oligarchy and democracy), democracy (equivalent to modern ochlocracy) was the worst because it was ruled by emotional people.⁵⁹ As a student of Plato, Aristotle followed Plato's arguments about rationality and political regimes. However, he was friendlier to religion than Plato was. Aristotle thought that a king should be religious too because "if men think that a ruler is religious and has a reverence for the gods, they are less afraid of suffering injustice at his hands, and they are less disposed to conspire against him." Therefore, an office responsible for administering religious rituals is an indispensable part of a state. The public should pay for religious worship and a portion of public land should be used to the service of the gods.⁶⁰

It is this Greek rational culture with which the evangelists of the apostolic time and the ante-Nicene church grew up. They adapted their theologies to the rational Greek culture to convert the heathens. Luke wrote his Gospel and the Acts to a Christian gentile, Theophilus, and Paul called himself "an apostle of Gentiles."⁶¹ In their writings addressed to Roman officials, Clement of Alexandria, Clement of Rome, and Justin Martyr repeatedly cited Plato to support their arguments. Their "rational arguments," however, fell on deaf ears.

St. Augustine proved himself as a master of rationality by his classic theological work, the *City of God*, and an exterminator of emotion and desires by another classic theological work, the *Confessions*. St. Thomas Aquinas brought rationality to its zenith as a model of theological works. Still, one would wonder how many ordinary Christians nowadays actually read these rational theological works.⁶²

After Renaissance, the supremacy of rationality took yet another transformation: it became an intellectual Frankenstein separated from its mother theology and drove theology into the closet of the private sphere. Spinoza and John Locke pioneered the intellectual movement of the separation of state and church. Immanuel Kant constructed a "rational church" which could only exist on paper.⁶³ From then on, the incarnation of rationality (science and technology) became the panacea to cure all human problems — physical, social and even spiritual.

Therefore, when ecological problems surfaced, not only did few ecologists seek help from Christianity, many, such as Lynn White, even blamed

---

59. Plato, *Republic*, 49–55, 206.
60. Aristotle, *Complete Works of Aristotle*, 1834, 2039, 2087, 2108, 2110.
61. Rom 11:13.
62. Augustine, *Confessions*; *City*; Thomas Aquinas.
63. Spinoza, *Treatise*; Locke, *A Letter*; Kant, *Religion*.

it for creating ecological problems in the first place. With the continuous lightning-fast advancement of science and technology, some rationalists are promoting Transhumanism (or "Posthumanism") to solve ecological problems. They correctly pinpoint the root of ecological problems, i.e., the humans. It is the quantity of human population and the unlimited desires of human nature that make our ecology unsustainable. Science and technology can help us prevent the incoming ecological crises. On the one hand, the population can be rapidly reduced by the forcible application of birth-control devices and abortion to poor people, many of whom tend to produce more babies than wealthy people. On the other hand, new drugs, genome technologies, and artificial intelligence can speed up human evolution and create a new species of hominids called "transhumans," "posthumans," or "inhumans" who are entirely rational and have no need for emotion and religiosity, which they determine as irrational. In fact, many proponents of Transhumanism worship Nietzsche as their Pope.[64]

Although growing in popularity, particularly among scientists and neuroscientists, Transhumanism is still regarded as a pop science and strongly criticized by philosophers and humanists. Few ecologists would go so far as to endorse the Transhumanist solutions to ecological crises for a very simple reason: they are not human and humanistic. This book shall proceed with the assumptions of human natures of rationality, emotion and religiosity, and discuss their corresponding ecological institutions of democracy, capitalism and church. However, first, let us examine these human natures as they appear in the Bible in the next chapter.

Summary

This chapter aims to construct a micro foundation of ecological behaviors through theories and findings of cognitive science and institutionalism. Among the major findings of neuroscience, are: rationality, emotion and spirituality are all parts of human nature; by nature and nurture, individuals are different from one another in terms of their relative capacities of rationality, emotion and spirituality; rationality is often the slave of emotion; spirituality may regulate both rationality and emotion; human behaviors consist of both routines and adaptations; and humans employ their capacities of rationality,

---

64. On Transhumanism, see More and Vita-More, *Transhumanist*, Seidel, *Inhuman*. For a comprehensive critic of Transhumanism from a Christian perspective, see Cole-Turner, *Transhumanism*.

emotion and spirituality to pursue survival, happiness and greed. An effective ecological institution needs to be built on all these human natures. However, most current ecological theories and programs are overreliant on individual rationality, which easily leads to collective irrationality of ecological problems. If religious institutions, which specialize in spiritual behaviors, were the root of ecological problems, they cannot but be a significant part of the solution. But even if religious institutions become participants of ecological programs, they are subject to the same constraints imposed by human natures, thus, limiting their impact on ecological programs. The alternative of the rationality-based Transhumanism would only exacerbate ecological problems along with the destruction of humanities.

3.

Neurotheological Human

THE PREVIOUS CHAPTER DISCUSSES neuroscience findings concerning the human natures of emotion, rationality and spirituality, and their relationships with ecological institutions. This chapter applies the typology of human natures to the Bible to demonstrate that the Bible promotes a balanced development of human nature on which practical ecological programs can be built. This argument is based on the assumptions that God created both nature and natural law for the sake of humans, and that science and theology should not be considered as unrelated "two books": one about the scientific law, the other, ethics. As Jürgen Moltmann suggests: "Theologically, the book of nature was always read in the light of Holy Scripture . . . We must, of course, be able to reverse this order of things too, and must be able to read the Bible in the light of the book of nature . . . Only that which is compatible with scientific reason or which opens up for science new horizons of interpretation can count as divine revelation."[1] Science and theology are and should always be compatible with each other because God cannot contradict Himself, although being the creator of the universe God reserves the ultimate sovereignty to modify or suspend natural law according to His providence on the believers.

As theologian Fraser Watts proposes, "it really is central to theology to have a perspective on human nature. The vast majority of religious doctrines, at least in the monotheisms, is about the interaction between God and humanity."[2] Christian theology is and should be based on the Bible. If the Bible provides only a partial understanding of human nature, then any

1. Moltmann, *Sun*, 196.
2. Watts, "Psychology," 4855.

theology derived from the Bible is, at its best, a partial prescription for human behaviors, or a self-destructive mythology at its worst. Either way, Christians probably would not have survived the tribulations in different places of the world over the past two thousand years.

The neuro-institutional approach of this book cannot but take an anthropocentric position on ecology, which is consistent with the above assumption that God created both nature and natural law for the sake of humans. This position differs from the Deep Ecology theorists who prefer biocentrism or ecocentrism, which treat the biosphere or the ecology equally with, if not more important than, humans. It also differs from the Eastern Orthodoxy's cosmic spiritual ecology which treats human salvation as a part, not the center, of cosmic transfiguration.[3] This chapter will explain these differences.

So, can we find evidence of neuroscientific arguments in the Bible? The answer is not only a "yes," but we can argue that almost the entire Bible can be consistently interpreted by the neuroscientific arguments presented in chapter 2 of this book. In the following, the unit of analysis of the Bible is the chapter, not verse, because the sheer number of the latter is beyond the scope of this chapter. The total number of Biblical chapters is close to 1,200. It is easier to observe a major neurotheological theme in a chapter than a verse, although exemplary verses of each chapter will be highlighted in the following discussion. Biblical chapters are grouped into three categories: God brain (GB), emotional brain (EB), and rational brain (RB). However, even a casual reader of these chapters would find that these Biblical chapters often cover more than one category. In fact, most Biblical chapters cover all three categories of GB, EB and RB. For analytical purpose, however, it is still possible to locate one of the three major themes in these Biblical chapters (see Appendix 3.1). The criteria for categorizing Biblical chapters are explained at the beginning of each subsection below.

Before we proceed to the discussion of rational, emotional and God brains, a fundamental controversy about the origin of humans needs to be resolved before human brain is analyzed. Atheist biologists argue that humanity is evolved from primates (monkeys and apes). Conservative evangelicals insist that God created human, so says the Bible. Can a new Biblical exegesis provide a reasonable compromise between these two contradictory arguments? I think so.

---

3. For Deep Ecology, see Barnhill and Gottlieb, *Deep Ecology*. For Eastern Orthodoxy's ecological spirituality, see Chryssavgis and Foltz, *Toward an Ecology*.

Section 1 of this chapter discusses how Biblical verses can be reinterpreted to make evolution theory compatible with Creationism. Once we are confident that the scientific man is compatible with the theological man, sections 2 to 4 explain how Biblical chapters can be categorized into subjects of spirituality, emotion and rationality. Section 5 demonstrates that the Bible keeps a relatively balanced teaching about spirituality, emotion and rationality. This chapter completes the construction of a micro foundation of ecotheology, based on which macro ecotheologies about the institutions of the church, capitalism and democracy can be evaluated, which are the subjects of chapters 4 to 6. For most Christian readers, the following sections may look like "reading the Bible in a year" déjà vu. However, Biblical verses and stories are re-wired and re-interpreted to show their relevance to human natures. So, please bear with me.

Neurotheological Origin of Human

Traditional evolution theory traced the origin of the modern human race to about six million years ago when the first "human" developed distinctive traits apart from apes. What are these distinctive traits? Most evolution scientists think that it is the size and complexity of the brain. Some argue that humans began to walk on two legs (bipedal), which required a lot of energy, which stimulated the human brain to grow to aid its access to more supplies of food and protein. The growth of brain size enabled humans to invent sharp tools for hunting and killing wild animals as well as defending themselves against other predators. Other scientists, particularly neuroscientists, argue that size does not matter so much. Rather, it is the "fold" or "wiring" of the human brain that matters. For instance, the Neanderthals had a bigger brain and body than Homo sapiens. However, Homo sapiens developed more sophisticated weapons with which they annihilated the Neanderthals; probably the first "ethnic cleansing" in human history. In particular, the development of language capability enabled Homo sapiens to accurately communicate with one another, organize large-scale societies, develop new technologies, accurately pass survival information to the next generation, and thus prevail over all other animals in the world.

The term "Homo sapiens" was coined by Swedish zoologist Carl Linnaeus (1707-1778) in 1758. In biological classification, Homo sapiens is a Species of Homo, which in turn is a Genus of hominidae that is a Family of haplorhini, which belongs to the Order of primates. Among other physical features, Homo sapiens are distinguishable from other species of Homo in the size of the skull, particularly in the frontal lobe, which earned this species the name "Home sapiens" (man of wisdom).

About ten years ago, textbooks on anthropology assumed a linear line of human evolution using the analogy of a single tree.[4] They considered that Homo sapiens (250,000 to 300,000 years ago) and Homo Neanderthalensis (330,000 to 24,000 years ago) shared the same ancestor of Homo Heidelbergensis (1 million years ago). They furthermore surmised that Homo erectus shared the same ancestor of Homo Ergaster (1.8-1.7 million to 600,000 years ago), and Homo Habilis shared the same ancestor of Australopithecus Garhi (2.5 million years ago). They furthermore posited that Australopithecus Africanus and Australopithecus Aethiopicus shared the same ancestor of Australopithecus Anamensis (4 million years ago), who might be a descendant of Sahelanthropus Tchadensis (6 million years ago), who (or which) first developed a set of human DNAs different from apes.[5]

Later on, because of the discovery of new fossils and more accurate dating technology (e.g., carbon-14 dating, electron spin resonance dating, and uranium-series dating), the older linear tree map is not only frequently challenged and re-drawn, but more recently replaced by the hypothesis of multiple lineages, using the analogy of "bushes." Each one of the above fossils might come from different ancestors, other than the one found to exist earlier. The earlier human ancestors turned out to be extinct and had no direct genetic relationship with Homo sapiens. They might belong to different "bushes" of ancestral lines. Recently, some anthropologists even suggest that "If we want to be objective, we shall almost certainly have to scrap the iconic list of names in which hominid fossil specimens have historically been trapped, and start from the beginning by hypothesizing morphs, building testable theories of relatedness, and rethinking genera and species."[6]

According to the latest studies of human fossils and DNAs, they trace the "scientific Adam" and "scientific Eve" of the modern human race to the Homo sapiens about 60,000 years ago in East Africa. Earlier findings that human fossils are directly or indirectly related to the Australopithecus species have been questioned with regards to their relationships to the modern human. One example is the Neanderthals, whom some researchers believed

---

4. For instance, Scarre, *Human*, 58.

5. Historian Michael Cook put Homo sapiens between 130,000 and 50,000 years ago, with more confidence on the latter dating. Cook, *Brief History,* 8–9.

6. Schwartz and Tattersall, "Defining," 931–32.

co-existed with Homo sapiens in Western Europe from 40,000 to 24,000 years ago. Neanderthals were first regarded as the ancestor of Homo sapiens, until the hypothesis was rejected and they were found to be partial ancestors of some Homo sapiens.[7] In fact, the extinction of the Neanderthals and other "human" species might be due to combined deadly assaults of repeated glaciers, great floods, and, finally, ethnic cleansing by the Homo sapiens during the last glacier period about 110,000 to 12,000 years ago. In 2015, the discovery of Homo Naledi fossils in the Rising Star Cave in South Africa may throw away all hitherto human fossils and point to a unique lineage of the modern human race.[8] While the jury is still not out concerning the identification of the first human among evolution scientists, the Bible seems to have a different story to tell about human origin.

About the origin of the human race, the Bible says that on the sixth day of creation, "God created man in His own image, in the image of God He created him; male and female."[9] Although humans were created on the same day, woman was created after man: "Then the LORD God formed man of dust from the ground, and breathed into his nostrils the breath of life; and man became a living being." This man, named Adam, probably could not handle all the assignments God ordered, so God created a more capable companion, a woman named Eve, to help him do his jobs.[10] Furthermore, Eve was not made anew from dust, but from one of Adam's ribs, signaling a genetic relationship between Eve and Adam.

How do we reconcile the Biblical and biological accounts of the human origin? Theologians have different answers to the question, ranging from a total denial of any legitimacy of evolutionary explanation in the Bible to a total acceptance of evolutionary explanation in the Bible. Others take different degrees of literal explanation of the Bible to make evolutionary evidence compatible with Biblical verses. Barrett and Caneday conduct a comprehensive survey of the literature and group them into four perspectives on the Biblical origin of the human race: no historical Adam (Evolutionary Creation), a historical Adam (Archetypal Creation), a historical Adam (Old-earth Creation),

---

7. Tattershall and Schwartz, "Hominids," 7117–19.

8. Asu, "Institute of Human Origins."

9. Gen 1:27. The Biblical version cited here is the New American Standard Bible (NASB; 1995), unless otherwise noted. In the following paragraphs, verses from the same book of the Bible will be grouped together in their citation form.

10. Gen 2:7, 20–23.

and a historical Adam (Young-earth Creation); each represented by Denis O. Lamoureux, John H. Walton, C. John Collins, and William D. Barrick.[11]

The Evolutionary Creation perspective maintains that God created humans, but He created humans by a slow evolutionary process. The literal interpretation of the Adam story is based on "ancient conceptualization of biological origins," and is as erroneous as the conceptualizations of the 3-tier universe and the flat earth by Biblical authors. The Archetypal Creation perspective holds that Adam and Eve are historical figures. However, they are better explained as archetypes of human spirituality and sin rather than the biological origins of modern humans. Archetypes do not rule out the possibility that Adam and Eve were two real persons. The Old-earth Creation perspective upholds Adam and Eve as two real persons, the first humans created by God, but they were created much earlier than the literal interpretation of the Bible would suggest. More importantly, a biological explanation is not appropriate for the interpretation of the Adam story, which is all about the religious relationship between God and humans. Finally, the Young-earth Creation perspective insists on the literal interpretation of the six-day creation and the whole Adam story, without any room for flexibility given to the evolutionary evidence. Adam and Eve were two real persons, period! Proponents of this perspective worry that the inerrancy of the Bible is at stake if it yields an inch of ground to evolution theory.

Combining the strengths of the above perspectives, I offer four basic principles for the reconciliation of Biblical verses and evolution evidence concerning the human origin. First, the inerrancy of the Bible is assumed, but human interpretations of the Bible may have flaws. As neuro-institutional humans, we simply do not have full capability and information to understand the exact meaning of every word and every verse of the Bible written in Hebrew and Greek. The best strategy of exegesis, therefore, is to combine the most credible interpretations and treat it as the least erroneous interpretation, which may be replaced by a better interpretation in the future. Secondly, Genesis chapters 1 to 11 are usually treated as pre-historical documents based on oral mythologies passed down by Abraham, edited by Moses, and recorded by theologians of much later generations. These mythologies were written to convey important religious and ethical teachings, often at the expense of historical and grammatical clarity (not errors though). Thirdly, authors of the Bible were constrained by their scientific knowledge when they wrote down what God revealed to them about nature and natural law. It is as unfair to ask

11. Barrett and Caneday, *Four Views*.

scientists to elaborate the ethics of the Big Bang theory as to ask the authors of the Bible to write DNAs and quantum physics into the creation story. Lastly, the Trinitarian God and Jewish teachers (patriarchs, prophets, and apostles) seemed fond of parables and archetypes as pedagogical tools. Therefore, some verses and stories probably should be interpreted as such and not as scientific data published in the journal of *Science*.[12]

With these four principles of exegesis in mind, the biological and Biblical accounts of the human origin can now be made compatible. That is, Genesis 1-11 should be interpreted as pre-historical mythologies filled with parables to lay down the fundamental religious and ethical catechism of Judo-Christianity, often at the expense of historical and grammatical clarity (but not errors). Genesis consists of five stories about human origins that are consistent with the evolution theory: the creation of man and woman; Cain killed Abel; the other human species in the genealogy from Adam to Noah; the Great Flood; and the intercontinental migration of human species described in the story of the Babel tower.

First, the humans God created as described by Gen 1:27 are probably not the human species of the "Lucy" genre of the Australopithecus 3.2 million years ago,[13] but the descendants of the Homo sapiens of 200,000 years ago (the Omo1 and Omo2 skeletons in the Ethiopian Omo River).[14] In the eyes of Genesis's authors, Lucy and her/its genre, as well as other Hominids, were probably categorized as monkeys or apes that God created in the morning of the sixth day before He created Adam. Who were the first "humans"? When did it happen? Are they the "scientific Adam" and "scientific Eve?" We do not know. However, God picked them out of other Homo sapiens and "created" them with "dust" and "breath."

How do we interpret Gen 2:7 that "God formed man of the dust of the ground, and breathed into his nostrils the breath of life; and man became a living soul"? To the author of Genesis, there was no way he could describe the creation of man in the modern scientific way. He could only use the terms of "dust" and "breath" as the construction materials. What do exactly "dust" and "breath" mean? We do not know. They could be anything modern sciences refer to: DNAs, chemical compounds, or re-wiring of brain circuits. Similarly,

12. For a seminal work of neo-evangelical exegesis principles, see Osborne, *Hermeneutical*.

13. Ghosh, "First human." Lucy is the common name referring to a set of bone fragments, AL 288-1, found in the Awash Valley of the Afar Triangle in Ethiopia. It is regarded as the earliest hominin (genus Homo).

14. Hopkin, "Ethiopia."

Eve was created from Adam's rib. What does the "rib" mean? Could it refer to a shared new DNA with Adam? The author of the Bible could not have known, nor can we be sure. The bottom line is that God caused Adam and Eve to be created. They could be real persons or, more likely, archetypes.

The second Biblical story of the human origin consistent with the evolution theory comes later in Genesis; it surfaced after the story about Cain killing Abel. Cain, a keeper of flocks, was first born to Adam and Eve. Abel, a tiller of the ground, was Cain's brother. In their performance of a religious ritual, God had regard for Abel and his offering, but not for Cain and Cain's offering.[15] Coincidentally, anthropologists discovered that Homo sapiens living in the Herto Village by the Awash River of Ethiopia probably practiced mortuary rituals around 160,000 years ago. About 40,000 years ago, Neanderthals and other Homo sapiens in the Middle Paleolithic and Upper Paleolithic developed sophisticated religious artifacts, along with language, drawing and rituals.[16]

Out of jealousy, Cain killed Abel. God discovered the murder and expelled Cain from where he had tilled. Cain begged God for mercy on his life. He explained it to God: "Behold, You have driven me this day from the face of the ground; and from Your face I will be hidden, and I will be a vagrant and a wanderer on the earth, and *whoever* finds me will kill me."[17] This verse offers the first clue of human origin in the Bible. Who was this "whoever" in the verse? After Adam and Eve were brought to life, Genesis 1-3 never mentioned that there was a fifth human-being other than Adam, Eve, Cain and Abel. Was this "whoever" another human species in existence prior to or concurrently with the human species of Eve and Adam?

In addition, following the Archetypal Creation perspective, the story of Cain killing Abel could be describing the centennial wars between gatherer-hunter nomads (Abel) and agricultural tribes (Cain) in the early history of Homo sapiens, not of other species of Homo erectus.[18] Anthropologists have concluded that in most of these wars, agricultural tribes usually won due to their larger population and more advanced social organizations. So, it was Cain who killed Abel, not the other way around. As to the dating of the story of Cain killing Abel, it could not have been earlier than the emergence of human agriculture 11,500 years ago. It also means that there is a gap of tens

---

15. Gen 4:2-4.
16. Trinkaus and Shipman, *Neanderthals*.
17. Gen 4:14.
18. Diamond, *Guns*, chaps. 4-6.

of thousands of years between the creation of Adam and Eve and the story of Cain killing Abel. Cain and Abel were descendants of Adam and Eve, but thousands of years apart.

The third Biblical story of human origin consistent with the evolution theory is in Genesis 5 as a prelude to Noah's story. At the beginning of Genesis 5, the author reconfirmed God's creation of man and woman. "In the day when God created man, He made him in the likeness of God. He created them male and female, and He blessed them and named them Man in the day when they were created." After a long list of genealogy from Adam to Noah (probably more likely to be archetypes or tribes than real persons), a strange mythology about human races was introduced in Genesis 6. "[T]he sons of God saw that the daughters of men were beautiful; and they took wives for themselves, whomever they chose." Furthermore, "[t]he Nephilim were on the earth in those days, and also afterward, when the sons of God came in to the daughters of men, and they bore children to them. Those were the mighty men who were of old, men of renown." [19] Who were these "sons of God," "the Nephilim," and the "mighty men of renown"? The latest findings about the Neanderthals might be consistent with these Biblical verses. Many of them were found to be taller and stronger than the Homo sapiens who came to Europe later and was probably responsible for the ethnic cleansing of the Neanderthals. These stories about the 'sons of God," "Nephilim," and the "mighty men of renown" could have happened before the story of Cain and Abel. Or, they were describing the events related to other descendants of Adam and Eve. Exact dating and sequencing was not a major concern for the authors of Gen 1-11. They were more interested in the proper relationships between God and humans.

The fourth Biblical story of human origin consistent with the evolution theory is what happened after the Great Flood. The flood destroyed all living creatures on land. All human races, including the "whoevers,""sons of God,""the Nephilim," the "mighty men of renown," and even the descendants of Adam and Eve, with the exception of the Noah family (Homo sapiens), perished in the Great Flood, which might be archetypes of all the great floods in the last glacier period from 110,000 to 12,000 years ago. The evangelical story of human origin is remarkably consistent with evolution theory in that humans were under constant selection processes. Their difference lies in the selection criteria: by natural environment according to evolution theology, and by God for their religious and moral values.

19. Gen 5:1-2; 6:2-4.

Lastly, Genesis 11 ends the mythology about human origin with yet another mythology which probably described this intercontinental migration. "Now the whole earth used the same language and the same words" is probably a sentence alluding to the common origin of Homo sapiens in Africa. However, the migrant Homo sapiens developed their own languages and religions. In the eyes of Biblical authors, this is not good. Therefore, through a mythology about a high tower (Babel) which migrant Homo sapiens built probably for religious purposes, "the LORD confused the language of the whole earth; and from there the LORD scattered them abroad over the face of the whole earth."[20]

By this far of reading, conservative evangelists might have raised their hands high up in the air and cried wolf: "This neurotheological account of human origin is tantamount to a denial of God's existence and creation. Is the Biblical creation story only a myth created in and by the human mind where God is only a fictional figure?" No, the above neurotheological account does not refute the existence of God, nor the role of God in creation. As clearly stated in Genesis, it was God who created the universe and humans. However, how He created them and how fast, we are not sure. On the one hand, the authors of Genesis simply did not have the scientific knowledge to record the creation method and process. Thus, they would have used ambiguous Hebrew words of "dust," "rib," "fresh," and "breath/wind" to describe the materials God used to make a human, and used words of "day" and "generations" to describe God's perspective of His time or of His sequence of creation. A neo-evangelical theology may safely assume that God created other species of genus Homo and other primates with different materials or lack of certain materials (implied by the word "breath/wind") to build the frontal and parietal lobes of Homo sapiens. If conservative evangelists truly want to be "literal" about the Bible, they should be aware that the Hebrew language is often "literally" ambiguous across context and time. Some Hebrew words had different meanings and even pronunciations in different historical periods and locations. On the other hand, if God had told the authors of Genesis in modern biological jargons, they probably would be very much confused and frightened by these scientific languages. Thus, what is an acceptable compromise between biology and the Bible is the possibility that Genesis was describing the origin of Homo sapiens (Adam and Eve), but not the first genus Homo (Lucy) or other primates.

20. Gen 11:1, 9.

Once we establish a truce between creationism and evolutionism about human origin, similar exegetical methods are applied to what exists inside human brain in the following sections. Not surprisingly, among the 1,189 Biblical chapters, with the exception of only a handful of chapters that deal with genealogy or greetings, most chapters address rules and behaviors related to the Godly, emotional and rational brains. Appendix 3.1 summarizes these Biblical chapters.

God Brain in the Bible

Those Biblical chapters related to the God brain aim to arouse the believers' feelings of a transcendent, omnipotent, omnipresent and glorious God. Most of these Biblical chapters overlap with those of emotional brain and rational brain because God is always present in the latter two categories of chapters. However, chapters of the God brain are distinctive from the other two categories by the relatively non-personal presence of God in these chapters. God is transcendent, omnipotent, omnipresent and glorious for and by His own sake. The personal God, either via emotional feeling or rational reasoning, is not prominent in these chapters of the God brain.

With so much emphasis on God in the Bible, it might come out as a surprise to God-centered theologians that the number of such chapters is only about 120 out of the total 1,189 chapters, less than ten percent. This number lends support to the theological arguments that the Christian God is mainly a personal God and that the Bible is about God as much as, if not more, about Man.

For instance, Genesis 1:1-25 describes the omnipotent God creating the universe, time, and earth. Not until the last five verses of Genesis 1 was Man brought to a relationship with God. The book of Job further reveals a transcendent God who is beyond personal emotion and rational thinking. The good old Job thought that this God was his personal God and he followed all the religious rituals and moral codes God prescribed for him. This "personal" God rewarded him handsomely with ten children, 7,000 sheep, 3,000 camels, 500 yokes of oxen and 500 female donkeys. Satan challenged God in a way that modern neuroscientist would do in an experiment: Does Job obey God because God is transcendent and glorious for His own sake or because God is a personal God who bestows favors to devoted believers? God accepted the challenge and let Satan torment Job at will. When Job suffered from Satan's torture and lost everything, he felt God was doing injustice to him and was so aloof about his predicaments. He complained to God in his mind. Job's friends thought likewise. They thought Job must have done something wrong in his mind or behaviors that deserve God's harsh punishment. They urged Job to repent, but Job refused to do so. Both sides engaged in an endless debate about the personal God until God directly spoke to Job in chapter 38 about His transcendence. "Where were you when I laid the foundation of the earth? Tell Me, if you have understanding. Who set its measurements? Since you know. Or who stretched the line on it? On what were its bases sunk? Or who laid its cornerstone?" After these opening statements, God continued to bombard Job with numerous questions of creation and natural law to expose Job's minuscule rationality. Finally, Job gave up as any rational human would and realized that God was not just his personal God but much more a transcendental God who is above all creation and natural law: "I know that You can do all things, and that no purpose of Yours can be thwarted. Who is this that hides counsel without knowledge? Therefore I have declared that which I did not understand, things too wonderful for me, which I did not know ... Therefore I retract, and I repent in dust and ashes." Only after Job understood God's transcendence did God become Job's personal God again by rewarding him with another ten children, 14,000 sheep, 6,000 camels, 1,000 yokes of oxen and 1,000 female donkeys.[21]

The Psalm contains about eighteen chapters praising God's transcendence, omnipotence and glory. A few examples are illustrated here. "The voice of the LORD is upon the waters; The God of glory thunders, The LORD is over many waters ... The voice of the LORD hews out flames of fire." "Before the mountains were born or You gave birth to the earth and the world, even from everlasting to everlasting, You are God. You turn man back into dust and say, 'Return, O children of men. For a thousand years in Your sight are like yesterday when it passes by, or as a watch in the night.'" The Psalmist urged all believers, angels, hosts, creatures, and the universe to praise God for His creation and His natural law, including the human law governing "kings of the earth and all peoples; princes and all judges of the earth."[22]

The Ecclesiastes explicitly ridicules the limits of human rationality and emotional desires to live a peaceful and joyful life. "Vanity of vanities," says the Preacher, "Vanity of vanities! All is vanity!" For those who seek comprehensive knowledge about the world, the Preacher advised them to stop the nonsense, because "that which has been is that which will be, and that which

---

21. Job 1:2–3; 38:4–6; 42:2–6; 42:12–13.
22. Pss 29:3, 7; 90:2–41; 48:11.

has been done is that which will be done. So there is nothing new under the sun." Contemporary professors certainly can benefit from the Preacher's another reminder that "the writing of many books is endless, and excessive devotion to books is wearying to the body." For those who work their hearts out to accumulate wealth, the Preacher proclaimed their vanity because "riches being hoarded by their owner to his hurt." He further warned the wealthy people that "a man to whom God has given riches and wealth and honor so that his soul lacks nothing of all that he desires; yet God has not empowered him to eat from them, for a foreigner enjoys them. This is vanity and a severe affliction." What is the alternative to rational and emotional means to live a peaceful and joyful life? The Preacher concluded: "Fear God and keep His commandments, because this applies to every person."[23] It is this admonition against the human obsession with rationality and emotion that the word "vanity" is applied to criticism in chapters 4 to 6 of those ecological programs which rely too much on rational solution and succumb too much to emotion (e.g., to encourage the consumption of green technology).

The fact that God is sometimes above human rationality and emotion is revealed in the book of Jonah. Jonah was an ethnocentric (nationalist) prophet who projected his nationalism to God as a nationalist God exclusively of and for the Israelis. He could not understand why the Israeli God would send him to the Assyrian capital of Nineveh to proclaim God's forthcoming destruction of this sinful city. The Assyrians had been Israel's archenemy for generations. After the reluctant prophet had proclaimed the message in Nineveh, the Assyrians repented and were spared from destruction. Jonah had every ethno-rational and ethno-emotional reason to be mad with God, which he did. At the end of the book of Jonah, God patiently explained to him about His universal and transcendental nature: "should I not have compassion on Nineveh, the great city in which there are more than 120,000 persons who do not know the difference between their right and left hand, as well as many animals?"[24] God is not only the God of the Israelites, but also the God of humans, and even of all creatures.

Moving from the transcendental God in the OT, the Gospel of John aims to make the argument that Jesus is God and is, therefore, also transcendent, omnipresent, omnipotent and glory. At the beginning of the Gospel of John, the author employed thirty-four verses to elaborate the Trinitarian nature of

---

23. Eccl 1:2, 1:9; 12:12; 5:13; 6:2; 12:13.

24. John 4:11.

Jesus.[25] However, the Greek text of John 1:1 summarizes this Trinitarian theology: "In the beginning was the Word, and the Word was with God, and the Word was God." The Greek text rendered: "Ἐν ἀρχῇ ἦν ὁ λόγος, καὶ ὁ λόγος ἦν πρὸς τὸν θεόν, καὶ θεὸς ἦν ὁ λόγος." The NASB edition (and other English versions) does not quite capture the real meaning of the Greek text due to the limitations of English grammar. First, the equative verb, ἦν (*ein*), is an imperfect tense, meaning an action which was going on for a while, and should not be translated in aorist tense which means that the action occurred and finished in the past. So, a better translation should be something like: "In the beginning, there had been the Word, and the Word had been with God." That is, the Word (Jesus) had been there when God created the universe. The Word was NOT created by God along with the universe. God cannot and does not create Himself. Secondly, the last part of the verse "the Word was God" is not a full presentation of the Greek textual meaning either. For one thing, it should be translated as "the Word had been God." For another, the "God" (θεός; *theos*) does not have an article and is likely to denote a quality of God, not the substance of God. So, the Greek text is better rendered as "the Word had been Godly (or, of God)." In the NT, most verses use "God" to refer to the first persona of the Trinitarian God, especially when the second (Jesus) or third (Spirit) persona is mentioned in the same verse. With an article, "God" usually denotes the Trinitarian God or to gods of other religions.[26] Finally, let us not ignore the "and" (καί; *kai*) in the verse. There are two "and"s in the verse, which means that the three parts of the verse should be linked closely, if not as identical in content. These two instances of *kai* establish solidly the Trinitarian and transcendental nature of Jesus, which no other human can share.

The Hebrews further elaborates on the holiness, transcendence and Trinitarian nature of Jesus. First, the theological status of Jesus is categorically above all angels and all the prophets in the OT. With regard to the angels, Jesus is the One "whom He (God) appointed heir of all things through whom (Jesus) also He (God) made the world. Moreover, He (Jesus) is the radiance of His (God's) glory and the exact representation of His (God's) nature, and upholds all things by the word of His (God's) power. When He (Jesus) had made purification of sins, He sat down at the right hand of the Majesty on high, having become as much better than the angels, as He has inherited a more excellent name than they." In connection with the great prophets like

---

25. John 1:34.
26. Wallace, *Greek Grammar*, 257-259, 266-269.

Moses, they were only good servants of God. No matter how good they were, they remain servants. However, Jesus belongs to a different category, as He was the son of God. So the author of the book of Hebrews makes a clear distinction: "Moses was faithful in all His house as a servant, for a testimony of those things which were to be spoken later; but Christ was faithful as a Son over His house— whose house we are, if we hold fast our confidence and the boast of our hope firm until the end."[27]

The book of Hebrews continues to address the unique status of Jesus over other great priests like Aaron. To function as a priest for the Israelis, Aaron was appointed by Moses. However, Jesus was appointed, according to the order of Melchizedek, by God as the one and only one priest for all humans. Jesus is "a high priest, holy, innocent, undefiled, separated from sinners and exalted above the heavens, who does not need daily, like those high priests, to offer up sacrifices, first for His own sins and then for the sins of the people, because this He did once for all when He offered up Himself."[28]

Lastly, the transcendence of the Holy Spirit is frequently mentioned in the New Testament, not in chapters though, but in many verses. The presence of the Holy Spirit in the NT takes four forms: the Holy Spirit gives power to the receiver (Jesus or believers); the Holy Spirit is holy and the truth; the Holy Spirit is from God; and the Holy Spirit dwells in the receiver (Jesus or believers). We will come back to the first form when we discuss the emotional brain, because most of these verses, particularly those verses in the book of Acts, describe the relationships between the Holy Spirit and His receiver.

In addition to the frequent entitlement of the Spirit with the word "Holy" (ἅγιος; *hagios*), several NT verses mentions the holiness of the Holy Spirit in other manners. "Go therefore and make disciples of all the nations, baptizing them in the name of the Father and the Son and the Holy Spirit," says Matt 28:19 about the Trinitarian nature of the Holy Spirit. "Whoever blasphemes against the Holy Spirit never has forgiveness, but is guilty of an eternal sin," says Mar 3:29 about the holiness of the Holy Spirit; so does Luke 12:10. Other verses (particularly in the Gospel of John) refer to the Holy Spirit as the "truth" (ἀλήθεια; *aleitheia*): "The Spirit of truth, whom the world cannot receive"; "When the Helper comes, whom I will send to you from the Father, that is the Spirit of truth who proceeds from the Father"; and "when He, the Spirit of truth, comes, He will guide you into all the truth."[29]

27. Heb 1:2–4; 3:5–6.
28. Heb 5:10; 7:26–27.
29. John 14:17; 15:26; 16:13.

These verses in the Gospel of John, and many more verses in other books of the NT, also elevate the religious status of the Holy Spirit to that of God by explicitly mentioning that the Holy Spirit is from God. These other verses include: "Therefore having been exalted to the right hand of God, and having received from the Father the promise of the Holy Spirit, He (Jesus) has poured forth this which you both see and hear"; "And we are witnesses of these things; and so is the Holy Spirit, whom God has given to those who obey Him"; "You know of Jesus of Nazareth, how God anointed Him with the Holy Spirit and with power";[30] "For to us God revealed them through the Spirit"; "But a natural man does not accept the things of the Spirit of God"; "the Holy Spirit who is in you, whom you have from God";[31] "The grace of the LORD Jesus Christ, and the love of God, and the fellowship of the Holy Spirit, be with you all";[32] "Do not grieve the Holy Spirit of God";[33] and "he who rejects this is not rejecting man but the God who gives His Holy Spirit to you."[34]

What is most relevant to the Biblical neurotheology is the reference to the Holy Spirit residing in the receiver (Jesus or the believers). "Immediately coming up out of the water, He (Jesus) saw the heavens opening, and the Spirit like a dove descending upon Him";[35] "you will receive power when the Holy Spirit has come upon you"; "Then they began laying their hands on them, and they were receiving the Holy Spirit"; "the Holy Spirit fell upon all those who were listening to the message"; "when Paul had laid his hands upon them, the Holy Spirit came on them";[36] "through the Holy Spirit who dwells in us, the treasure which has been entrusted to you";[37] "whom (Spirit) He poured out upon us richly through Jesus Christ our Savior";[38] and "who also sealed us and gave us the Spirit in our hearts as a pledge."[39]

The Bible does not clearly state where in the human body the Holy Spirit stays. Moreover, it is very likely that most authors of the Bible thought it was the human heart where the Holy Spirit stayed; for instance, "who also sealed

---

30. Acts 2:33; 5:32; 10:38.
31. 1Cor 2:10; 2:14; 6:19.
32. 2Cor 13:14.
33. Eph 4:30.
34. 1Thess 4:8.
35. Mark 1:10; see also Luke 3:22 and John 1:32 for the same reference.
36. Acts 1:8; 8:17; 10:44; 19:6.
37. 2Tim 1:14.
38. Titus 3:6.
39. 2Cor 1:22.

us and gave us the Spirit in our hearts as a pledge." Given the limited medical knowledge at the time, this primitive conjecture is not a surprise. Many ancient philosophers made the same mistake. However, most of these verses in the NT point out that the brain is probably either the entry point or the location where the Holy Spirit stays.[40] Particularly, in most of these verses, the use of Greek grammar of accusative nouns, instead of genitive or dative nouns, as receivers of the Holy Spirit implies that the Holy Spirit literally enters the human body instead of staying above or on (upon) it.[41] For instance, in Mark 1:10 "Immediately coming up out of the water, He saw the heavens opening, and the Spirit like a dove descending upon Him," the NASB renders "descending upon Him." However, the Greek text is καταβαῖνον εἰς αὐτόν. Not only the accusative noun of αὐτόν (Him; *auton*) is used, the preposition εἰς (*eis*) is often translated as "into." So, the correct translation should be: "the Spirit like a dove descending *into* Him." Similarly, "when Paul had laid his hands upon them (the Ephesian believers), the Holy Spirit came on them" (Act 19:6). The first "them" is a dative noun αὐτοῖς (*autois*), so the translation "hands upon them" is correct; Paul's hands cannot enter inside the believers. However, the second "them" is a prepositional phrase with an accusative noun ἐπ' αὐτούς (*ep autous*), the NASB translation "the Holy Spirit came on them" is incorrect, and it should be "the Holy Spirit came *into (or inside)* them." In sum, if there is a suitable and comfortable suite in the human brain to host the Holy Spirit, the parietal lobe is probably the best choice.

Now, according to the Bible, the human brain may host the Holy Spirit, it may also host evil spirits. There are three logical relations between the Holy Spirit and evil spirits existing in the human brain: (1) the Holy Spirit is present while evil spirits are not; (2) the Holy Spirit is not present while evil spirits are; and (3) both the Holy Spirit and evil spirits are present. Biblical verses support the first two relations, but never the third. The Bible indicates that those prophets, apostles and believers, once received the Holy Spirit, would not be possessed by evil spirits. Only those who never received the Holy Spirit and those whose Holy Spirit left them, would evil spirits be able to enter their brain. Those possessed people on whom Jesus and His apostles performed exorcism were all non-Christians.[42]

There are a couple of probable exceptions in the Bible, but these exceptions only prove the rules. The case of Saul is an exception that proves the

---

40. Mark 1:10; Acts 8:17, 19:6.
41. Wallace, *Greek Grammar*, 369–371, 376.
42. Matt 9:32-34; Mark 1:21-28; Luke 4:31-37; Acts 8:7, 10:38, 16:18; 19:12.

rule. Saul received the Spirit after Samuel anointed him as the king of Israel. But after he repeatedly disobeyed Samuel, the Spirit left him first, then, the evil spirit entered his mind.[43] Was Peter possessed when Jesus scolded him by saying "Get behind Me, Satan! You are a stumbling block to Me; for you are not setting your mind on God's interests, but man's"?[44] Probably not. For one thing, Jesus was probably referring to the demonic idea in Peter's mind, rather than the demon in his mind. Otherwise, a simple exorcism performed by Jesus on Peter would do. For another, the Holy Spirit had not yet descended upon the believers until the Pentecostal. So was the case of Judah. "Satan entered into Judas . . . he went away and discussed with the chief priests and officers how he might betray Him to them."[45] Again, if Satan literally entered into Judas' mind, then, Judas should not be held responsible for conspiracy against Jesus; a simple exorcism by Jesus would do. Likewise, is the case of Ananias and his wife, Sapphira.[46]

Emotional Brain in the Bible

There are about 340 Biblical chapters that discuss the personal relationships between God and human emotion. These chapters can be further divided into two categories: (1) Mutually beneficial relations between God and human emotion; (2) God provides grace and protection to His believers against or beyond considerations of justice and human rationality.

The first category constitutes the overwhelming majority of these Biblical chapters. They describe or stipulate mutually beneficial relations between God and human emotion. On the one hand, God provides protection, grace and blessings to His believers to satisfy their emotional needs, such as safety, food, property, happiness, a unique personal relationship with God in the form of father and children. On the other hand, believers are urged to love, praise, talk and sing to God to please God. God blessed "happiness" is such an important theme in the Bible that it occurs in one hundred and seven verses in twenty forms.[47] Even when Jesus, His disciples, and ante-Nicene martyrs were suffering from Roman and Jewish persecutions, they continued to en-

---

43. 1Sam 10:9; 16:14.

44. Matt 16:23.

45. Luke 22:3–4.

46. Acts 5:1–11.

47. BibleWorks, search "μακάριος" (*makarios*) in NT and LXX. The Hebrew equivalent of μακάριος is אַשְׁרֵי (*ashireii*).

courage Christians to be happy in a transcendental view: "to seek happiness in sadness, pleasure in pain, joy in sorrow, ecstasy in death."[48]

The final stage (day) of God's creation is the creation of humans. "God said, "Let Us make man in Our image, according to Our likeness; and let them rule over . . . (everything) on the earth."[49] Two things stand out in these relationships between God and humans. One, humans belong to a different category of creation than other creatures; only humans were created according to God's image. Other animals, including apes and chimpanzees, were created by God, but not according to God's image. Second, no other animal than humans were delegated by God the exclusive authority to "rule over" the earth.

The personal and exclusive relationship between God and humans is further elaborated in Gen 2, "Then the LORD God formed man of dust from the ground, and breathed into his nostrils the breath of life; and man became a living being."[50] The life of humans was derived from God's breath. No other animal received God's breath as humans did. Afterwards, this man was placed in the Garden of Eden, and a woman of the same human species created for him.

However, this personal and exclusive relationship between God and humans soon turned sour because of unconstrained human desires justified by human rationality, which will be discussed in the next section dealing with the rational brain. God avenged on human betrayal with the Great Flood that destroyed most of the human race except for the family of Noah. After the flood had receded, God established a covenant with Noah to reassure His personal relationship with human and His delegation to human the authority to rule over the earth. "God blessed Noah and his sons and said to them, 'Be fruitful and multiply, and fill the earth. The fear of you and the terror of you will be on every beast of the earth and on every bird of the sky; with everything that creeps on the ground, and all the fish of the sea, into your hand they are given.'"[51]

The metaphor of the Tower of Babel probably describes the migration process of humans (descendants of Noah) to other parts of the world and the establishment of new religions once they arrived in there. God chose the obedient Abram to renew His covenant with humans: "I will make you a great nation, and I will bless you, and make your name great, and so you shall be

48. McMahon, *Happiness*, 76–96, 83.
49. Gen 1:26.
50. Gen 2:7.
51. Gen 9:1–2.

a blessing [...] And in you all the families of the earth will be blessed." This covenant is personal and exclusive between God and His human believers: "I am God Almighty; Walk before Me, and be blameless. I will establish My covenant between Me and you, and I will multiply you exceedingly." The covenant of protection and blessings between God and His believers was passed down from Abraham to Isaac and to Jacob. To Isaac, God explained the continuity of the covenant: "sojourn in this land and I will be with you and bless you, for to you and to your descendants I will give all these lands, and I will establish the oath which I swore to your father Abraham. I will multiply your descendants as the stars of heaven, and will give your descendants all these lands; and by your descendants all the nations of the earth shall be blessed, because Abraham obeyed Me and kept My charge, My commandments, My statutes and My laws." To Jacob, God reiterated the covenant: "I am God Almighty; be fruitful and multiply; a nation and a company of nations shall come from you, and kings shall come forth from you. The land which I gave to Abraham and Isaac, I will give it to you, and I will give the land to your descendants after you."[52]

The story of Joseph speaks of a lonely but firm believer who had the slightest idea about God and repeatedly experienced fatal threats to his life. First, was his brothers' attempt on his life, followed by the seductive wife of an Egyptian officer, and culminated in the interpretation of Pharaoh's dreams. Nevertheless, God not only protected against these threats but also turned these threats into opportunities of great fortunes for Joseph. Furthermore, with God's blessings, not only Joseph finally rose to the powerful position, second only to Pharaoh, but also the whole family of Jacob found a safe haven in Egypt during a great famine, and "multiplied" rapidly there afterwards. Thus, God's covenants with Abraham, Isaac and Jacob were carefully preserved.[53]

The beginning of the Exodus started with both a blessing and an omen for the Israelis. About four hundred years after the family of Jacob settled in Egypt, the Israelis rapidly multiplied from a familial group about forty members to a nation (ethnic group) of about two million.[54] However, this blessing of God became an omen when "a new king arose over Egypt, who did not know Joseph." This new king was probably a foreign (Hyksos) ruler who

---

52. Gen 11; 9:1–2; 17: 1–2; 26: 3–5; 35:11–12.

53. Gen 37, 39–41

54. Exod 12: 40–41. Moses conducted a census the second year after the Exodus and counted the total Israeli male population to be 603,550 (Num 1: 45–46). If the average Israeli family had four members at that time, the total population could easily add up to over two million.

overthrew the royal family of Pharaoh around 1,730 BC. The Hyksos dynasties worried that "the people of the sons of Israel are more and mightier than we." They worried even more that the Israelis might form a political coalition with the royal family of Pharaoh to expel the Hyksos. Thus, the new kings mistreated Israelis and implemented ethnic cleansing.[55]

God bestowed providence upon Israelis by cultivating a mighty leader, Moses, for them. Moses, first, barely escaped from the ethnic cleansing, then, was miraculously rescued and adopted by a princess of the new royal family, who called themselves Pharaohs. Moses received a solid education and leadership training in the royal family that no other Israelis could. He probably found out his ethnic origin as he grew up and tried to make a connection with his own people by killing an Egyptian who killed an Israeli. However, the Israelis were not ready to trust someone who grew up in the royal family and soon exposed his vigilante crime. Moses fled to the desert, partly because of his exposed crime, but more likely because he had inadvertently gotten involved in a succession struggle within the royal family.[56]

As in the case of Joseph, in which the hardship a firm believer experienced often turns out to be a personal blessing from God, Moses emerged from the desert as a competent and respectable leader at eighty years old. Upon God's calling, he went back to Egypt to challenge the new Pharaoh by repeatedly quoting from God's instruction: "Let My people go."[57]

Then how could Moses, a leader of weaponless slaves, challenge the powerful Pharaoh to "Let My people go"? Here came the personal blessing from God again in the forms of Ten Plaques and the crossing of the Red Sea.[58] Notable among the Ten is the description that all Ten Plaques smite the Egyptians without causing any harm to any Israelis. The timing of the crossing of the Red Sea to allow two million Israelis a safe passage and the precise ending of the departed sea to destroy the pursuing Egyptian army are anecdotal to the thesis that God's protection and blessing are personal and exclusive to His believers only. Moreover, God's destruction of the natural world or human beings is done so for the ultimate purpose for the salvation of human souls.

55. Exod 1:8, 122; Hamilton, *Exodus*, 6–10.

56. Hamilton, *Exodus*, 28–32.

57. Exod 5:1, 7:2, 7:16, 8:1, 8:20, 9:1, 9:13, 10:3.

58. Gen 7–14. There is a debate about where the Red Sea is located and how the two million Israelis crossed the sea Hamilton, *Exodus*. 217-219. A compromise among these alternative explanations is that the Israelis crossed a river spout east of Rameses. It was a miracle, nevertheless, because of the timing of drying and flooding to destroy the pursuing Egyptian army.

God did not lead the Israelis out of Egypt only to die in the wilderness where water and food were in shortage and local tribes were guarding their turfs judiciously. God had promised the Israelis the final destination of exodus would be a "land flowing with milk and honey."[59] God was supposed to take full responsibility to provide water, food and safety throughout the journey. Thus, "the LORD was going before them in a pillar of cloud by day to lead them on the way, and in a pillar of fire by night to give them light, that they might travel by day and by night." When they could not find water, God made the bitter water of Marah drinkable and made spring come out of the rock. When they could not find staple food and meat, God provided plenty of quails and daily manna to them. When the local tribes of Amaleks, Canaanites, Amorites, Bashans and Midianites fought with the Israelis, God helped Israelis to defeat them.[60]

In the OT, the personal relationship between God and His believers was revealed not only in God's grace, but also in religious rituals. Although the books of Exodus and Numbers also contain scattered verses of religious rituals, they are summed up and expanded in Deuteronomy, particularly from chapters 12 to 20. By participating in religious rituals, believers are able to feel all kinds of religious emotions: transcendence and holiness of God, the unity of self with God, musical excitement and calmness, body movement, partaking food, relief from daily pressure, joy in singing and prayer, and the smell of incense and burned sacrifices. Even the taboos in food, fasting and holidays would generate a feeling of religious devotion and holiness.

Moses died before the Israelis crossed the Jordan River and entered "the land flowing with milk and honey." He had appointed a competent successor, Joshua, to complete his mission of exodus. The process of occupying Palestine re-iterates the theme that the relationship between God and His believers was both personal and exclusive. Mimicking Moses's miraculous crossing of the Red Sea, Joshua led the Israelis across the Jordan River also with a miracle: the water of the Jordan River was cut off at the moment Israeli priests placed their feet into the water. The water, flowing down from the upstream, simply "stood in one heap" just like the Red Sea departed. After all the Israelis had crossed the river, the water flowed again. Before the Israelis started their military campaign, God ordered another ceremony of circumcision to renew His covenant with a new generation of Israelis. Afterwards, it was simply blood and corpses flying over the remaining pages of the book of Joshua. The

---

59. Exod 3:8, 3:17, 13:5, 33:3.

60. Exod 13:21; 15:23; 17:6-16; Num 20:2-13; 21-24.

brutality of these battles is evidenced by repeated references to the phrases "they utterly destroyed everything with the edge of the sword," or "they slew them until no one was left of those who survived or escaped," "the sons of Israel had finished slaying them with a very great slaughter, until they were destroyed," and "He (Joshua) left no survivor." With these descriptions, the Bible espouses a relationship between God and His believers that were so personal and exclusive that modern apologetics have trouble defending the rationale of ruthless ethnic cleansing during this occupation process. Joshua summarized the book for the Israelis with the often-quoted verse that upheld this personal relationship between God and His believers: "You will not be able to serve the LORD, for He is a holy God. He is a jealous God; He will not forgive your transgression or your sins. If you forsake the LORD and serve foreign gods, then He will turn and do you harm and consume you after He has done good to you." The Israelis reconfirmed this personal relationship by an obedient reply: "No, but we will serve the LORD."[61]

The book of Ruth takes a major turn in explaining the personal relationship between God and His believers. It does so by two shifts. First, it shifts the unit of analysis from the ethnic group level to the more "personal" individual level with the focus on Ruth herself. Secondly, it shifts from the ethnic line of Israelis to an "infidel" woman who was married to an Israeli. Despite her different ethnic/religious origin, Ruth received personal blessings from God only because she became the wife of a believer in God and was converted to a believer in God as well. After her husband had died in a foreign land, she told her mother-in-law that "your people shall be my people, and your God, my God." She moved, with her mother-in-law, back to Bethlehem and was blessed by God to marry "a man of great wealth," Boaz. Not only did she live happily ever after in this rich family, but she was also able to bear a child she was unable to have with her former husband. Furthermore, this child was no other person but the grandfather of King David. Without Ruth, the rest of the Old Testament would have to be re-written, so would the whole New Testament. It is all because of an infidel woman, at a critical moment, made a critical choice to establish a personal relationship with God. What could the relationship between God and His believers be more "personal" than this?[62]

The books of 1 Samuel and 2 Samuel elaborate on the personal relationships between God and David in more details than any other person in the Bible. David was a nobody born to a shepherd family of eight brothers. Then,

61. Deut 13:15; 20:13; Jos 3:14–17; 6:21; 8:22; 10:28–40; 11:8–22; 24:19–21.
62. Ruth 1:16; 2:1; 4:17.

for no reason (neither did he express his solid faith in God, nor was it because of his wisdom and physical strength), he was chosen and anointed by Samuel to be the next legitimate king of Israel after Saul. He was chosen and anointed by Samuel only because God told Samuel "how long will you grieve over Saul, since I have rejected him from being king over Israel? Fill your horn with oil and go; I will send you to Jesse the Bethlehemite, for I have selected a king for Myself among his sons," that is David. This blessing to David, however, seemed rather a curse to David once Saul knew about this potential threat to his throne and his heirs. Saul attempted several times to thwart God's plan by murdering David but to no avail. David was driven to foreign lands and suffered all kinds of hardships, during which time he wrote a good portion of Psalms to praise God for ceaselessly protecting him. Finally, God's will prevailed over Saul's religious rebellion by ending his life on a battlefield with the Philistines.[63]

After he had succeeded Saul as the king of Israel, David continued to face external and internal threats to his throne. However, with his confidence in God, he diffused these threats one by one and finally earned the political and religious legitimacy of Israelis.

"Then all the tribes of Israel came to David at Hebron and said, 'Behold, we are your bone and your flesh. Previously, when Saul was king over us, you were the one who led Israel out and in. And the LORD said to you, "You will shepherd My people Israel, and you will be a ruler over Israel"'." In appreciation of God's providence, David planned the construction of the Holy Temple. God returned David's loyalty by making a personal covenant with David that "your house and your kingdom shall endure before Me forever; your throne shall be established forever." The covenant was carried over from King David in the Old Testament to his descendant Jesus in the New Testament.[64]

Like the book of Ruth, the book of Esther tells a story about a faithful female believer who played a critical role in the continuation of God's relationship with the Israelis. Unlike the book of Ruth, this time it was about the possibility of an Israeli genocide. Under the reign of the Persian king Ahasuerus, a Jewish high-ranking official Mordecai got involved in a fierce political struggle with another high-ranking official Haman of a historically hostile ethnic group. Thus, the personal power struggle soon deteriorated into an ethnic war. The monotheism of the Jewish people turned out to be a cause

63. 1Sam 16:1; 19–31.
64. 2Sam 5: 1–2; 7:16.

of an incoming ethnic cleansing ordered by the king who had promoted a cult of emperor worship recommended by the hostile official. Queen Esther of Jewish origin asked the Jewish people to fast for her for three days and nights before she risked her life to intervene in this political mess. Through a sophisticated plot, Esther framed Haman for harassing her and brought about Haman's execution. Building on Haman's death, Mordecai persuaded the king to allow the Jewish people to exercise ethnic cleansing on Homan's people. They even set up a religious holiday (Purim) to celebrate this revenge.[65]

In describing the personal relationships between God and His believers, what distinguishes the book of Esther from other books is the absence of God in the whole book. God did not explicitly pick Esther to be the queen in preparation for the showdown between the two ethnic groups. God did not explicitly order Mordecai to get involved in a power struggle with Haman. God did not tell Mordecai and Esther how to frame their political enemy. Nor did God instruct Mordecai to implement ethnic cleansing to avenge his ethnic enemies. However, the very absence of God in all these critical moments provides an even stronger promise to His believers that the personal covenant between God and His people will always be kept intact with or without God's explicit presence during crises.

Most chapters of the book of Psalm are about David's prayers to God in a time of personal crises either as results of enemy attack or as results of personal wrongdoings. Whichever the cause, the Psalmists pleaded God for personal protection or abundant mercy. Sometimes, the Psalmists reminded God of His covenant with the believers. Thus, the book of Psalm is frequently used in churches to provide comfort and assurance to believers that hardships will pass away, and God will walk with His believers through these hardships.

When its neighbors attacked Israel, God told the kings of Israel that "Ask of Me, and I will surely give the nations as your inheritance, and the very ends of the earth as our possession. You shall break them with a rod of iron, you shall shatter them like earthenware." When King Saul incessantly sought the life of David, David pleaded to God "O my God; set me securely on high away from those who rise up against me." When his own son Absalom attacked King David, he pleaded to God, "Arise, O LORD; save me, O my God! For You have smitten all my enemies on the cheek; You have shattered the teeth of the wicked." When the Psalmist sinned against God, he still could plead to God for forgiveness, atonement and personal protection: "O LORD, do not rebuke me in Your anger, Nor chasten me in Your wrath . . . Return,

65. Esth 2–3; 4:16; 5–7; 9:17–22.

O LORD, rescue my soul; save me because of Your loving kindness." The Psalmist always had confidence in his personal relationship with God: "The LORD is the portion of my inheritance and my cup; You support my lot."[66]

These themes of personal relationships between God and His believers repeat in other chapters of the book of Psalm (see Appendix 3.1). A synthesis of these themes is represented by Psalm 23, the most familiar Psalm among believers: "The LORD is my shepherd, I shall not want ... He restores my soul; He guides me in the paths of righteousness For His name's sake ... You prepare a table before me in the presence of my enemies; You have anointed my head with oil; my cup overflows. 6 Surely goodness and loving kindness will follow me all the days of my life, and I will dwell in the house of the LORD forever."[67]

Around 587 BC when the Babylonians attacked Jerusalem, the nearby tribe Edom, who were related to Israelis by blood,[68] did not come to help the Israelis. Even worse, they took advantage of the Babylonian invasion, looted Jerusalem, captured Israeli refugees, and turned them to the enemy. Therefore, Prophet Obadiah condemned Edom to ethnic extinction. He also extended his condemnation to all nations who attacked Jerusalem. Despite the demise of Israeli kingdom, Obadiah promised that "the deliverers will ascend Mount Zion to judge the mountain of Esau, and the kingdom will be the LORD's."[69]

The personal relationship between God and His believers in the OT is replaced by an even more personal relationship between Jesus and His disciples in the NT, because Jesus was physically present with them. The four Gospels of Matthew, Mark, Luke and John provided about twenty-four stories in which Jesus healed the leper, the paralytic, the blind, the mute, the lunatic, the sick and those possessed by demons; He even raised people from the dead.[70] These stories of healing and exorcism describe Jesus as a personal God who is always tentative to the emotional needs of believers.

---

66. Pss 2:8–9; 59:1; 3:7; 6:1,4; 16:5.

67. Pss 23: 1, 3–6.

68. Gen 25:30; 36:1, 8.

69. Obad 1:10–14, 21.

70. The following verses record these healing and exorcism in chronological order. Citations in the parentheses are the same stories cited by different Gospels: John 4:46–54; Mark1:21-28 (Luke 4:31–37); Matt 8:14–17 (Mark1:29–34; Luke 4:38–41); Matt 2:4 (Mark1:40–45; John 5:12–16); Matt 9:1-8 (Mark2:1–12); John 5:17–26); John (5:1–47); Matt 12:9–14 (Mark3:1–6); Luke 6:6–11; Matt 12: 15–21 (Mark3:7–12; Luke 6:17–19); Matt 8:5–13 (Luke 7:1–0); Luke 7:11-17; Matt 8:28–34 (Mark5:1–20; John 8:26–39); Matt 9:18-26 (Luke 5:21–43; John 8:41–56); Matt 9:27–31; Matt 9:32–34; Matt 14:34-36

While Jesus presented Himself as a loving and caring personal God to believers in the Gospels, He presented Himself as a personal God seeking justice and vengeance for His believers in the book of Revelation. Once Jesus unleashes the judgments of the Seven Trumpets and Seven Bowls, only the true believers will be protected from all these natural and supernatural disasters. Once Jesus completes judgments of the living humans and creatures, all believers of the past will come to life. Then, God takes over to judge the dead and evil spirits. Afterwards, God re-creates a new heaven and a new earth, and reserves them to be populated jointly by His believers and the Trinitarian God; while "for the cowardly and unbelieving and abominable and murderers and immoral persons and sorcerers and idolaters and all liars, their part will be in the lake that burns with fire and brimstone, which is the second death."[71] In chapter 4 of this book, I will comment on current ecotheologies for their lack of attention to the dual characteristics of the personal relationships between the Trinitarian God and humans. They dwell on the positive emotion but not the negative one.

The above Biblical chapters highlight the importance and tenacity of personal relationships between God and His believers. However, should the importance and tenacity of such relationships be maintained when they conflict with God's laws or human rationality? Will God break His covenant with His believers if they break His laws? Should His believers break this covenant when they face threats on their lives? The following Biblical chapters reconfirm the importance and tenacity of personal relationships between God and His believers in these situations.

By most human standards, Jacob was no better than a scoundrel in his whole life. Starting from his birth, he held the heel of his twin brother Esau, posing a potential complication to his mother's life. As a child, Jacob stayed at home while Esau did the hunting to bring food on the table. Jacob cheated Esau for the latter's birthright with a bowl of lentil stew. When his father Isaac was dying on his bed and ready to give the last blessings on his sons, Jacob cheated Isaac for the firstborn blessings. In fear of Esau's revenge, Jacob fled to his uncle's place. He cheated his uncle for a larger and healthier portion of his herd, and ran away with these possessions along with two daughters of his uncle. On his way home, Jacob put his wives and children before himself to

---

(Mark6:53–56); Matt 15:21–31 (Mark7:24–37); Matt 16:5–12 (Mark8:14–26); Matt 17:14–21 (Mark9:14–29); John 9:37–43); John 9:1–41; Luke 13:10–17; Luke 14:1–24; Luke 17:12–19; Matt 20:29–34 (Mark10:46–52); John 18:35–43).

71. Rev 21:8.

meet his revengeful twin brother Esau. What a man, a husband and a father? As he grew old, he spoiled his youngest son Joseph and caused Joseph's later hardships.[72]

Why did such a terrible scoundrel receive God's abundant blessings nevertheless? It is all because God had made personal covenants with Jacob's father Isaac and grandfather Abraham that their descendants will become a big ethnic group. It is all because God promised Jacob's mother Rebekah during pregnancy that "two nations are in your womb; and two peoples will be separated from your body; and one people shall be stronger than the other; and the older shall serve the younger." And it is all because Jacob knew too well about God's personal relationships with His believers that he never stopped reminding God of His covenants by offering frequent sacrifices to God.[73]

Similarly, the Israelis committed all kinds of sin against God that deserved ethnic cleansing, but God held His last temper to wipe them out because He had made personal covenants with Abraham, Isaac and Jacob to protect their descendants. God sent Moses to bring them out of Egypt, but the Israelis did not appreciate this help; they cursed Moses and Aaron: "May the LORD look upon you and judge you, for you have made us odious in Pharaoh's sight and in the sight of his servants, to put a sword in their hand to kill us." How did God respond to this complaint? After re-iterating His covenants with Abraham, Isaac and Jacob, God ordered Moses to execute the Ten Plaques as instructed. Witnessing the Ten Plaques and passing through the Red Sea, were the Israelis now happy with God's providence? No. Only two months after they left Egypt, they wanted to go back. They complained to Moses and Aaron that "would that we had died by the LORD's hand in the land of Egypt, when we sat by the pots of meat, when we ate bread to the full; for you have brought us out into this wilderness to kill this whole assembly with hunger." What did God do to them? God provided plenty of manna and quails to the Israelis. But while God and Moses were working on setting up religious laws on Mount Sinai, the Israelis were making a golden calf and having orgies, so God told Moses that He had had enough and wanted to destroy them. Moses quickly reminded God of His personal covenants with Abraham, Isaac and Jacob that should never be broken. "So the LORD changed His mind about the harm which He said He would do to His people." Thereafter, the Israelis continued to complain and sin against God. God punished

---

72. Gen 25:24–33; 27–32.

73. Gen 25:23.

them frequently but always stopped short of terminating them when Moses reminded Him of the covenants.[74]

The Psalmists probably realized that God's anger toward His sinful people is constrained by His personal covenants. Therefore, they taught their people to appeal to God's mercy over His justice. This is the theme of many chapters of the book of Psalm. Ps 51, written after David's affair with Bathsheba, is an exemplar of this theme: "Be gracious to me, O God, according to Your loving kindness; According to the greatness of Your compassion blot out my transgressions." "Deliver me from blood guiltiness, O God, because He is the God of my salvation."[75]

Song of Songs employs a theatrical format to describe God's patience with the Israelis, despite their religious adultery with foreign gods. The Jewish exegetical tradition singles out three repeated verses (Song 2:7, 3:5 and 8:4) as the core of this theological message. Zionists regard these verses as God's promises to restore the Kingdom of Israel. Through the mouth of the shepherd, God patiently called on the adulterous Israelis to voluntarily re-establish their personal relationships: "I adjure you, O daughters of Jerusalem, by the gazelles or by the hinds of the field, that you do not arouse or awaken my love until she pleases."[76]

The book of Lamentation picks up the theme of national suffering from the book of Psalm. The Kingdom of Israel ceased to exist in 587 BC at the hand of the Babylon Empire. Prophet Jeremiah, the author of the book, made no excuse for the Israeli suffering. The gist of Lam 1-4 is that Israelis deserve all kinds of national suffering because "Jerusalem sinned greatly." Israelis committed religious and physical adultery; prophets told lies and priests dishonored the temple; and the kings and officials disregarded social justice. Israelis deserve all kinds of suffering because "the LORD is righteous." But after the Israelis received all the punishment their deserved, God will come to rescue and restore Israelis. "Restore us to You, O LORD, that we may be restored; renew our days as of old." God will not forget us forever and will not forsake us so long, Jeremiah prophesized. After all, God is the personal God of His believers and His believers only. All the enemies who brought down the kingdom of Israel would ultimately suffer more than the Israelis.[77]

---

74. Exod 2:23–25; 5:21; 16:3; 32:10, 13–14.
75. Pss 51:1, 14.
76. Ravitzky and Swirsky, *Messianism*, 40-78, 211–33.
77. Lam 1:8, 9, 18; 4:6; 5:21.

The book of Habakkuk was written before the book of Lamentation, but both addressed to a similar theological issue concerning the relationship between God and His believers. Why would God employ an even more sinful, veracious, and pagan people (the Chaldeans and the Babylonians) to punish God's own people? Was not God the God of Israelis and Israelis only? Why did not God punish Israelis via Israeli prophets and priests, or by His might hands?

Habakkuk thought that his arguments and prayers could probably change God's mind about employing the Chaldeans to punish the Israelis. However, he was not confident that God would change His mind. What Habakkuk was confident about was that in the end, God would still be the God of Israelis. "Though the fig tree should not blossom and there be no fruit on the vines, though the yield of the olive should fail and the fields produce no food, though the flock should be cut off from the fold and there be no cattle in the stalls," Habakkuk prayed for the Israelis, "Yet I will exult in the LORD, I will rejoice in the God of my salvation."[78] Probably in response to Habakkuk's prayer but still according to His plan, God sent Babylonians to defeat the Chaldeans. But the Israelis refused to repent their sins. So, the Babylonian empire finally annexed the Kingdom of Israel.

In retrospect, the demise of the Kingdom of Israel turned out to be a blessing in disguise to the Israelis as a Godly people. It was during the exile in Babylon, Israelis re-created the religion of Jehovah and purified the belief. Even more importantly, Israelis would now take Messiah more seriously because they could not and dared not expect the restoration of a secular Kingdom of Israel in the near future. Through the visions of the four angels riding horses, four craftsmen, a man holding a measuring line, and Joshua, the high priest, Prophet Zechariah, proclaimed to the Israelis that their sins were forgiven by God; not because the Israelis had done something good to earn it, but because of God's grace. In addition to the atonement of sin, God promised the coming of Messiah to restore the faith community (but not necessarily the secular Kingdom of Israel). Prophet Zechariah proclaimed: "Rejoice greatly, O daughter of Zion! Shout in triumph, O daughter of Jerusalem! Behold, your king is coming to you; He is just and endowed with salvation, humble, and mounted on a donkey, Even on a colt, the foal of a donkey."[79]

As Zechariah prophesized, God sent Jesus the Messiah to save the sinners and opened a new chapter about the personal relationship between God

78. Hab 3:17–18.

79. Zech 9:9.

and His believers. On the one hand, Jesus as a Trinitarian God continued God's grace toward his believers by healing the sick and exorcizing the devils. On the other hand, Jesus as a human was called by God to prevail over human emotions to serve God. The personal relationship between God and His believers is thus re-enforced on both ends through the exemplars set by Jesus.

The birth of Jesus was a great challenge to Jesus' parents Mary and Joseph. It would be "rational" for Mary to turn down the angel's request for a virgin birth of Jesus, which could have resulted in her immediate death by stoning. It would be "rational" for Joseph to send Mary away secretly for her pre-marital pregnancy, instead of making themselves a laughing stock in the eyes of their relatives. But their passion toward God prevailed over human rationality and together they embarked on a treacherous journey to an uncertain destination.[80]

The virgin birth did not give Jesus a head-start in His ministry either. In His childhood, Jesus probably had to suffer emotionally and physically from the humiliation of virgin birth in a manger. After being tempted three times by Satan in the desert, Jesus embarked on an even more treacherous journey to a certain destination of death. According to human "rationality," Jesus could have settled a marvelous deal with Satan to be the leader of the Jewish community (the second temptation) or, even better, the leader of secular kingdoms (the third temptation). However, Jesus traded these temptations with his crucifixion. How "irrational" He was! In fact, He was entirely rational in the sense that His parietal lobe probably redefined the variables in His rational equation in both space and time. He was maximizing spiritual and material interests both on earth and in heaven; and the time frame of these values is forever, not contemporary.

The disciples of Jesus seemed to make a "rational" decision upon his crucifixion: they fled from the crucifixion process and seemed ready to give up on Him in the first few days following the crucifixion. After all, their master was gone, and similar death penalties might befall them. But the resurrection of Jesus changed all their rational calculation. Similar to Jesus, their parietal lobe received a shock treatment by the resurrection of Jesus and re-rout former "rational" circuits in the brain. They were now ready to consolidate Jesus' ministry at all costs. Furthermore, they took up the even more challenging Great Commission to proselytize the nations.[81]

During the ministry of Jesus, Judaism was not interested in proselytizing the nations for both theological and political reasons. For theological reasons,

---

80. Matt 1:18–25.

81. Matt 26–28; Mark14–16; Luke 22–24; John 12–21.

Judaism was a covenant between God and Jewish people only, and "being a Jew" was defined by both Jewish bloodline and faith in Jehovah. A few people from other ethnic groups joined the religion, such as Tamar, Rahab and Ruth. But Judaism since exile in Babylon did not encourage inter-marriage, not to mention about proselytizing.[82] For political reason, Judaism became a minority religion after exile. Any attempt of aggressive proselytizing might be regarded by the emperor and the majority religion as politically threatening.

Jewish Christians might have both religious and political reasons in mind when they challenged Paul's evangelical ministry among the nations. But the Holy Spirit, probably residing in their parietal lobe, transformed their religious and political calculation by an enlarged temporal and spatial framework. Theologically, the religion would no longer be limited to the Jewish people; and the supreme God was transformed into Trinitarian God, in Whom the Holy Spirit now played a prominent role in proselytizing. Politically, the apostles divided the Kingdom of Israel into two parts. The secular Kingdom of Israel was gone and temporally irrelevant to Christianity, while Christians should actively construct the heavenly Kingdom of Israel, which would be the Church. Unfortunately, the Jews sought the help of the Roman Empire to crush Christians. Nevertheless "irrational" martyrs were not deterred, and their Spirit-inspired rationality was passed on to other Christians. In a few centuries, they grew from a minority within the minority religion of Judaism to become the majority religion of the Roman Empire.

Rational Brain in the Bible

Anthropologists and neurotheologians assume that it was the evolutionary breakthrough of the human frontal lobe that differentiated Homo sapiens from other genus Homo and empowered Homo sapiens to rule the world. The major function of frontal lobe is rational thinking by which Homo sapiens developed sophisticated social norms, rules and institutions to regulate individual behaviors for the benefit of collective security and welfare. When individuals violated these norms, rules and institutions, they received punishment by their leaders. The Bible, especially the Old Testament, contains numerous chapters elaborating God's laws and punishments on transgressors. These 350 chapters demonstrate that God is not just love, as portrayed above, He is also justice; His love is just.

82. Matt 1; Ezra 10; Neh 13

Martin Luther explained the original sin as a result of the free will that God irrevocably gave to man and woman once they were created.[83] At their own free will, Eve and Adam ate the "forbidden fruit" of wisdom and were driven out of the Garden of Eden by God. From a neurotheological perspective, it was simply the result of a greedy emotional brain that overpowered rational brain. Being a slave to the emotional brain, the rational brain had little choice but to justify Eve's and Adam's behaviors. Eve first ate the fruit of wisdom because she was all emotional and greedy. She "saw that the tree was good for food, and that it was a delight to the eyes, and that the tree was desirable to make one wise." Then, her rational brain accepted the Snake's rhetorical remark that if they ate it they "surely will not die!" Adam did not even bother to use his rational brain to resist eating the fruit. When God confronted Adam for his transgression, he employed his rational brain and tried to blame it on both Eve and God: "The woman whom You gave to be with me, she gave me from the tree, and I ate." Being afraid of punishment, Eve's rational brain worked in full gear as well to passing the blame onto the Snake. However, neither excuses convinced the omniscient and just God; both Adam and Eve were driven out of the Garden.[84]

In the case of Adam and Eve, there was first a clear law given by God to Adam and Eve not to eat the wisdom fruit. But the next story about Sodom's sin has been under both rational and emotional debate since the early 1980s between conservative churches and liberal churches. What was exactly Sodom's "sin"? God told Abraham that "the outcry of Sodom and Gomorrah is indeed great, and their sin is exceedingly grave." Conservative churches claim that the sin was homosexuality. Liberal churches counter-claim that the sin was either inhospitality to strangers or rough (group) sex they intended to impose on strangers.[85] Either way, it was the emotional brain of Sodomites that was running excessively wild so that they violated one of God's death-warranted laws.

To maintain order and cohesion in an exodus group of more than two million people consisting of Israelis and other ethnic minorities, Moses promulgated a sophisticated, rational legal system. The legal system was immediately challenged by both Israeli leaders and ethnic minorities who had different degrees or kinds of emotional needs. In the case of the golden calf, Aaron's

---

83. Luther, *Bondage*.

84. Gen 3:4, 6, 12–13.

85. Gen 18:20. For theological debate about the sin of Sodom, see the representative works of Boswell, *Christianity and Homosexuality*, and Gagnon, *Bible and Homosexual*.

greed for religious leadership coincided with the sexual liberation mood of the people, plus the ethnic minority's preference for religious pluralism, formed a political-religious coalition to challenge the Mosaic law which was under construction. Aaron was spared after the golden calf incident, but his insatiable appetite for power remained. He and his sister Miriam conspired to discredit Moses for his interracial marriage. The leaders of priestly Levi tribe, envious of Moses and Aaron's leadership role in both religious and political hierarchies, plotted a coup against them. At Shittim, Israelis challenged the law because they "play(ed) the harlot with the daughters of Moab" and "bowed down to their gods." In all these challenges to Moses and his legal system, God decisively sided with Moses and severely punished the transgressors.[86]

The book of Deuteronomy, particularly from chapters 21 to 33, reiterates and expands on the laws in Exodus and Numbers. Moses sums up the consequences of these laws: prosper or perish. Prosper if these laws are obeyed, "I command you today to love the LORD your God, to walk in His ways and to keep His commandments and His statutes and His judgments, that you may live and multiply, and that the LORD your God may bless you in the land where you are entering to possess it." Perish if laws are defiled, "But if your heart turns away and you will not obey, but are drawn away and worship other gods and serve them, I declare to you today that you shall surely perish."[87]

These laws were reiterated by political leaders, priests and prophets throughout the history of the Kingdom of Israel. Those who dared to challenge these laws faced the consequence of severe punishment. The faithful and the greatest king of Israel, David, committed adultery with Bathsheba and murdered her husband Uriah. Court prophet Nathan found out and cursed David. Soon after, God "struck the child that Uriah's widow bore to David" and started a series of sibling murders and coups in his palace to punish David's adultery and murder.[88]

Upon his succession to the throne, Solomon built the temple for God and promoted rituals of worship. God was pleased and rewarded him with national prosperity and strength. But national prosperity and strength spoiled Solomon. "He had seven hundred wives, princesses, and three hundred concubines, and his wives turned his heart away" from God.[89] He began to promote

---

86. Num 1 25:1–2.
87. Deut 30:16–18.
88. 2Sam 12–20.
89. 1Kgs 11:3.

polytheism both in his palace and nation-wide. For his moral and religious crimes, God split the Kingdom of Israel into two upon Solomon's death, and ultimately destroyed the Kingdom of Israel for its moral and religious crimes.

Political and religious leaders learned the importance of God's laws during exile. They were determined not to repeat the same mistakes their ancestors did. Prophets Ezra and Nehemiah concentrated their efforts to rebuild the religion as a whole. Ezra built the temple, Nehemiah built Jerusalem's wall, and both promulgated a strict version of Moses laws to strengthen not just the physical but also the spiritual capability of the Israeli people.[90]

The book of Psalm is mostly about prayer and God's blessing, and therefore, is a guidebook for believers to strengthen their personal relations with God. However, the book of Psalm is equally a book about God's law and judgment, thus serving the purpose of strengthening the rationality of believers. Among the chapters cited in Appendix 3.1,[91] chapters 1 and 119 are anecdotal. Chapter 1 starts with a reminder of law and rationality: "How blessed is the man who does not walk in the counsel of the wicked, nor stand in the path of sinners, nor sit in the seat of scoffers! But his delight is in the law of the LORD, and in His law he meditates day and night."[92] The 176 verses of Psalm 119 merely elaborate and expand upon Psalm 1 and probably create and strengthen the neurocircuits between the emotional and rational brains of believers.

The book of Proverbs is a book of wisdom and rationality. It encourages believers to think rationally in order to live a long life and a life of prosperity in a world that is full of temptation and entrapment. The Proverbs will enable believers to "know wisdom and instruction, to discern the sayings of understanding, to receive instruction in wise behavior, righteousness, justice and equity; to give prudence to the naive, to the youth knowledge and discretion." Despite all its practical advice contained in Proverbs, however, the ultimate wisdom comes from God and God's laws. "The fear of the LORD is the beginning of wisdom, and the knowledge of the Holy One is understanding." Ironically, the king of wisdom Solomon and the alleged author of Proverbs failed to adhere to the true wisdom and fell into the very temptation and entrapment Proverbs had warned.[93]

90. Ezra 3–10; Neh 1–13.

91. Chapters of Psalm that emphasize law and rationality include Pss 1, 14, 15, 19, 36, 37, 50, 52, 53, 58, 72–76, 81–83, 101, 111, 112, 119, 132, 137.

92. Ps 1:1–2.

93. Prov 1:2–4; 9:10.

The Prophets continued to remind the Israelis the importance and consequences of abiding by God's law. The rational calculation for the Israelis as a nation is simple: prosperity or perish is contingent upon whether the nation follows God's law. Few Israeli prophets could provide a more profound witness to this rational calculation than Ezekiel. He was both a prophet and a priest. He witnessed the Babylonian invasion in Jerusalem and was in exile, along with other Israelis, until he died in a foreign land. He exhorted Israelis to renew religious life by strictly following God's law. Israelis had to pay for their polytheism, apostasy, moral corruption, and injustice; so, they did through exile. Amid Israeli perish, however, Ezekiel also frequently provided hope and promised prosperity, if Israelis decided to return to God's law. God would never leave Israelis alone, even during the exile: "Thus says the Lord GOD, 'Though I had removed them far away among the nations and though I had scattered them among the countries, yet I was a sanctuary for them a little while in the countries where they had gone.'" At the end of punishment, "I will take you from the nations, gather you from all the lands and bring you into your own land," God promised. But how to make sure that His believers do not break God's law again? God declared, "I will put My Spirit within you and cause you to walk in My statutes, and you will be careful to observe My ordinances." A rational God is not separable from a personal God, vice versa.[94]

Ezekiel's allusion to the Holy Spirit provided a critical link between the OT and the NT. Although the Gospels devoted a large portion to describe the love of Jesus, the apostles spared no time to complement the love of Jesus with God's law through their Holy Spirit. Heresies emerged immediately among the churches Paul established. In his second letter to Thessalonians, Paul warned against the heretic member of the church "who opposes and exalts himself above every so-called god or object of worship, so that he takes his seat in the temple of God, displaying himself as being God." How will Jesus deal with this person? "The Lord will slay with the breath of His mouth and bring to an end by the appearance of His coming." How could believers keep God's law? Through the Holy Spirit, said Paul, "because God has chosen you from the beginning for salvation through sanctification by the Spirit and faith in the truth." Paul repeated this message against heresies in his first letter to Timothy. In the church at Ephesus, some church leaders "taught strange doctrines . . . pay attention to myths and endless genealogies, which give rise to mere speculation rather than furthering the administration of God which

---

94. Ezek 11:16; 36:24, 27.

is by faith." For those who violate God's law, Paul would hand them over to Satan, so that they will be taught not to blaspheme.[95]

In addition to religious orthodoxy, the apostles need to develop new codes of conduct, based on God's law, to strengthen the governance of a growing church. The apostles devoted several letters to address such issues, such as 1 Timothy 2-6, 2 Timothy 2-4, Titus 1-3, Philemon, James 1-5, 1 Peter 2-3, 1 John 1-5, 2 John, and 3 John. They covered issues of personal integrity, marriage, gender equality, selection of church leaders, relationships among church members, treatment of disadvantaged members, dealing with non-believers, church-state relations, and relations between belief and work.

Since God's law and God's judgment are not separable, the NT also devotes a significant portion to the issue of God's judgment. Peter warned the believers that "it is time for judgment to begin with the household of God; and if it begins with us first, what will be the outcome for those who do not obey the gospel of God?" He continued the theme of judgment in 2 Peter: "But the day of the LORD will come like a thief, in which the heavens will pass away with a roar and the elements will be destroyed with intense heat, and the earth and its works will be burned up."[96] In the Bible, the most complete treatment of the LORD's final judgment is in Revelation. Jesus will personally take up the judgment plan and execute it with perfect precision. The unbelievers, the sorcerers, the immoral persons, the murderers, the idolaters, the liars, the apostasies, the devil and evil spirits, all will be thrown into the lake of fire and sulfur. Only the sincere believers will be allowed to reside in the New Heaven and the New Earth with the Trinitarian God.

In addition to the above Biblical chapters that promote religious laws and intimidate transgressors, the Bible also contains several chapters that encourage His believers to control their emotional brain for the sake of God and His law. Abraham was one hundred years old and his wife Sarah was ninety years old when they were told that they could finally have a child of their own the next year. The birth of Isaac must have brought them joy, pride and serenity, but not for long. When Isaac became a teenager, God tested Abraham to offer Isaac as a living sacrifice to God. Abraham had not done anything wrong, nor had Isaac. But their essential emotional needs took second place when obedience to God was required. Although Genesis does not explain why Moses performed the sacrificial ceremony and almost did murder his only child, Hebrews 11:19 provides an explanation: "(Abraham) considered that

---

95. 2Thess 2:4, 8, 13; 1Tim 1:3–4, 20.
96. 1Pet 4:17; 2Pet 3:10.

God is able to raise people even from the dead, from which he also received him back as a type." With his faith in and past experiences of God's omnipotence, Abraham successful overcame the generic urge to protect his child. It was a rational decision derived from the God brain.

The authors of the Proverbs probably realized how powerful and destructive human greed could be thus they devoted several chapters of warning. Echoing Psalm 1:1, Proverb 4:14-15 teach believers how to deal with temptations; just avoid them: "Do not enter the path of the wicked and do not proceed in the way of evil men. Avoid it, do not pass by it; turn away from it and pass on." Extra-marital desires are most destructive, because "the lips of an adulteress drip honey and smoother than oil is her speech; but in the end, she is bitter as wormwood, sharp as a two-edged sword." Instead, spend your sexual desires exclusively on your wife, says Proverbs.[97] As if they could not say enough about the destructive force of adultery and fornication, the authors of Proverbs repeated the same message in Pro 6-7.

While Proverbs provided moral codes to believers living under the protection of the Kingdom of Israel, the book of Daniel provided models of believers living in a precarious land ruled by a foreign ruler. The happiness and greed of believers were no longer the major concern of religious leaders. The very survival of the Israelis was under constant threat from the dominant and competing tribes in the foreign land. Daniel and his friends were put to a test when they were children. To eat or not to eat? It was the question. They decided to suppress their emotional desires for meat sacrificed to foreign gods and, instead, to religiously eat clean vegetables only. But they were put to a much more severe test when they grew up to be servants to the emperor. To worship or not to worship? It was the question. This time they decided to suppress their fear for their lives and not worship the golden image erected by the emperor; instead, they accepted the punishment to be thrown into a furnace of blazing fire. An angel of God rescued them from the fire and exonerated them. Although Daniel's role and religiosity in this incident remains a theological debate (he was not thrown into the furnace), he expressed his religious commitment to God by publicly challenging King Belshazzar who desecrated holy vessels taken from the Jewish temple in Jerusalem. In fact, he cursed King Belshazzar and resulted in the King's death that very night. Daniel did not withhold his religious commitment either to the new Mede king, Darius, who ordered all citizens not to bow to any god except the king for thirty days, or be thrown into a lions' den. Daniel suppressed his fear for his life and continued

---

97. Prov 5:3–4, 15–23.

his routine worship to God, three times a day. He was thrown into the lions' den, but God sent angels to shut the lions' mouths. He came out the den unscathed and exonerated. The book of Daniel seemed to provide exemplars of martyrs for Christian believers under Roman rule.

The book of Haggai faced a different sort of emotional desires of the believers. Should they allocate their time and resources to furnish their houses and daily needs or to build the holy temple? Most Israelis chose the former in the early years of Darius rule. Therefore, Jewish prophets and priests urged Israelis to complete the construction of the temple, and in response, Israelis completed the project in four years. The book of Haggai is probably one of the favorite books for church leaders who want to build a church structure. They encourage donations by citing the verse: "I will shake all the nations; and they will come with the wealth of all nations, and I will fill this house with glory, says the LORD of hosts."[98]

No one else in the Bible sets a better exemplar of controlling human desires than Jesus. The devil knew too well what human's major weaknesses were: physical desires, religious pride, and political greed. It tempted Jesus on all three fronts, but Jesus successfully rejected these temptations by His unshakable commitment to God. Jesus foresaw similar hardships His believers would face after His death. Therefore, He proclaimed detailed rules, judgments and a doomsday to encourage His believers to accept life-threatening challenges for the sake of spiritual salvation.[99]

Among the apostles, Paul was probably the best person to talk about controlling desires; he was tempted by human desires all the time. He had a good study of human desires in general. But he understood that he himself was no exception to his observations. He admitted that he was not only a sinner but "the foremost of all sinners." He saw "a different law in the members of my body, waging war against the law of my mind and making me a prisoner of the law of sin which is in my members." In neurotheological terms, Paul certainly had a powerful emotional brain that bothered him all the time. He knew that "nothing good dwells in me, that is, in my flesh; for the willing is present in me, but the doing of the good is not." He cried out loud: "Wretched man that I am! Who will set me free from the body of this death?" Fortunately, his God brain prevailed over his emotional brain. "Thanks be to God through Jesus

---

98. Hag 2:7.
99. Matt 4: 1–11; Mark 1 1–14; Luke 4:1–13;

Christ our Lord! So then, on the one hand I myself with my mind am serving the law of God, but on the other, with my flesh the law of sin."[100]

How to deal with runaway emotions? Paul spent much space in letters to churches. In his first letter to the Corinthians, Paul provided detailed instructions about desires, marriage, idolatry, rituals, and spiritual pride. Similar instructions were echoed in his letters to the Ephesians, the Colossians, and to Timothy.[101]

But we know from neurotheology that rationality is only a slave to emotional brain. How could Pauline rational moral codes be effective means to contain the emotional brain? Paul seemed to realize this loophole in his argument. The force for law-bidding must come from another source other than rationality or law; that is, from the God brain. This is probably the reason why he also distinguished himself from other apostles who emphasized so much about law and rationality, such as Peter and Jacob. Paul's central theme in the Epistle to the Romans is that one cannot follow law or do any good deed without the help of the Trinity God. In his letters, Paul repeatedly employed the phrase "by faith" (ἐκ πίστεως, *ek pisteus*; διὰ πίστεως, *dia pisteus*)[102] to teach believers how to overcome emotional challenges; that is, by making a connection to the God brain.[103]

Balanced Brain in the Bible

So far, Biblical chapters have been put into the categories of God brain, emotional brain and rational brain by their relative emphasis on one type of the brain or the other. But taken as a whole, the Bible teaches its readers to develop all three brains in a balanced way and to strengthen the interconnections (via growing dendrites and axons) among brain parts. The following 370 Biblical chapters are such examples.

The story of the Great Flood begins with God's punishment of human sins (RB), continues with God's blessings of Noah (EB), and ends with God's

---

100. 1Tim 1:15-16; Rom 7:18, 23–25.

101. 1Cor 1–15; Eph 4–6; Col 2–3; 1Thess 4–5.

102. Although ἐκ may be translated as "because of," most of the contexts point to the translation of "by" as an instrument. διὰ can also be translated as "because," but it is not a common usage, and the contexts still prefer the translation of "by" (Wallace, *Greek Grammar*, 368-369, 371-372).

103. Rom 1:17, 3:22, 3:28, 3:30, 3:31, 4:11, 4:13, 4:18, 4:20, 5:1, 5:2, 9:30, 15:13; 2Co 4:13; Gal 2:16, 2:20, 3:8, 3:11, 3:14, 3:22, 3:23, 3:24, 3:25, 3:26; Eph 2:8, 3:12; Phil 3:9; Col 3:12; 1Thess 1:13; 2Thess 1:1, 2:13; 1Tim 1:2; 2Tim 3:15

creation of a new world sealed by the rainbow sign (GB). The transcendence, mercy and justice of God is summarized in God's proclamation to Noah: "When the bow is in the cloud, then I will look upon it, to remember the everlasting covenant between God and every living creature of all flesh that is on the earth [...] This is the sign of the covenant which I have established between Me and all flesh that is on the earth."[104]

Before Moses died, he recounted and taught the Israelis God's glory (GB), blessings (EB), laws and punishments (RB) in the forty years of their exodus. He concluded all these lessons with the Song of Moses, in which God self-proclaimed: "I, I am He, and there is no god besides Me; it is I who put to death and give life. I have wounded and it is I who heal, and there is no one who can deliver from My hand."[105] This is God of omnipotence, passion and justice.

The omnipotence, passion and justice of God created cycles of blessings and judgments upon Israelis in the book of Judges. God would bestow blessings on Israelis by sending a competent leader (judge) to defeat the enemy. But after receiving blessings, Israelis immediately disobeyed God's law. God implemented judgment on Israelis by allowing the enemy to attack Israelis. Israelis suffered greatly, repented sincerely, and asked for God's blessings. Accordingly, God bestowed blessings. This continued for four hundred years, with twelve judges appointed by God to save the Israelis.

This cycle of blessing and judgment was repeated in the rule of Samuel, who was a prophet, priest and judge. At the end of Samuel's rule, the Israelis were tired of the cycles. They attributed the cause of the cycles to the lack of a secular kingdom for the Israelis; they wanted a secular solution, not a religious solution. Despite God's warning that a secular solution would never work, the Israelis insisted on having one. So, God tried to make the best out of a terrible solution; He appointed a "good" king (a secular judge) to govern the faith community.[106]

But the first king, Saul, failed to reconcile the irreconcilable dual responsibilities of political and religious leaders. In the end, the "temptation" and "rational thinking" of political leadership overwhelmed the duties of religious leadership. Saul would have been a perfect king for the Israelis; he was handsome, taller than any of the people, hand-picked by Samuel as instructed by God, and given the Spirit of the LORD. He led the Israelis to defeat their

104. Gen 9:16–17.
105. Deut 32:39.
106. Isa 1–8.

neighbors. But in fear of losing political support from the Israelis before a war, he disobeyed God's commandment. From then on, it was all downhill. Based on his "rational thinking," he disobeyed God's instruction how to fight a war. Based on his "rational thinking" and emotional obsession with his throne, he sought the life of David, who was appointed by God to succeed Saul. He killed Ahimelech the priest and most of his family members out of a suspicion that Ahimelech was aiding David's escape. Finally, he sought military advice from a medium and paid the price with his own life and lives of his three sons.

The cycles of blessing and judgment continued throughout the history of the Kingdom of Israel. "Good" kings were blessed, such as Hezekiah and Josiah of Juda, who sincerely followed God's law and reformed the religion. But they were rare; all other kings of Judah and Israel were notorious for disobeying God's law. The secular kingdom was proven not compatible with the spiritual kingdom, because the secular kingdom always tilted the kings toward political rationality and emotion at the expense of God's law and compassion. In the end of these cycles, God destroyed both the secular kingdoms of Judah and Israel, and compelled the Israelis to live as a pure religious community, and to live a balanced and interconnected life of rationality, emotion and God.

Several chapters of the book of Psalm address a balanced teaching of rationality, emotion and God.[107] Psalm 18 is exemplary. The first part of Psalm begins with an emotional appeal to God's protection, "the LORD delivered him from the hand of all his enemies and from the hand of Saul. And he said, "I love You, O LORD, my strength." Then, the second part of Psalm praises the omnipotence and transcendence of God. The emotional appeal is repeated from 18:16 to 18:19. Then, the justice and judgment of God fills the verses of Psalm 18: 19-28. The theme of personal God re-appears from 18:29 to the end of Psalm 18.

Most of the chapters in the Prophets also devote relatively equal portions to strengthen the believers' brains of rationality, emotion and God. Isaiah 9 provides a gist of the book of Isaiah. God presents Himself as a personal God to the Israelis from verses 9:1 to 9:5, in which God promises to destroy the enemies of Israelis. Verses 9:8 to 9:21 present God as a rational God to the Israelis, Who executes continuous and severe judgments on the rebellious Israelis without mercy. But the critical verses and the most cited verses of Isa 9 are verses 9:6-7, which describe the omnipotence and transcendence of Triune God: "For a child will be born to us, a son will be given to us; and the

---

107. Pss 9–12, 17, 18, 25, 26, 31, 33, 34, 78, 89, 94, 98, 99, 106, 107

government will rest on His shoulders; and His name will be called Wonderful Counselor, Mighty God, Eternal Father, Prince of Peace. There will be no end to the increase of His government or of peace, on the throne of David and over his kingdom, to establish it and to uphold it with justice and righteousness from then on and forevermore. The zeal of the LORD of hosts will accomplish this." Similar themes of rationality, emotion and God are repeated in a balanced way in other Prophets.[108]

The balanced teaching of rationality, emotion and God in the OT is materialized in the balanced life of Jesus. He showed His compassion over the sick and possessed; He taught moral codes to His believers; and He tried to convince the Jews that He is Triune God, the Messiah they had expected. The Gospels of Matthew, Luke, and John address these issues evenly.[109] For instance, the Eight Beatitudes can be grouped into teachings of rationality, emotion and God, although theologians may have exegetical disagreements over the definition of the Beatitudes. "Blessed are the poor in spirit, for theirs is the kingdom of heaven." "Blessed are those who have been persecuted for the sake of righteousness, for theirs is the kingdom of heaven," and "Blessed are you when people insult you and persecute you, and falsely say all kinds of evil against you because of Me" are probably teachings about God. "Blessed are those who mourn, for they shall be comforted," "Blessed are the gentle, for they shall inherit the earth," "Blessed are the merciful, for they shall receive mercy," "Blessed are the peacemakers, for they shall be called sons of God" are probably teachings about compassion. And "Blessed are those who hunger and thirst for righteousness, for they shall be satisfied" and "Blessed are the pure in heart, for they shall see God" are probably teachings about rationality.[110]

Lastly, the Bible teaches not only a balanced development of rationality, emotion and God, but also the inter-connection among the three. In neuroscientific terms, it stimulates not only the individual growth of neurons in the frontal lobe, limbic system and parietal lobe, but also the "circuits" among these brain parts through the growth of dendrites and axons of each neuron across these brain parts. In Rom 3-15, Gal 3-6, and Phi 1-4, the doctrine of "righteousness by faith" seems to serve this neurotheological purpose. All human races are condemned to death because human nature is inherently sinful, Paul says. Could they escape the punishment by following rational law? No, they never could, because their evil emotion would enslave their

---

108. Isa 1–66; Jer 1–52; Hos 1–14; Joel 1–3; Amos 1–9; Mic 1–7; Zeph 1–3; Mal 1–4.
109. Matt 5–7; 10–16; 17–25; Luke 4–21; John 4–1.
110. Matt 5:3–9.

rationality and could only make things worse, as Paul explains: "by the works of the Law no flesh will be justified in His sight; for through the Law comes the knowledge of sin." So, how does one get out of the bad "circuits" connecting evil emotion and self-justification? "By faith in Jesus Christ," Paul proclaims the solution, "because in the forbearance of God He passed over the sins previously committed . . . so that He would be just and the justifier of the one who has faith in Jesus."[111] In neurotheological terms, evil emotion needs to be cleansed by the filter of the God brain, and rationality should be re-directed from evil emotion to the God brain. Only when the electrical and chemical signals sent by, or going through, the God brain, could believers receive powerful and correct help to become righteousness.

Together with chapter 2, this chapter finishes the discussion on the neurotheological foundation of human behaviors. The next three chapters put this neurotheological human in the institutional context of the church, capitalism and democracy.

Summary

This chapter completes the construction of a micro foundation of ecotheology. It first demonstrates that evolution theory is compatible with creationism with regard to the origin of modern humans. The Bible studies the same human and human natures as science does. Sections 2 to 4 explain how Biblical chapters can be categorized into subjects of spirituality, emotion and rationality. With so much emphasis on God in the Bible, it might come out as a surprise to God-centered theologians that the number of chapters about God's glory and attributes is only about 100 out of the total 1,189 chapters. This number lends support to the theological arguments that Christian God is mainly a personal God and that the Bible is about God as much as, if not more, about Man. There are about 300 Biblical chapters, almost three times that of about God, which discuss the personal relationships between God and human emotion. Emotion is indeed the slave master of human behaviors, isn't it? To control human emotion, the Bible spends another 300 or so chapters to encourage the believers to pursue wisdom and obey laws. However, the Bible sets up a model man as the One who has a balanced and integrated personality of spirituality, rationality and emotion. This emphasis is often embedded in other Biblical chapters on spirituality, rationality and emotion respectively. Moreover, there are about 400 chapters which teach a balanced development

111. Rom 3:20, 26.

of spirituality, rationality and emotion. Therefore, any ecotheology about the institutions of church, capitalism and democracy also needs to be based on a balanced view of individual spirituality, rationality and emotion, which is the main theme running through the next three chapters of this book.

4.

Church and Post-Ecotheology

"Who has believed our message? And to whom has the arm of the LORD been revealed?" (Isa 53:1)

"The scribes and the Pharisees have seated themselves in the chair of Moses; therefore all that they tell you, do and observe, but do not do according to their deeds; for they say things, and do not do them." (Matt 23:2-3)

ALTHOUGH ECOLOGISTS HAVE WRITTEN numerous volumes about the imminent ecological crises, and how to avoid them, since the 1960s, the same challenge Isaiah and Jesus raised could be raised again by those ecologists in the world today. Immediately after reading a good ecological book or upon hearing an ecologically correct speech, most middle-class consumers would resume their habits of destroying the ecology in their daily routines: run air conditioners all day long, go to a buffet every weekend, travel to a foreign country every half-year, buy new cell phones every other year, shop for new dresses and shoes every month, purchase a new car every four years, and move to a bigger house every ten years. Former American Vice-President, Al Gore, is a good example. He delivered one of the most persuasive presentations on ecology in the film "An Inconvenient Truth" (2006). However, he lived in a mansion of 10,000 square meters which consumed electricity of 221,000 kWh, 20 times of the national average.

The same question Isaiah and Jesus raised could be raised again by ecotheologians to most Christians today. Although ecotheologians have written numerous volumes about ecological crises and how to avoid them, most Christians simply choose to ignore those words of wisdom. Immediately after reading a good ecological book or hearing an ecologically correct sermon, most church members and pastors would resume their habits of destroying the ecology in their daily routines, much as other non-Christians would.

Furthermore, the same question Isaiah and Jesus raised could be raised again by the author of Revelation and Christian scientists to these very theologians themselves. Most ecotheologians develop their arguments based on the assumption of sustainable development as if they could postpone or prevent the coming of the Parousia. Revelation and scientific evidence of incoming ecological meltdown find a little room in their majestic ivory tower. Al Gore's "Inconvenient Truth" is about the restoration of a dying ecology when there is still time, while the Bible's "Inconvenient Truth" is about total annihilation of a dying ecology in preparation for a new one. Both science and the Bible patently state that we are already living in the age of post-ecology.

This chapter will first evaluate Chinese ecotheories as re-discovered by Western ecotheorists. The second section exposes the limits of current ecotheologies, as represented by the works of Jürgen Moltmann and Pope Benedict XVI. The third section of this chapter systematically studies all the Biblical verses directly related to the ecology and post-ecology to present the holistic ecological view of the Bible. The fourth section constructs a neuro-institutional post-ecotheology to address to the above questions and lay down the theological foundation for chapters 5 and 6. The last section summarizes the major arguments of this chapter.

Re-discovered Chinese Ecotheories

By definition, the ecology is a post-modernity issue, and the threat of global ecological crises was not recognized by Western ecologists until the 1960s. It was also the time some Western ecologists looked for non-Christian religious and philosophical sources to serve as their ideological foundations, because Lynn White accused Christianity for its original sin in creating ecological crises, as discussed in chapter 1 of this book. However, no Chinese ecologist existed in the 1960s and 1970s to lend support to Western ecotheories. The Chinese were still struggling against the challenges of economic modernization. In fact, from 1966 to 1976, the Chinese communist regime was waging the Cultural Revolution to annihilate traditional Chinese religions, including Confucianism, Daoism and Buddhism. How could these religions spare time to talk about the ecology? It was not until the late 1990s when Western ecotheories were imported to China did some Chinese intellectuals begin to re-discover ecological statements in their traditional religions through these Western theoretical lenses.

Impressed by the "China Rising" in the past few decades, a few Western ecotheorists once again look to Chinese religions and philosophies for solutions to ecological crises. Among other things, they find that the Daoist arguments of harmony between humans and nature (*tianren heyi*, 天人合一), geomancy (*fengshui*, 風水), limited exploitation of natural resources, meditation, and living a simple life are consistent with the principles of modern ecological programs.[1] They also find that the Chinese Buddhist precepts of equality among all creatures (*zhongsheng pingdeng*, 眾生平等), releasing captive animals (*fangsheng*, 放生), vegetarianism, (more) meditation, and living a simpler life than the Daoists would recommend are inspirational to promoting ecological consciousness. Both Daoism and Buddhism prescribe anti-anthropocentrism in opposition to the anthropocentrism of Christianity.[2]

As a by-product of "China Rising," pollution, food safety, deforestation, internal ecological refugees caused by economic development projects also caught the attention of Chinese intellectuals and government leaders. "If Western ecologists said there is something ecologically correct in Chinese religions, there must be something worth looking into," a few Chinese intellectuals thought. So, they dig into the Collection of Daoism (*Daozang*, 道藏) which consists of 5,485 volumes and about 60,000,000 words, or the Collection of Chinese Buddhism (*Zhonghua Dazangjing*, 中華大藏經) which contains 230,000 volumes and more than 100 million words. It is not hard to find a significant amount of ecological statements in these Collections. However, not many Chinese intellectuals have developed additional insights other than what those Western ecologists had told them.[3] Even worse, some of the ecological statements in these Collections turn out not very ecological at all.

There are a number of major problems with Chinese ecotheories. First, there is too much emphasis on meditation but little on action. According to their conclusions, if one mediates long enough the harmony between humans and nature, the holiness of nature, or nirvana, all ecological crises could be meditated away. Could they? Secondly, even if some made concrete

1. On Daoist ecotheories, see Hathaway, *Tao*; Kim, *Theology*; Miller, *Green Religion*.

2. On Buddhist ecotheories, see Coleman, *Awake*; Henning, *Buddhism and Deep Ecology*; Kaza and Kraft, *Dharma Rain*; Payne, *How Much*; Tucker and Williams, *Buddhism and Ecology*. For ecotheories in other Asian traditions, including China, see Callicott and McRae, *Environmental Philosophy*.

3. Recent Chinese ecotheories include Bi, "Theory and Practice"; Chen, "On Taoist"; Sun, "Inspiration"; and Yang, 'spirit."

suggestions concerning actions, they might be unrealistic or counterproductive for modern societies. For instance, if we all follow the dressing codes of Buddhist monks or nuns, the fashion business in Milan, Paris, and New York would probably collapse overnight. If we stop buying new home appliances and send broken ones to repair shops, what would happen to Wall Street? If we all become vegetarians . . . how many would? And what are its impacts on poultry, fishing, and cattle industries? Would the release of captive animals destroy local ecological balance or lead them to death if they are misplaced? Does the release encourage the business of catch-and-release as being promoted by some temples? If we are forbidden to kill any insects, how do we keep crops healthy and humans from diseases? Do the Buddhists accept modern medicine most of which are tested on laboratory animals before they go on the market? Does not the Daoist practice of alchemy often include elements harvested from endangered species for their mystical natural and spiritual powers? Does not readjusting building outlooks and office furniture to meet *fengshui* requirements waste resources? As Yi-fu Tuan had cautioned in as early as 1968 about the "discrepancies between environmental attitude and behavior" in China, could Buddhist monks and Daoist priests live up to these ecological standards?[4] Has not Ven. Yongxin 釋永信, the abbot of the largest Chinese Buddhist temple *Shaolinshi* 少林寺, been criticized for his luxurious lifestyle and sexual misconducts? Finally, even if everything said above is theoretically correct, it does not mean we can resolve the collective action problems of the ecology. So far, Confucianism, Buddhism and Daoism have not offered institutional solutions to solve national or international ecological crises in the (post-) modern era.

This is not to say that Confucianism, Buddhism and Daoism have nothing to contribute to the global ecological movement. For one thing, the Chinese need to find ideological justifications in their traditional cultures for the ecological programs they desperately need. For another, God did occasionally teach His believers through the mouths of non-believers to remind them the truths, or complementary to the truths in the Bible. For instance, Jethro, the priest of Midian and Moses' father-in-law, offered suggestions to set up the administrative system of leaders of thousands, of hundreds, of fifties and of tens. Balaam, the priest of Moab, blessed the Israelis. And the spirit of Cyrus, king of Persia, was stirred up by God to help the Israelis rebuild their temple.[5] For the same theological reason, Christians can be reminded of God's creation

4. Tuan, "Discrepancies."
5. Exod 18:21; Num 22–24; Ezra 1:1–4.

by the Chinese harmony between humans and nature, of God's teaching of living a simple life (but not too extremely a frugal life), of God's ultimate plan of salvation by Daoist and Buddhist meditation, and of Messiah's Parousia by the Buddhist eschatology about Maitreya Buddha. In particular, as soon as Buddhism arrived in China, the Buddhist eschatology was merged with Daoism and Confucianism and became a major religious justification for peasant revolutions until 1911.[6] Nevertheless, Christians should not dwell too much on Chinese religions and lose their core theological doctrines of Trinity, Parousia, and integrating faith with action. Unfortunately, many Western ecotheologians seem to take the wrong elements from Chinese religions to develop their ecotheologies, as will be discussed in the next section.

However, there are at least two attributes of Chinese religions, which both Western and Chinese ecotheorists have missed, that will contribute to the self-reflection of Western ecotheologies.[7] The first attribute is religious tolerance. Ever since the end of the Buddhist Four Great Tribulations (*sanwu yidi zhi huo,* 三武一帝之禍) in 955 AD, China has not experienced significant religious wars as in Western societies. Confucianism, Buddhism and Daoism were freely practiced in the royal courts, local governments and families. Their syncretistic natures certainly helped to maintain the peace, but they also maintained their distinctiveness from one another. Christian churches do not and cannot adopt theological syncretism. But there is plenty of room to engage in democratic ecological dialogue among different social classes within the church, among different Christian denominations, and between Christianity and other religions. Chapter 6 will build on this thesis of religious tolerance.

The other attribute of Chinese religions, which may contribute to contemporary ecological programs, is their relative distance from major political controversies. Chinese Buddhism learned this the hard way. When it arrived from Tibet to China in large quantity around the fifth century, it carried with it the Tibetan Buddhist tradition of a religious state as Catholicism in the Middle Ages. It challenged the Confucian and Daoist cultures as well as the religious legitimacy of the Chinese dynasties. It was even involved in some palace coups. The religious coalitions of Confucianism and Daoism fought back and inspired the Buddhist Four Great Tribulations. In order to survive in the Chinese political-religious environment, Chinese Buddhism

---

6. Lee, "Daoist Tribulation."

7. For the history of Chinese state-religion relations, see Goossaert and Palmer, *Religious Question*; Lagerwey, *China*; and Kuo, *Religion and Nationalism.*

abandoned the Tibetan political Buddhism, and afterwards made friends with Confucianism and Daoism. Thus, although the Chinese state was a "religious state," there was never a state religion to super-impose its religious and moral codes on the state. Confucianism did serve as a political "orthopraxy" for all religions. However, it did not forbid the emperors, state officials, aristocrats and peasants from practicing other religions. Keeping a safe distance between religion and state in the Chinese religious history may remind the Christians of their Biblical duty of building a spiritual "kingdom on earth," not a secular "kingdom on earth," when they engage in ecological programs. This is the subject of chapter 6.

Vanity of Ecotheologies

> "You ask and do not receive, because you ask with wrong motives, so that you may spend it on your pleasures." (Jas 4:3)

"Is It Too Late?" is the title of a 1972 book written by a pioneer in ecotheology, John B. Cobb, Jr. Given the scientific data and projections available at his time, the conclusion of the book was resoundingly pessimistic: it is too late! However, as any good pastor, priest and theologian would do, Cobb prescribed the standard solution to all despair and pessimism in a Christian's life: HOPE. "It is the belief in this Spirit, the giver of life and love, that is the basis of hope. In spite of all the destructive forces we let loose against life on this planet, the Spirit of Life is at work in ever new and unforeseeable ways, countering and circumventing the obstacles we put in its path."[8]

In the 1995 revised version of this book, Cobb reaffirmed his dilemma: "it is already too late. That is, there were possibilities for a happy future in 1970 that no longer exist today." The change he had hoped for has come in the form of growing consensus and action in the world over the importance of environmental issues. After citing some ambivalent evidence of such change, however, he wavered back to pessimism: "It would be possible to list other encouraging signs of change. It would also be possible to point too much that is profoundly disappointing and discouraging. The fate of the Earth remains unsure."[9] The Afterword of the 1995 edition no longer mentions the word "hope" or "spirit." Will the hope take longer to come? Alternatively, is it possible that Christian theologians have hoped for something contrary to

8. Cobb, *Is It Too Late*, 81.
9. Cobb, *Is It Too Late*, 83–85.

what the Trinitarian God has planned for the world? Do we "ask with wrong motives, so that (we) may spend it on (our) pleasures," as James 4:3 says?

Jürgen Moltmann and Pope Benedict XVI respectively are probably the most prominent Protestant and Catholic ecotheologians today. Although making a significant contribution to ecotheology, their contribution to ecological practice is limited at their best and maybe counter-productive at their worst. Their ecotheologies are not much different from Cobb's forty years ago. In fact, most of the current ecotheologies exhibit limits and side-effects that provide short-term comfort to average Christians at the expense of long-term spiritual welfare.

Jürgen Moltmann publishes several works on ecotheology, among which *Sun of Righteousness, Arise! God's Future for Humanity and the Earth* is the focus of our discussion.[10] The book starts with a discussion of the general decline of traditional European churches in the twentieth century, and the rebirth of independent churches in the twenty-first century. As compared to traditional churches, these independent churches place more emphases on the resurrection of Jesus Christ and the coming of the kingdom of God on earth. These two emphases are related: the resurrection of Jesus "is inclusive, open to the world, and embraces the universe, an event not merely human and historical but cosmic too: the beginning of the new creation of all things."[11] The new creation of the world is not necessarily another Christendom. "This does not mean the churchification of the world; what is in view are Christ's cosmic dimensions . . . Christianity is designed to be the healing beginning of the healed creation in the midst of a disrupted and sick world."[12] The kingdom of God is about righteousness, justice and love, not about monotheism; in fact, Christianity is not monotheistic.[13] Neither will the resurrection of the natural world through resurrected Jesus Christ lead to the literal New Heaven and New Earth described in the book of Revelation, or to the kingdom of God coming down from heaven, but to "this-worldliness of the new creation of all things. God does not save his creation for heaven; he renews the earth. God's kingdom is the kingdom of the resurrection on earth."[14]

---

10. Moltmann, *Sun*. Moltmann's earlier works related to ecology include: Moltmann, *God*; *Spirit*; *Source*.

11. Moltmann, *Sun*, 55.

12. Moltmann, *Sun*, 69.

13. Moltmann, *Sun*, chapters 10–12.

14. Moltmann, *Sun*, 72 and chapter 9.

What about the total destruction of the existing world described in the book of Revelation? Moltmann argues that "the idea that the world will end with God's final judgment is not originally a Christian concept, and not even a biblical one."[15] The resurrection, or "sunrise," of Christ is to repair the existing world by righteousness, justice and love. The judgment is not about vengeance against sinners and non-believers, or about the annihilation of the physical world, but about raising up the victims and educating the perpetrators.[16] Once all the disrupted conditions in creation are made right, "the new creation can stand on the firm ground of righteousness and justice, and can endure to eternity."[17] There is no need for the New Heaven and New Earth.

How do we bring about righteousness, justice and love in this world? Moltmann prescribes a "new Trinitarian thinking and experience." Trinity is not just a spiritual concept, but a social program to save the world. A Trinitarian community is "one without privileges, and one where liberties are not infringed. The persons can be persons only in community; the community can be free only in its personal members. It ought to be possible to harmonize personal liberty and just community if we look at the triune God and his resonance in the church, provided that the church, ecumenically united."[18]

Once the church is ecumenically united, Christians can proselytize the model of the Trinitarian community to the entire world. How can each Christian think and experience the Trinitarian God? Here comes Moltmann's famous Theology of Meditation and Hope: seeing, recognizing, wondering, contemplating, and perceiving that will enable us to enter the light of truth, face to face with Trinitarian God.[19] Following the above diagnosis and prescription, all human beings will live happily ever after, and ecological crises no more to be worried. Amen!

From the neuro-institutional perspective, Jürgen Moltmann's ecotheology seems to put a major emphasis on strengthening the linkages between God brain and rational brain so that Christians may sanctify ecological values. As Christian psychiatrist, Mark R. McMinn, correctly remarks: "Unlike meditation in Eastern religions, where the goal is to empty one's mind, the goal of Christian meditation is to fill one's mind with an awareness of God's presence." "Our inner life, shaped by God's transformation of our character

---

15. Moltmann, *Sun*, 127.
16. Moltmann, *Sun*, chapter 13.
17. Moltmann, *Sun*, 141.
18. Moltmann, *Sun*, 163.
19. Moltmann, *Sun*, chapter 15.

through Scripture and other means, is our greatest resource in helping hurting people."[20] With their experiment on college students who practiced Zen Buddhist meditation, Canadian neuroscientists Veronique A. Taylor reconfirms many similar studies that mindfulness meditation can promote emotional stability. In particular, he finds that "experienced meditators had increased connectivity between certain default mode network religions (e.g., dorsomedial prefrontal cortex [rational brain] and right inferior parietal lobule [God brain], compared to beginner meditators."[21] This emotional stability after meditation is undoubtedly an important first step toward a solution to ecological problems. However, a first step is not a complete solution to ecological problems, especially if the first step is stepping on a wrong path.

There are at least six major problems with Moltmann's ecotheology that make it both empirical and theologically unsound. First, "faith apart from works is barren."[22] Meditation (seeing, recognizing, wondering, contemplating, and perception) does not necessarily produce action, while prevention of ecological crises requires concrete actions with or without meditation. Even if meditation could produce action, Moltmann does not specify which concrete actions are appropriate; he talks only about general principles of ecological actions.

Secondly, suppose a Christian is motivated by Moltmann's book and is ready to take ecological actions. However, she immediately faces the collective-action problem of ecological goods: that she cannot do it alone and whatever action she takes, it amounts to a drop of clean water in a polluted lake unless other people do take similar ecological actions. She would soon feel frustrated and return to the much easy job of ecological meditation. Yes, meditation could be ecological as long as it is practiced at home without an air conditioner on.

Thirdly, an ecotheology based on the resurrection of Jesus is a non-starter for resolving ecological crises. On the one hand, if Jesus had already been resurrected two thousand years ago, then why does He need to be resurrected again? There is no second resurrection of Jesus in the Bible, only the Second Coming of Jesus (Parousia). On the other hand, it does not generate the sense of urgency required for coping with imminent ecological crises. Psychological experiments show that most people are risk-averse, put more value on losses than on gains, and prefer immediate consumption to future consumption.

20. McMinn, *Psychology*.
21. Taylor et al. "Impacts," 4-14.
22. Jas 2:20.

Moltmann is correct to argue that the resurrection of Jesus indeed brings hope to Christians who are suffering. However, most contemporary Christians are not suffering in their material life, although an effective ecological program will cause them material suffering. Why do they ever want to hope for the resurrection of Jesus when they enjoy so much their present material life?

Fourthly, Moltmann's appeal to an ecumenical church across boundaries of religions may achieve so little in ecological programs, while costing so much in church unity. Unified ecological actions require unified ecotheologies, but not necessarily a unified or ecumenical church, if it is ever possible. Furthermore, most of other religions probably do not care if Christianity gives up on its monotheism or not. They probably do care if some Christian theologians promote various conspiracies of "One God, Many Christs" and demote their supreme gods down to Christian Christs under Christian God.[23] Thus, Moltmann's appeal to an ecumenical church across boundaries of religions may kindle all kinds of religious wars and distract their efforts to save the earth.

Lastly, the goal of Moltmann's ecological program is neither Biblical nor psychologically possible. If everything he envisions goes smoothly, the result will be "the new creation can stand on the firm ground of righteousness and justice, and can endure to eternity." How could this not be Biblical? The catch is that Moltmann's "new creation" is the result of human effort to improve the existing world and keep it sustainable to eternity; it is an "earthly kingdom *like* heaven." It is not the result of God's new creation of another "kingdom *of* heaven on earth" after a destruction of the existing world. Even if Moltmann's analogy of Jesus' resurrection is applicable here, Jesus' resurrection only occurred after His body was dead. If the analogy of resurrection is relevant here, the current world needs to be totally destroyed before the New Heaven and New Earth arrives. After meticulously examining thirty-two Biblical verses related to the eschatology of Jesus and fifty-eight verses on the arrival of the kingdom of God, theologian Dale C. Allison convincingly argues that "our choice is not between apocalyptic Jesus and some other Jesus; it is between an apocalyptic Jesus and no Jesus at all . . ." and that the kingdom of God is "a realm as well as a reign; it is a place and time yet to come in which God will reign supreme."[24]

This distorted Biblical assumption of a savable world through Christian hope and action is not only the core of Moltmann's, and that of his followers like Frederick Herzog, ecotheology. It is also that of his critics, like George

---

23. Dupuis, *Toward*.
24. Allison, *Constructing Jesus*, 33–47, 164–201.

Weigel and Oliver O"Donovan, who debate with Moltmann on the ecological role of the state without challenging his assumption of a savable world.[25]

Furthermore, for Moltmann, righteousness and justice are not only spiritual but also social and political; but in the Bible, they are spiritual only. Righteousness and justice as a social-political program are the inventions of the Enlightenment program based on human rationality. According to the findings of neurotheology, human rationality is only a slave to the human emotion. Are there not as many definitions of righteousness and justice as there are personalities, cultures, and time periods? Can ordinary citizen with only bounded rationality understand and pursue so many social and political issues which may or may not have a direct relationship with the ecology? Therefore, Moltmann's "new creation" is probably a political mirage at its best and a new "crusade" at its worst in the sense that most crusades failed to reach Constantinople because crusaders devastated one another on the road.

Followers of Moltmann's ecotheology, the South African theologians Jakub Urbaniak and Elijah Otu, probably expand his logic and expose his difficulties more than other students of Moltmann's. They correctly see the coming reign of God via Jesus incarnated in the body of the church and cosmic nature. Though, their ecotheology is not anthropocentric nor monotheism, but rather pantheist and religiously pluralistic, and part of the Deep Ecology school.[26] They suggest a "theological matrix for the postulated inter-species, and indeed universal (cosmic) solidarity in the eschatological expectation, a solidarity with all flesh including both living creatures and, mutatis mutandis, the very basic physical stuff." Furthermore, they appeal to all the "comrades of the kingdom" to become "particularly clear-sighted and sensitive to the suffering of the creatures of God, the marginalization of the poor, women, black, LGBTI people, etcetera, and the great ecological dangers alike," although they do not elaborate on how to take concrete actions on these complicated agendas.[27]

The other major ecotheological work is the "Green Pope" Benedict XVI's *The Garden of God: Toward a Human Ecology*. It is a collection of Pope Benedict's fifty-five ecological speeches and messages addressed to different walks

---

25. Herzog, *Justice*; Weigel, "Political"; O'Donovan, *Desire*; cited from Webb, "Eschatology," 500–17.

26. Among other qualities, Barnhill and Gottlieb, *Deep*, 6. define Deep Ecology to include "an emphasis on the intrinsic value of nature (biocentrism or ecocentrism); a tendency to value all things in nature equally (biocentric egalitarianism); . . . a tendency to look to other cultures (especially Asian and indigenous) as sources of insight."

27. Urbaniak and Out, "How," 7-8.

of life. Therefore, it is not as academic as Moltmann's ecotheology. Nevertheless, several major arguments can be discerned in the book.

First, Moltmann was a colleague of Pope Benedict at Tübingen Theological Seminary before the latter became the Pope. Following the tradition of St. Francis of Assisi, the Pope starts his ecological meditation with the sanctification of the earth, which "mirror the creative love of God" and "is indeed a precious gift of the Creator who, in designing its intrinsic order, has given us bearing that guide us as stewards of his creation." Resonating Moltmann's ecotheology of resurrection, Pope Benedict urges Christians to "contemplate the cosmos and its marvels in light of the creative work of the Father and the redemptive work of Christ, who by his death and Resurrection has reconciled with God." All Christians should 'seriously cultivate the mental openness that is dictated by love and rooted in faith . . . [to witness] their sense of responsibility for the safeguard of creation."[28]

Secondly, the book promotes a Human Ecology. Ecological crises are "the consequences of an inhumane concept of development . . . [which is] limited to the technical-economic aspect [and] obscuring the moral-religious dimension." A Human Ecology is both narrower and broader than secular ecology in the sense that it is human-centered instead of nature-centered, and it is concerned not only with ecological values but also human values like peace, economic development, basic needs, equitable distribution of resources, morality, family values, social justice, intergenerational solidarity, and human rights. This Human Ecology assumes that "humanity is indeed capable of carrying out its grave duty to hand on the earth to future generations."[29]

Thirdly, the combination of faith and science would lead Christians to appreciate creation and Human Ecology and engage in ecological practices. "God has given us two books: the book of sacred scripture and the book of nature." Therefore, the construction of a Human Ecology requires both faith and reason. The Holy Spirit "comes to meet us through creation and its beauty," and strengthens the faith in Human Ecology; while "nature is truly structured in a mathematical way, and that our mathematics, invented by our human mind, is truly the instrument for working with nature, to put it at our service, to use it through technology."[30]

---

28. Urbaniak and Out, "How," 12, 33–34, 42–44, 51–52, 84–85.

29. Urbaniak and Out, "How," 14–16, 18, 34, 38–52, 73–75, 98–99, 104, 134–135, 139–196.

30. Urbaniak and Out, "How," 5, 91, 108, 125-133.

Finally, Pope Benedict makes concrete suggestions about ecological practices. He promotes more modest lifestyles, reductions in energy consumption, improvements in energy efficiency, and he denounces "consumerist mentality" which causes "the excessive and arbitrary consumption of resources." Particularly, he promotes "a strategic revitalization of agriculture" not only for the sake of meeting the poor's basic needs but also for cultural reasons. He promotes "personal responsibility along with a social dimension of rural activities based on the undying values of hospitality, solidarity, and sharing the toil of labor."[31]

Pope Benedict's ecological statements are consistent with various Catholic ecotheologies since the Second Vatican Council (1962-1965) began to discuss ecological issues. They are shaped by the major theological emphases of the Second Vatican Council, namely, expanded tolerance of theological diversity and promotion of social justice. Accordingly, two major principles of ecotheology are laid down at the Council: "respect for Earth and the biotic community . . . as God's creations; and provision of steps to ensure that from the goods of creation human needs would be met as people worked together for the common good." Human "domination" over nature is first replaced by human "dominion" and finally replaced by "stewardship." In more concrete terms, a Catholic ecotheology consists of "sacramental universe," "Christian's essential duty to care for creation," "understanding of bioregional issues," "sacredness and dignity of all creation," "the relationship between environmental degradation and human poverty," "a shift from anthropocentric dominion to stewardship-caretaking perspective," and "a relational consciousness about humanity's interdependence with other creatures within creation."[32]

Speaking to the general audience, Pope Benedict's ecotheology covers more theological and empirical issues than Moltmann's. However, several debates can be raised about the Pope's arguments. First, like the problem with Moltmann's ecotheology, the Pope's ecotheology is built on the book of Genesis, not Revelation; on the resurrection of Jesus, and not on the Parousia of Jesus. Among the fifty-five speeches in Pope Benedict's book, only one briefly talks about the relationship between ecology and Revelation. The title of the speech is "Creation Is Marked by Finitude." He quotes from Mark 13:31, "Heaven and earth will pass away, but my words will not pass," to start this speech. He soon switches direction to the creation ecology without

---

31. Urbaniak and Out, "How," 46, 48, 109-111, 198-200, 204,
32. Hart, *Environmental Theology*, 8, 60, 101.

elaborating the implications of a finite nature, what "will pass away" means for ecotheology?[33]

Secondly, although an improvement over Moltmann, the Pope still relies too much on meditation while ignoring the collective-action problem in practice, even within the Church. Archbishop Jean-Louis Bruguès, who writes the foreword for Pope Benedict's ecological book, cited three examples of Vatican's ecological actions: photovoltaic panels were installed on the roof of the principal auditorium of the Vatican; its dining rooms were powered by a solar cooling system; and it cultivated a several-hundred-acre climatic forest in Bükk (Hungary) in order to become the first climatically neutral country.[34] The problems with these "ecological" actions are: did the Vatican actually reduce the "excessive and arbitrary consumption" of electricity in the spacious auditorium and dining rooms? Could the Vatican not use these rooms without air-conditioning as they were originally designed? Moreover, why does the earth need another "several-hundred-acre climatic forest" to be cultivated so that the forest would provide a valuable quota to offset Vatican's current pollution or to be traded in the global carbon-dioxide market, i.e., to encourage more pollution?[35] By 2016, the project was not yet implemented, probably a good news for the earth.

An article recently published in *The Catholic World Report*, "Catholics, the Environment, and a "Culture of Waste," enumerated the ecotheology of Popes Benedict and Francis (named after the great ecotheologian, St. Francis of Assisi). Two readers' comments immediately followed this report. The one from India complained: "In India . . . all festival announcements and information about saints, posters on Church matters are printed in thick plastic sheets (which are called flex banners here) and after used one time thrown away to pollute the earth . . . Community dinners arranged at Church premises invariably uses plastic throw-away plates, cups, etc., which are then happily thrown away as nonperishable waste forever. Learned priests and prelates . . . seem to be totally unaware that polluting the earth is a mortal sin as announced by our former Pope Benedict." The other comment was from Sri Lanka: "I could not agree more with what our friend in India says. I believe there should be a group appointed by the church, in each Diocese, to educate each parish and advise them on how to conduct such occasion. Banana leaves

---

33. Hart, *Environmental Theology*, 36–38.
34. Hart, *Environmental Theology*, ix.
35. Struck, "Carbon Offsets."

are great to eat off!"³⁶ Apparently, the collective-action problem of ecological crises persists in these "individually-rational" Catholic churches, despite the inspirational appeals by the Popes. What the Church needs to do next, as the Sri Lankan Catholic suggested, is to set up an institution to educate and monitor the priests.

Thirdly, while Moltmann strayed away from an orthodox ecotheology by proposing a non-monotheist ecumenical church, Pope Benedict might have strayed away by expanding too much the political agenda of his ecotheology. Both Moltmann and Pope Benedict seem to converge on the interpretation of the New Heaven and New Earth as a renewal of the current heaven and earth and make them eternal for future generations. If the current world is savable, the Church must play a vital role in public life. But which aspect of public life? Only those related to ecology? No. On Pope Benedict's ecological agenda, natural ecology is subsumed under Human Ecology which includes peace, economic development, basic needs, morality, family values, social justice, intergenerational solidarity, equitable distribution of resources, and human rights. Can an ordinary, bounded-rationality Christian engage in ecological actions with a profound or clear understanding of all these social-political goals in mind, if these goals can ever be well defined? Have not these social-political goals seriously divided liberal Christians and fundamentalist Christians in Western societies since the 1980s? Will ecological crises suddenly bring about a happy reunion of the liberals and the fundamentalists in the near future? Will his program, if successful, result in the unification of the church and the state at the global scale: the Third Christendom?

Pope Benedict's ecotheology probably is a succinct summary of theologies of ecojustice, which ultimately encounter the above practical questions at the local church level. Take for example Michael S. Northcott's theology of ecojustice. He blames secular modernity for creating ecological crises by undermining traditional culture and religion which had maintained harmonious human relations with nature. In Hebrew and Christian traditions, there are plenty of norms, rules and practices which help keep these harmonious relations. But which part of the Christian human relations are cogent to ecology? Instead of those verses cited in most ecotheological works in chapter 3 of this book, Northcott focuses on those related to justice and equity. He argues that "excessive inequalities between humans are not only opposed to divine justice, which is enshrined in the law of the covenant community, but also to the natural law of the land and of created order." Justice is "crucial to an

---

36. Ziegler, "Catholics."

ecological perspective on human society" because "the oppression of the poor is intricately connected with the destruction of environments and habitats throughout human history as well as in the contemporary developing world. The just distribution of those biophysical goods which make for human flourishing ... is essential to a civil society in which crime and social disorder are minimized, and in which the poor do not have to steal, or to destroy their environment, in order to provide for their children," and "justice requires that those abstract economic and technological forces which construct human life and society in the modern world must be subjected to democratic control."[37]

The ecotheologies of Moltmann and Pope Benedict are the most prominent among contemporary ecotheologians. In addition to them, there are probably as many ecotheologies as there are stars in the sky. According to Willis Jenkins' contribution, which follows that of Laurel Kearns, there are three "practical strategies" of ecotheology: ecojustice, Christian stewardship, and ecological spirituality.[38] Ecojustice theologies "rely on a view of sanctification in which grace illuminates creation's integrity. Stewardship theologies rely on tropes of redemption, where an encounter with God creates vocational responsibilities to care for creation [...] [Theologies of ecological spirituality] appropriate themes of deification, by which personal creativity brings all creation into the gift of union with God."[39]

Prominent theologians of ecojustice include James Gustafson, Larry L. Rasmussen, Michael S. Northcott, H. Paul Santmire, Lisa Sideris, and Jürgen Moltmann.[40] Major theologians of Christian stewardship include R.J. Berry, Calvin B. DeWitt, Au Sable Institute, J. David Cassel, Richard T. Wright, Susan Power Bratton, Holmes Rolston III, E. Calvin Beisner, and Ronald Cole-Turner.[41] Representative theologians of ecological spirituality include Thomas Berry, Matthew Fox, Gordon Lathrop, Charles Murphy, Pierre Teilhard de Chardin, and Orthodox theologians Philip Sherrard and Patriarch Ignatius IV of Antioch. Representative theologians emphasize mystical religious experiences rather than religious doctrines, sacramental and liturgical sensibilities

---

37. Northcott, *Environments*, 264-265, 314-315.

38. Kearns, "Saving," 55-70; Jenkins, *Ecologies*; Cassel, "Stewardship."

39. Jenkins, *Ecologies*, 19.

40. Gustafson, *Ethics*; Rasmussen, *Earth*; Northcott, *Environments*; Santmire, *Brother*; Sideris, *Environmental*.

41. Berry, *Environmental Stewardship*; DeWitt, *Caring for Creation*; Au Sable Institute, "Au Sable"; Bratton, *Christianity*; Rolston, *Conserving*; Beisner, *Where Garden*; Cole-Turner, *New Genesis*.

rather than rational theological analyses, and cosmic transformation rather than anthropocentric salvation.[42]

After Jenkins carefully examined these three practical strategies, he proposed his theology of ecological grace, which is, in essence, a combination and adaptation of these three practical strategies.[43] Although he replaces "meditation" with "lamentation," "sanctification" with "grace," and "resurrection" with "restoration," his major lines of arguments are not significantly different from that of these three practical strategies. After all, these three practical strategies differ among themselves not in kind but degree, and not in Biblical truth but relative emphasis. Most Christians probably cannot tell the difference between "sanctified creation's integrity" (ecojustice) from "creation's union with God" (ecological spirituality). Nor would theologians of ecojustice and ecological spirituality disagree with the stewardship theologians' proposition that Christians have a sacred responsibility to restore ecological balance.[44]

For instance, Richard Bauckham claims that his ecotheology is enlightened by Jürgen Moltmann, who, according to Jenkins, is a theologian of ecojustice. However, Bauckham's ecotheology clearly belongs to the genre of ecological spirituality, as he follows closely the arguments of Mathew Fox and Francis of Assisi, who, according to Jenkins, are theologians of ecological spirituality.[45] Although he is somewhat critical of the stewardship theology for being anthropocentric, Bauckham concludes his "theology of biodiversity" or "creation mysticism" with propositions similar to the stewardship theology like "humans have 'dominion' (caring responsibility) for other living creature," "dominion begins from appreciating God's valuation of his creation," and "dominion is to be exercised in letting be just as much as in intervention."[46] In fact, if not somewhat constrained by the ecojustice theology and the stewardship theology, Baulkham's "theocentric creation" may lead theologically unsophisticated lay believers to stray into the limbo of deism, animism, or

---

42. Berry, *Dream*; Fox, *Creation Spirituality*; Lathrop, *Holy Ground*; Murphy, *At Home*; Chardin, *Phenomenon*; Chryssavgis and Foltz, *Toward*, 4–5.

43. Jenkins, *Ecologies*, chapter 12.

44. Dyke disagrees with the term and content of "responsible stewardship" which may "merely be a hidden new way to affirm human dominion, human arrogance and anthropocentrism." Instead, he suggests "reluctant interference" or "careful interference." Dyk, "Responsible."

45. Bauckham, *Living*.

46. Bauckham, *Living*, 227–29.

pantheism.⁴⁷ What is the good of saving the natural world, if we could, when many believers stray into the pantheist natural world?

Some ecotheologians propose to label human behavior against nature as a "social sin" in order to discourage Christian believers from polluting the environment.⁴⁸ Catholic theologian Jame Schaefer calls the sin against God's creation not only as a "social sin" but as a "planetary sin."⁴⁹ Based on the ecotheology of spirituality, this is potentially a powerful tool to intimidate ecological perpetrators. After all, if God brain has a powerful control over rational brain and emotional brain, what could be more effective an ecological measure than telling sincere Christians that polluting the environment is as bad as blasphemy against God? Or, that you cannot go the heaven because you drank bottled water at a theological conference the other day.

There are several problems with this method. First, by adding a new Commandment to the Bible, this method risks "taking the name of the LORD your God in vain."⁵⁰ Secondly, it might unintentionally put the Second Coming of Jesus in this category because He will destroy the current natural world as described in Revelation. He is the One and only One who is capable of committing this "planetary sin" by Himself. Thirdly, it imposes an unbearable burden on average Christians who cannot know the exact boundary of this sin. Am I committing an ecological sin because I use plastic products at home, take my station wagon to work instead of walking, read a paperback book instead of an electronic version, and eat chicken and fish instead of vegetables? Is the Green Patriarch or the Green Pope themselves free from these sins in his everyday life? Fourthly, it cannot resolve the collective action problem of ecological crises when other Christian believers or believers of other religions do not accept this radical view of ecological sin.

These criticisms apply to similar ecotheological projects which push to the extreme on issues of social justice and religious pluralism. For instance, the Earth Bible Project proposes six major hermeneutic principles of ecotheology: Intrinsic worth of the universe and its components; Interconnectedness (and interdependence) of all living beings; Voice of the Earth as a subject, rejoicing or speaking against injustice; Purpose of the universe and all its components in a dynamic cosmic design; Mutual custodianship acting as partners with

---

47. Similar stray into theological grey areas is the work by Jay B. McDaniel who introduces the concept of "panentheism" between theism and pantheism. McDaniel, *With*.

48. Nash, *Loving Nature*.

49. Schaefer, "Environmental," 69–94.

50. Exod 20:7.

Earth, rather than rulers; Active resistance of Earth and its components in the struggle for justice.[51] Anthropocentric creation and Parousia can hardly find their footprints in these six principles

Can feminist ecotheologies help amend these ecotheological problems? Probably not. In fact, they probably make ecological problems even more complex by bringing in additional controversies of social justice and pantheism. For instance, Mary Mellor's feminist ecology correctly assumes that there is "a connection between the exploitation and degradation of the natural world and the subordination and oppression of women." It is true that often women, particularly those in developing countries, suffer the most from ecological crises. However, she hastily blames the intrinsic patriarchy in Christianity and rationalism for both sins. It is also true that men dominate most positions in church leadership and the scientific community. Nevertheless, it is not clear whether female church leaders or female scientists are naturally equipped with ecological genes stronger than those of men. Are women necessarily better "mediators" between nature and humans than men?[52] Ecological philosopher Andrew Dobson provides more criticisms of ecofeminism,[53] which need not be repeated here.

Adapting to this line of feminist ecology, feminist theologian Catherine Keller highly endorses Moltmann's ecotheology of hope, meditation, and social justice. However, she goes beyond Moltmann in three major ways. First, on the timing and scale of ecological doomsday, she is very optimistic: "There is still-time. Time to wake up . . . We can stop running Genesis backwards. The transition is a matter of degree, not of apocalyptic absolute. Indeed it is a matter of keeping the warming to two degrees Celsius." Secondly, she proposes to learn from "feminist and queer experience of relationality, failure and resilience" about how to embody and activate our intersectional webwork." What "intersectional webwork"? It is a webwork of all religions learning from one another and "collaborate in an ecumenical complexity." To make this point, she starts her argument and ends her conclusion with the Greek mythological story of Gaia (goddess of the earth).[54]

The theological contributions and weaknesses of these current ecotheologies are like Moltmann's and Pope Benedict's. That is, they rely too much on the book of Genesis to sanctify (or deify) the earth and humanity's

---

51. Nilsen, "Expanding," 667.
52. Mellor, *Feminism*, 1–2, 179–84, 188–90.
53. Dobson, *Green*, 176–87.
54. Keller, "Democracy," 4, 9, 11–15.

responsibility to manage the earth; they apply the analogy of the resurrection of Jesus to the renewal of the earth; they promote the meditation method to generate ecological devotion; and/or they expand ecological concerns to include other social and political agendas. Their common weaknesses include the downplaying of the judgment day in the book of Revelation, overlooking the collective-action problem, and placing too much hope on human rationality to construct/renovate a heaven-like secular kingdom on earth. Russell A. Butkus and Steven A. Kolmes summarize well that the common response of most ecotheologies "is action grounded in the hope and the conviction that the ecological future is, to some degree, in human hands." Furthermore, they continued, "that the reign of God refers to the renewal and restoration of all creation – inclusive of the human and natural worlds – is very likely one of the most important contributions of ecotheology."[55]

Frustrated by the indiscriminating, excessive, and impractical love promoted by many ecotheologists, Lisa H. Sideris constructs an evolutionary ecotheology which holds a "minimally interventionist ethic toward nature." She makes distinctions between wild and non-wild biotic communities (animals and plants), and recommends that human compassion for the latter can be treated as an extension of love and ethics among human beings. She continued that human compassion for the former should be limited, minimally interventionist, and should respect the natural, or God's, law of biological evolution and adaptation.[56]

Sideris' solution has not only greatly reduced the ecological responsibilities for Christians, but also left some ethical room for the Second Coming of Christ to destroy nature. After all, the wild biotic community falls within His ethical jurisdiction, not human's. However, her solution deals only with the relationships between humans and biotic communities, not among humans. Furthermore, this ethical room is not too big for Christ because He is going to destroy both the wild and non-wild biotic communities. Therefore, what we need for a Biblical ecotheology is to build on the Bible as a whole and keep all the relevant verses in balance. For this purpose, we need to systematically list and examine all those verses directly related to the ecology and post-ecology.

---

55. Butkus and Kolmes, *Environmental Science*, 135, 165.
56. Sideris, *Environmental*, chapter 6.

Biblical Verses of Ecology and Post-Ecology

This section analyzes about 120 Biblical verses or paragraphs that explicitly address issues related to the ecology. Starting with the most often cited verses by ecotheologians, I use the cross-reference function of the *BibleWorks* to locate more verses. Then, I divide these verses into two groups: those related to "God created the natural world and natural law" (GNL), and those related to "God delegated humans to manage the natural world" (HMN). These verses or paragraphs are listed in Appendix 4.1.

Most of these verses (about 100 out of 120) are related to the theme of what I call "God created the natural world and natural law" (GNL). "God" is the Trinitarian God, including Jesus who also participated in the creation. Most of these GNL verses re-iterate the creation story of the book of Genesis, and praise God for His omnipotence and providence in creating the natural world in addition to the natural laws which govern the natural world. No wonder the majority of ecotheologians construct their theologies based on the book of Genesis.

It is also not a coincidence that the majority of ecotheologians, especially those "ecojustice theologians" and "spirituality theologians," propose the meditation method or emphasize the ecological spirituality to resolve ecological crises. Most of these verses could stimulate the God brain and the emotional brain (as discussed in chapter 3 of this book), which would sanctify ecological goals and behaviors and would strongly motivate people to take ecological actions.

However, many of these GNL verses also deal with God's destruction of His creation, which most ecotheologians tend to ignore. Gen 6:7-7:24 describe how God, by the great flood, destroyed all lives on land except those in the ark. Chapters 7 to 10 and 12 of Exodus enumerate how God exercised His supernatural power in the ten plaques to punish the rebellious Pharaoh. In many chapters of the Psalms, the Psalmists praised God's creation of heaven and earth. However, immediately after the praise in Psalm 102:25, the Psalmist proclaimed that "all of them will wear out like a garment; like clothing You will change them and they will be changed." [57]Similar messages of God's destruction of His creation are proclaimed in Isa 34:4; 51:6; Joel 1:15; Mic 1:4; Nah 1:5; Matt 24:35, 37; Mark 13; 2Pe 2:5; 3:7, 10, 12; and particularly, in Rev 6, 8, 9, 16-20. Most ecotheologians seem to downplay these verses of destruction and jump from the creation of heaven and earth in Genesis

---

57. Ps 102:26.

directly to God's creation of the New Heaven and New Earth in Revelation as if these two are the same. According to them, God's New Heaven and New Earth is simply a renewal or repair of the old, just like a homeowner blowing off the dust on the furniture after a long vacation abroad; no destruction of the old furniture is needed. However, this renewal argument cannot account for these more than twenty verses/paragraphs of God's destruction.

The second part of Appendix 4.1 includes verses/paragraphs of "God delegates humans to manage the natural world" (HMN). There are only about twenty verses under this category as compared to more than eighty verses in the previous category of "God created the natural world and natural law." However, it is quite clear that through these verses, God gave humans the power and responsibility to govern the natural world. They also lend staunch support to theologies of ecological stewardship. Since management requires rational thinking, we can assume that these verses are useful in stimulating the God brain and the rational brain to generate practical ecological actions.

Among these twenty HMN verses, the most controversial one is Genesis 1:28. "God said to them, 'Be fruitful and multiply, and fill the earth, and subdue it; and rule over the fish of the sea and over the birds of the sky and over every living thing that moves on the earth.'" Lynn White cites this verse as the "historical roots of our ecologic crisis." He argues that anthropocentric Christians justify their abusive exploitation of the natural world because God gave humans the rights to "subdue" (כבש *kabshu*) and "rule over" (רָדָה; *radu*) the natural world.[58] In response, ecotheologians have re-translated these two OT terms to mean a responsible, balanced, self-restrained "governance" or "dominion" over the natural world.[59] The Septuagint translates "subdue" as κατακυριεύω (*katakurieuou*; become the master, gain dominion over, subdue, LORD over it, rule), and "rule over" as ἄρχω (*archou*; rule).

What about in the NT? In Hebrew 2:8: "You have put all things in *subjection* under his feet. For in *subjecting* all things to him, He left nothing that is not *subject* to him. But now we do not yet see all things *subjected* to him." What does "subjection" (ὑποκάτω; *hupokatou*) mean? It means "become subject," "subject oneself," "be subjected or subordinated, obey." In James 3:7, "For every species of beasts and birds, of reptiles and creatures of the sea, is *tamed* and has been *tamed* by the human race." The Greek word for "tamed" (δαμάζω; *damazou*) means exactly that, to: "subdue," "tame," and "control."

---

58. White, "Historical," 1203–07.

59. Bauckham, *Living*, 20–29.

Thus, the politically correct exegesis of these Hebrew and Greek words has evolved from "domination" to "dominion" to the contemporary keyword of "stewardship." Taken together, the original meanings of these OT and NT terms lend staunch support to the theology of stewardship that humans are delegated by God to subdue, rule over, and control all other creatures, including angels. Humans and all other creatures are not equal, as the theology of spirituality seems to imply. Humans are superior in rational thinking and theological status to all other creatures. God created both humans and all other creatures, but He did not do so equally. The stewardship theology is definitively anthropocentric if by anthropocentric we mean humans have a unique leadership status among all the creatures. However, it is not anthropocentric because these HMN verses and the theology of stewardship never suggest that humans have the ultimate authority to do whatever they like to all other creatures. These verses and the theology clearly spell out that the ultimate authority comes from God and God alone. In God, humans rule the world.

After reviewing recent German ecotheologies, Ulrich Körtner proposes a "responsibility-ethics model of ecological ethics." Based on the Biblical tradition of anthropomorphic creation, he disagrees with the anti-anthropocentric assumption of "ecologism" which "commits a naturalistic fallacy" and "reasons from an *is* to an *ought*." He argues that "even if ecological ethics declares all of the biosphere an object of ethical reflection and concern, it is always only the human who is and remains the subject of ethical judgment." Non-human life forms can be assigned an "intrinsic dignity" derived from creation, but it is different from and subordinate to human dignity. His ecotheology of "responsibility ethics" stipulates that "plants and animals, as well as the earthly biosphere in its totality, are objects of ethical reflection insofar as they are impacted by human actions and their consequences. The more non-human life is involved in human contexts of action, the greater the responsibility, although it is not a matter of reciprocally, that is, symmetrically, proportionate responsibilities."[60]

Having said these, a few counter-intuitive questions can be raised about the rule over the world. Does it include not only maintenance but also destruction? Since human authority to rule over the world comes from God and many of the GNL verses mention about God's destruction of the world, should humans follow God's will to destroy the world? Or, should humans obstruct God's plan of destruction and save the world because God created

---

60. Körtner, "Ecological," 3–4, 7–9.

it? If human authority to rule over the world comes from God, then, humans seem to have no choice but to follow God's plan either to save the world or to destroy the world. Most current ecotheologies do not see the latter paradox coming. This paradox will be dealt with in the next section.

Among these twenty HMN verses, there are six that link the management of the natural world with social justice.[61] Here, social justice is limited to charity works and holidays for all workers and domestic animals. These laws of Moses set up an institution, like the Sabbath, to enforce social justice as part of God's plan to govern the world. The authors of Pentateuch probably knew well that they could not rely only on human motivation or good will to uphold social justice, but rather on a stable and enforceable institution to do the job. What does this institution look like? Is it the state law? Probably not. These six verses do not provide too much detail, and the State of Israel was not yet established when these laws were written. It is fair to say that these six verses are religious norms designed for specific social purposes (charity and holidays) that constituting binding power toward the believers. Any ecotheology should exercise exegetical prudence over the political interpretation of these verses.

Furthermore, among these twenty HMN verses, only two verses belong to the New Testament, and neither has anything to do with social and political justice. Therefore, Jürgen Moltmann, Pope Benedict and other theologians of "ecojustice," who make social and political justice central to their ecotheologies, probably extrapolate too much from such few verses in the Bible.

Based on these 120 verses/paragraphs related to the ecology and post-ecology, what then does an ecotheology look like which is theologically sound and empirically practical to generate ecological motivation and behavior? The next section aims to construct such a theology.

Church and Post-Ecotheology

A neuro-institutional post-ecotheology develops its concrete actions based on, first, the above Biblical teachings about the holiness of nature and human responsibility to manage nature, as most ecotheologians suggest. However, a neuro-institutional post-ecotheology further relies on two inter-related principles of positive psychology at the individual and collective levels. At the individual level, Christians should take only those ecological actions which do not substantially reduce their overall happiness (happiness as defined in chapter

61. Exod 20:10; 23:10–11; Lev 19:9–10; 23:22; 24:19–20; Deut 5:14.

2 of this book). At the collective level, local churches should take only those ecological actions which do not substantially reduce their overall happiness and only when these ecological actions receive a consensus among congregation members. Both principles emphasize tolerance and compromise toward different ecological positions among individual Christians and churches. An ecological action which substantially reduces individual or collective happiness is not likely to garner persistent support but is likely to divide the church.

Since the overwhelming majority of the ecological verses in the Bible are related to the stimulation of the God brain and the emotional brain, theologians of ecological spirituality are correct to emphasize the importance of meditating the relationships among God, human, and the natural environment. However, this is only a first and partial step for the church to deal with ecological crises. It is the first step because rational meditation alone does not necessarily result in actions, while emotional meditation alone may result in radical actions prohibited by the Bible. This issue will be analyzed later in this section. It is a partial step because it relies too much on verses related to God's creation, while ignoring those verses about God's destruction of His creation. We need to bring the whole book of Revelation back to ecotheology.

Admittedly, the book of Revelation is probably one of the most controversial books in the Bible with regard to its authorship, canonical status, and exegesis of the multitude of supernatural phenomena, including the seven churches, seven seals, seven trumpets, seven bowls, Rapture, Great Harlot, Parousia, Armageddon, and the New Heaven and New Earth. Should they be interpreted literally, metaphorically, or spiritually? Does the book of Revelation have anything to do with the ecology? If the book of Revelation is interpreted only spiritually in its entirety, then, it is great news to the world! No physical judgments of the Seven Seals, Seven Trumpets, Seven Bowls, and Armageddon; these are just spiritual battles all Christians face in their daily life.[62] The world will not end, and Revelation is just one of the scary moral storybooks that Sunday school teachers use to intimidate naughty or sleepy kids.

Ecotheologians Daniel L. Brunner, Jennifer L. Butler, and A.J. Swoboda build their Evangelical Ecotheology on a revised version of the above spiritualized Revelation. Being Evangelical theologians, they cannot deny Revelation's literal implications of total destructions. However, Revelation's literal implications would deny the theological and empirical values of the long-term, comprehensive ecological programs they try to build. Therefore,

---

62. Aune, *Revelation*; Beale, *Book of Revelation*.

they re-interpret Revelation in half way between the spiritual and the literal: "Our Christian goal becomes not to escape into some postmortem destiny but to embrace God's kingdom in the present . . . Apocalypse, therefore, is not a future destructive judgment but a future creative judgment; God resurrects the world within which a new humanity will live."[63] Nevertheless, as chapter 1 of this book shows, there is growing convergence between scientific evidence and the book of Revelation. It is probably safer to take Revelation literally than spiritually in the near future.

If the book of Revelation is interpreted literally, most of the supernatural phenomena do correspond closely to ongoing and escalating ecological crises. The first and second horses represent domestic violence and international war; the third horse, inflation; and the fourth horse, hunger and plaque. The first bowl triggers a worldwide epidemic of foul and evil sores. The global warming, forest fire, and abnormal weather can be linked to the judgments of the first trumpet, the fourth trumpet, the fourth bowl, the fifth bowl and the seventh bowl. The second trumpet and the third trumpet are characterized by pollution in the ocean and the river; so are the second bowl and the third bowl. The fifth and sixth trumpets bring out mutated insects and animals. The fall of Babylon predicts the final collapse of global political order after a global war of Armageddon. Then, all humans in a new resurrected body will face the judgment of God sitting on the white throne. This new resurrected body, by definition, is a new body after the destruction of the old (death), not a repaired, revived body of the old. We do not know in appearance how similar the new body and the old body are. However, they are qualitatively different because the new body will live forever either in the lake of fire for non-Christians or in the New Heaven and New Earth for Christians. So is the world: "the first heaven and the first earth had passed away, and the sea was no more." Instead, New Jerusalem comes down out of heaven from God. It is not a repaired and revived product of the old Jerusalem. It does not even look alike to the old Jerusalem; especially as there is no more physical temple in New Jerusalem. Therefore, when God said, "Behold, I am making all things new" and "these words are trustworthy and true," He probably meant it in literal sense.[64] That is, the New Heaven and New Earth may look like the old heaven and earth, yet they are qualitatively different. The new comes about after the old is destroyed and thrown away.

63. Brunner et al., *Introducing*, 140.
64. Rev 21: 5.

Notably, all these horrible events are predestined by God and executed by Jesus Christ Himself. The four horsemen are "given" power to make war and cause death. In Greek grammar, "given" (ἐδόθη; *edothei*) is aorist passive and is interpreted as "sacred passive tense" to imply that God or Jesus Christ is the giver. Similarly, the angels of the seven trumpets and seven bowls are also "given" (ἐδόθησαν; *edotheisan*; also in aorist passive) these instruments of judgment by God to destroy God's creation. At Parousia, Jesus comes as a military commander, "in righteousness He judges and wages war . . . From His mouth comes a sharp sword, so that with it He may strike down the nations, and He will rule them with a rod of iron; and He treads the wine press of the fierce wrath of God, the Almighty."[65]

How do ecological Christians meditate the above destruction of God's creation ordered and executed by Trinitarian God Himself and take actions in response to this meditation? In addition to the peace, love and providence of God that theologians of ecological spirituality emphasized, we see the other face of God: judgment, fury and destruction. While the love of God's creation inspires Christians to love the damaged the natural world, or using Baukham's word, to "lament" the damaged the natural world, the destruction of God's creation by God Himself generates awe and fear of God's judgment.

Both sets of motivations are conducive to ecological actions. However, according to neuroscience, humans probably respond to the threat of life much more quickly and seriously than to peace and love. When the thalamus receives a threat signal, it immediately transmits it to the amygdala to react: fight or flight. Thus, the signals or peace or love may be more readily ignored or transmitted slowly to the anterior cingulate, which may not be a very strong area.

The ecological strategies in response to the dual attributes of God's love and judgment are different. Moltmann, Pope Benedict and most ecotheologians built their ecotheologies upon Genesis, skipped all the verses on the destruction of nature, and touched down directly on the New Heaven and New Earth of Revelation 20–21. It is quite logical for them to assume that the world is renewable. Since the world is renewable, their ecological strategy does not spell urgency. They treat the polluted world like a mixed-drug addict treating his bad habits: This year I will reduce my consumption of alcohol by 50percent from four bottles a day to 2 bottles, while I "meditate" or "lament" my healthy body before I took on the bad habit; my body can wait and is renewable. Next year I will cut down my consumption of marijuana by

---

65. Rev 6: 2–8; 19: 11, 15.

50percent from one kilogram to half a kilogram a day, while I "meditate" or "lament" the wonderful experience of smoking marijuana; my body can wait and is renewable. In the third and fourth years, I will deal with the more painful processes of cutting down on my daily consumption of heroin and ecstasy drugs. However, I have not figured out what to "meditate" and "lament." I am not in a hurry, because the body can wait and is renewable. Even though I am 180cm tall, weigh only 35 kilograms, suffer from all kinds of tumors due to decades of drug and alcohol abuses, I will continue to "meditate" and "lament" because my body can wait and is renewable. Hey, do not accuse me now for being lazy! Am I not doing something healthy to improve my health?

Typical of the above vanity is the long list of ecological actions provided by Gerald T. Gardner and Paul C. Stern, which includes carpool to work, tune-up the car, cut highway speed, set heating at 68 degrees Fahrenheit, buy a fuel-efficient car, and buy a more efficient air conditioner and refrigerator. Together, these actions would provide two percent in "improvement" in energy consumption.[66] But how much more new consumption of energy will be generated by buying these new efficient products? Why not take public transportation to work and delay buying new products until the old products become beyond repair?

Similarly, these ecotheologians propose ambiguous, piecemeal and moderate ecological actions to deal with the incoming ecological avalanches.[67] They start with "meditate" and "lament" what Genesis says. From the complexity of their archaic theology, the meditation and lamentation will probably take a while before the readers can take concrete ecological actions. What concrete ecological actions? They do not specify. Many churches begin to promote recycling bottles and paper products, bringing your utensils to church activities, purchasing "green" products, and turning off the lights when the church is not in service. These certainly contribute to the *slowdown* of the speed of deterioration of ecological crises. However, they do not *stop* the further deterioration of ecological crises. Particularly, if the church decides to hold more energy-consumption activities and build a larger church structure, the absolute amount of pollution and energy consumption may be more substantial than the status quo without taking these ecological actions.

---

66. Gardner and Stern, "Short List," 12–25.

67. For instance, Celia Deane-Drummond *Primer*, 120–121, develops a four-prong "theologically informed ecological ethics": liturgical transformation, global and local Ecclesial responsibility, practical steps in individual responsibility, and building a collective conscience. However, in the eyes of social scientists, these solutions are still too abstract and fragile to solve ecological crises.

Can the church, through meditation and lamentation, lead to more drastic ecological actions that are required to save the "renewable" world? Theoretically, it is possible. If all the Christians have as strong religious commitment to the ecology as the martyrs did to God in the first century, the world could be saved and renewable (let us ignore, for the moment, the scientific evidence about passing the point of no-return). The fact that the number of martyrs is small throughout Christian history does not bring much hope to such a theoretical possibility. If ecological martyrs are few, then there is a serious collective-action problem even within the church. If a few ecological martyrs stop using plastic plates and cups in church activities while all other church members continue to do so, these ecological martyrs cannot make a big dent on the pollution, and they only inconvenience themselves. If one or two churches are converted into ecological martyrs while other churches are not, the same result follows and may cause the transfer of church members from the ecological church to the non-ecological church. If the whole church community becomes martyrs while all other religions do not, the church community may suffer from a decline in their faith, while the world remains unrenewable. There is an ecological glass ceiling for what the ecotheology based on Genesis and resurrection can do. An alternative ecological strategy needs to be realized.

Ecotheologian Laura Ruth Yordy shares her frustration with the failure of the church in response to environmental crises. She lists five causes: "the ineffectiveness of education, the difficulty of implementing real change at the practical level, the relative powerlessness of church officials, the common vision of a church as a collection of individuals, rather than as an active moral subject . . . and congregations resist difficult environmental changes because the problem is posed as both overwhelming in nature and/or solvable by technology."[68]

The theological solution to her frustration and that of many churches is to adjust the ecological role of the church. Instead of setting too high a goal for herself as a participant in the ecological movement, the church should play only a "witness" to the Trinitarian God's "eschatological creation" which will restore "peace, abundance, justice, liberation, righteousness, and communion with God."[69] In practical terms, Yordy recommends that each church should define their ecological discipleship on her own terms, and put more emphasis on cultivating a way of life that praises and witnesses to God.

68. Yordy, *Green*, 11–12.
69. Yordy, *Green*, 44.

Yordy probably notices the contradictory messages conveyed by Genesis (creation) and Revelation (new creation after the total destruction of the old), and their implications for ecological practices at the local church level. New creation is too much a job, if ever possible, for any church or the church to accomplish. Besides, it is a job of the Trinitarian God, not of the church. The church is better fitted to play the more practical role of witness to new creation.

This book concurs with Yordy's re-orientation of the church's ecological role but goes further to propose an alternative theological strategy which builds an ecology more on Revelation than Genesis, and more on God's judgment than on God's love. The theological premise of this ecological strategy is that the world is not and should not be savable and renewable. It is both the Biblical truth and the empirical truth!

Admittedly, there can be two neuroscientific responses to this pessimistic ecological strategy: give up or give in, which corresponds to the fight or flight functions of the amygdala in the brain. If the world is not savable and renewable, why do we bother to engage in ecological actions which will turn out to be vanity anyway? Enjoy the world while it lasts until God destroys it! This response is too Stoic and brings shame to the church community as irresponsible as Lynn White described.

In fact, American liberal Christians (i.e., mainline churches) have prepared enough ammunition to fire at will at any conservative Christian (e.g., the Southern Baptists and the Cornwall Alliance) who disagree with their radical ecological agenda. They would cite Lynn White's statement about the original ecological sin committed by Christianity. When Christianity answered White's challenge by promoting the stewardship theology, some liberal Christians criticize them for not having enough enthusiasm toward ecological programs. Is it because conservative Christians do not worship nature as pantheists do? Alternatively, is it because conservative Christians welcome the fast arrival of End-times?[70]

To these charges, I plead guilty as charged. This book follows the conservative Christian view that many current ecotheologies are too close to pantheism to the comfort of ante-Nicene theology. If there is a hard choice between the ecology and pantheism, "and if it is disagreeable in your sight to serve the LORD, choose for yourselves today whom you will serve . . . but as for me and my house, we will serve the LORD."[71] Similarly, if there is a hard choice

---

70. Barker and Bearce, "Theology"; Zaleha and Szasz, "Why."

71. Josh 24:15.

between protecting the ecology and welcoming the Parousia, it is the latter that I must choose.

Furthermore, it is the mainline churches that are fast declining and degenerating, not so much the conservative churches. As a Chinese Christian, looking for a Biblical model of church in contemporary Western societies, on which model should I build my ecotheology? The practical answer seems to be clear. Finally, social scientists who are familiar with survey techniques would also notice a common gap between attitudes and actions. Conservative Christians may well be less concerned with ecological protection than liberal Christians or other religious believers. However, few studies so far have shown that liberal Christians or other religious believers live a life more ecologically friendly than conservative Christians do. On the list of an ecological litmus test would include our daily routines: wear imported cloth or locally made cloth, eat imported food or locally grown food, drive (an) imported car(s) or take a bus to work, and live in a small apartment or a spacious urban house?

Theologian Anna Case-Winters makes a good suggestion about how Christians see the inevitable end of the world. She is not happy with the fact that many theologians do not take seriously scientific confirmations of the creation's "perpetual perishing." Based on the relevant theological insights of Karl Barth, Miroslav Volf, Jürgen Moltmann, and process theology, she proposes a Christian eschatology which can incorporate scientific perspectives of the end of the world. That is, Christians hold and believe in constant and perpetual meaningful relationships to God before and after death. Upon death or the end of the world, we are "judged and transformed and redeemed according to divine ends." It is the faith we need to affirm in the process toward the end of the world whenever it comes that "God is the source, companion, and the end of all things, and [...] God will be working for good."[72]

However, for the sake of "political correctness," there is a response to the second charge. The second response to this pessimistic ecological strategy is to "give in," not in a passive sense of total capitulation to the evil of polluting the world but in the sense of active "adaptation" to the unrenewable world. This adaption involves both spiritual and empirical adaptation. Spiritual adaption refers to the reinterpretation, or as the literal meaning of Revelation unambiguously reveals, of the destruction of the world as a good sign for the fast realization of the New Heaven and New Earth, which the Christian community has longed for in the past two thousand years. "Forgetting what *lies* behind

---

72. Case-Winters, "The End."

and reaching forward to what *lies* ahead."[73] Genesis' creation is a point in the long past, at least 200,000 years ago, to be meditated and lamented. However, the Revelation's New Heaven and New Earth is the future to be cherished and rejoiced. In between, there are tribulations for Christians to endure. The main purpose of the Revelation or the NT is not to save the world but to encourage Christians to "be faithful until death" during the tribulations.[74] Even though the first heaven and earth created by God are sacred, the contemporary world is not sacred, need not be sacred, and never will be sacred; but the Christian faith is and will be forever. It is the spiritual world that needs to be saved, not the material world which is destined for total destruction.

Empirical adaption refers to a proper level of ecological actions and proper preparation for the tribulations. For the church, there are three possible types of practical adaptive actions to the doomsday scenario: to help accelerate ecological crises, to stop further deterioration of ecological crises, and to go along with the mainstream ecological policies and public opinion. The first adaptive action refers to measures that accelerate ecological crises, such as increased spending on consumer goods and use of non-recyclable products. If it is God's will to destroy the world, why don't we give Him a hand to accelerate it? No, we do not. God does not need our help on this matter, as described in the book of Revelation. He will do it just by Himself and do it well. It is one thing He destroys what He created, and it is another thing that we destroy what He created and is damaged by us. Two wrongs do not make a right. Furthermore, Christians are supposed to "respect what is right in the sight of all men. If possible, so far as it depends on you, be at peace with all men."[75] When ecological protection is a right thing in the sight of most societies nowadays, the church should not walk against it.

The second adaptive action refers to the immediate discontinuation of any consumption that is not related to basic needs of human living. Similar to the renewable-world strategy, this adaptive action calls for drastic measures to freeze or reverse ecological crises. However, unlike the renewable-world strategy which assumes that these drastic measures will achieve the goal of a renewable world, this second adaptive action does not make such a theological assumption. However, if not, any rational Christian would ask why we should bother to drastically sacrifice current consumption for a goal not strongly supported by the Bible? True. This second adaptive action is not likely to have a

73. Phil 3:13.
74. Rev 2:10.
75. Rom 12: 17–18.

strong theological nor popular support within the church, because it is against human nature.

The third adaptive action is to go along with mainstream ecological policies and public opinion. The general question about church-state relations will be discussed thoroughly in chapter 6 of this book. It suffices to summarize its conclusion that in the past thirty years in Western societies, the church (both Protestantism and Catholicism) has suffered from decline due to immature and unprofessional responses to controversial social and political issues, such as gender equality, abortion rights, evolution versus creationism, Muslim immigrants, and homosexual marriage. These issues alienate the church from the society, divide the church community, and cause intergenerational conflicts within the church. The church has benefitted nothing, but declined from active engagement in these social and political debates. The last thing the contemporary church needs is to actively engage in yet another divisive social and political issue like the ecology. Here, I propose that if the mainstream ecological policies call for a drastic reduction of consumption, go along with them. If the mainstream ecological policies promote only slow and piecemeal reforms, go along with them too. If the mainstream ecological policies conflict with one another, which is often the case, choose the least controversial policies (e.g., recycling). "Every person is to be in subjection to the governing authorities. For there is no authority except from God, and those which exist are established by God. Therefore whoever resists authority has opposed the ordinance of God; and they who have opposed will receive condemnation upon themselves. For rulers are not a cause of fear for good behavior, but for evil. Do you want to have no fear of authority? Do what is good and you will have praise from the same" (Rom 13: 1–3).

However, what if the government works against the ecology, say, hiring church members to a new coal factory (as Donald Trump addressed to a new coal mine in June 2017), what should the church do? The local church should encourage her members to look for other jobs but should not make a judgment on those who have no other choice but to take the coal factory job. In general, the church should go along with the prevailing world public opinion that everyone, regardless of their faith, takes some ecological actions as they see fit to their living conditions. Ecological action is an ethical behavior, but it does not and need not rank very high on the list of Christian ethics. The much more important Christian ethics than the ecology are evangelism and charity, which are also the major missions and specialties of the church. To keep a balance between the ecology and evangelism, Christians should not destroy nature to speed up Parousia, neither should they take drastic ecological actions which may impede evangelism. In fact, nothing we can do to speed up or slow down God's plan for Parousia and the ecology.

The adaptive action of the church also calls for a renewed emphasis on spiritual and physical forbearance during tribulations before the New Heaven and New Earth come. If the scientific forecasts and theological discussions in chapters 1 and 3 of this book are correct, ecotheologies should move from "pre-environmental" prescriptions of preventing global ecological crises from happening to "post-environmental" (or "post-ecology") prescriptions of surviving unstoppable ecological crises.[76] According to the literal interpretation of the Revelation, the natural and supernatural disasters caused by seven trumpets and seven bowls will fall only on non-Christians and strayed Christians. However, Christians will be indirectly affected by these hardships and directly persecuted by non-Christians due to their revenge on God's wrath. "And it was given to him to give breath to the image of the beast, so that the image of the beast would even speak and cause as many as do not worship the image of the beast to be killed . . . and he provides that no one will be able to buy or to sell, except the one who has the mark, either the name of the beast or the number of his name." As the mighty angel foretold: the judgments "will make your stomach bitter, but in your mouth it will be sweet as honey."[77]

Furthermore, some human-made tribulations other than those willed by God will have an impact on most Christians: all kinds of exotic illnesses caused by food with too many chemicals and bio-engineering, smog in the cities, and chemical and radioactive hazards at home, school and work environment. Humans will indeed live longer as medical technology continues to improve. Though, humans will also be likely to fall into more new/old illnesses at younger ages, which means spiritual and physical suffering will be longer in their whole life.

If the church believes that the contemporary world is doomed to utter destruction and is happening fast, then, tribulations to Christians are certainly an integral part of the judgment process. Therefore, the principal mission of the contemporary church is to revamp teaching on spiritual and physical forbearance in preparation for these tribulations. Come to Sunday services, attend Bible study sessions, join evangelical missions abroad, discontinue bad behaviors, and start regular exercise programs, if not self-defense technique

---

76. These two terms, "pre-environmental" and "post-environmental," are adapted from Dobson, *Green*.

77. Rev 10: 9; 13: 14–17.

lessons. In between these programs, take one or two lessons on the ecology and perform occasional community services to clean up the environment would suffice.

What about population growth? Should the church promote birth control for the sake of the ecology? After all, 9 billion people by 2050 is much more than the ecology can take. Wars within and among nations are likely to increase to worsen decreasing fresh water, arable land, living space, and other basic needs. A neuro-institutional post-ecotheology would suggest that it is not necessary to promote birth control within the church. The Bible never says so. On the contrary, God blesses His believers to have numerous children.[78] Besides, child-bearing is part of human needs for survival and happiness. However, it is up to the personal consideration of individual believers to decide how many children they plan to have and if they are of sufficient physical health to do so. An average of two to three children would probably fit the ecological standard of most countries. After all, there is still some room left in the New Heaven and New Earth.

One may raise the question: Does not the above neuro-institutional ecological strategy seem too complacent or apathetic to the worsening ecological crises? Yes and no. Yes, it is complacent and apathetic because the Bible does not encourage Christians to save the un-renewable world. No, it is not complacent and apathetic because Christians continue to participate in ecological activities as most of the communities do, but no more and no less. If the whole community at the levels of the village, city, county, state or international organization decides to take drastic measures to "save the world," this post-ecological strategy also encourages Christians to go along with them, but no more and no less. The church is not theologically, politically and administratively qualified to overcome the collective action problems of the ecology and to lead the crusade against ecological crises. Before the church can save the world, she must save herself first. The Western churches probably are deteriorating considerably faster than the world ecology.

The last sentence brings out the final component of the neuro-institutional post-ecotheology: the democratization of the church. The church's contemporary failure to produce a proper ecotheology is a mirror of the general failure of Western churches to respond to the fast-changing social, economic and political environment, as evidenced by the controversies over gender equality, abortion, creationism versus evolution, and homosexual marriage. If these failures are omens to what is to come, the Western churches are likely to

---

78. Gen 15:5; 22:17; Neh 9:23; Job 21:11; Ps 107:41; Isa 10:22; 48:19; Ezek 36:37.

get their whole body dirty again by jumping into the muddy ecological pool without sound theological foundation, political reasoning and a democratic church. What each church should do and can do depends on a collective decision by all members of the church based on a holistic understanding of the Bible, the priority of ethical behaviors, the capability of each church and each member of the church, and constructive dialogue with the local community and other churches. If they decide to "meditate" or "lament" the ecology forever without doing anything else, let them do so. If they decide to take drastic ecological actions, such as turning off air-conditioning forever, let them do so. If they decide to meditate one year and take drastic ecological action every other year, let them do so. Their decisions should not be dictated by the Pope, bishops, priests, pastors, or theologians (including this author) inventing an ecotheology in their soundproof, cozy ivory towers with their air-conditioners and computer gadgets running twenty-four hours a day.

For instance, in this chapter, the afore-mentioned debate in Catholic churches in India and Sri Lanka may follow the above suggestion to resolve their disagreement whether the local church should use plastic plates or banana-leaf plates at church activities. Church leaders should discuss these matters with their believers and make a collective decision. If the church collectively decides that local sanitary condition is a chief concern for the health of church members or guests, then, human health trumps ecological concern. Catholic believers from other churches should not have much say in this matter. Do these church members who decide to use plastic plates need to feel guilty about committing this "social sin" against God? Not at all! This "social sin" is constructed by contemporary theologians, not by God. As long as they can justify their choice by collective decision, Biblical verses and practical considerations, there is no "social sin" committed here.

Neither do the Popes at Vatican need to feel guilty about committing the "social sin" against God just because they routinely turn on air-conditioning in the vast church compound to receive guests, or frequently travel around the world with a large convoy of security guards to bless Catholics. They should be applauded for taking energy-saving measures which the church advisors recommended but not to be criticized for lack of more radical ecological measures.

We also need to bear in mind that individual Christians, inspired by the Holy Spirit, may take more conservative or radical actions toward ecological protection beyond the church standards. Should the church denounce or punish them for doing so? Providing their actions are legal, the church should probably refrain from judgment on their behaviors. After all, there is a risk that the judgment falls upon not only the individual but also upon the Holy Spirit.

However, former U.S. Vice President Al Gore's 10,000-square-feet mansion in Belle Meade area of Nashville, with air-conditioners running all-season long, is a somewhat different story. The mansion used "221,000 kWh of electricity in 2006, more than 20 times the national average of 10,656 kWh . . . and (he) spent more than $30,000 in combined electricity and natural gas bills in 2006."[79] He also owns at least three additional vacation houses. Again, he commits no "social sin" but rather an inappropriate behavior according to the ecological standards average Americans would adhere, not to mention about those ecological standards he championed for others in the "Inconvenient Truth." The criticism is fair and consistent with the post-ecotheology of this book in the sense that it compares Al Gore's energy consumption to the national average. Similarly, "Green Pope" Benedict's red Prada's shoes might not connote a message consistent with his message of a frugal life; he soon took notice of this inconsistency and never wore it again.[80] In a sense, most Christian ecologists cannot but be ecological "hypocrites" if they impose a set of stringent ecological standards on other people but fail to observe the same standards themselves.[81]

Summary

This chapter begins with an evaluation of Chinese Daoism and Buddhism which some Western ecotheorists regard as superior to Christian ecotheologies. However, the overall picture of Daoist and Buddhist ecotheories does not look better. Unfortunately, most Christian ecotheologies seem to echo the weaknesses of these Chinese ecotheories. As represented by the ecotheologies of Jürgen Moltmann and Pope Benedict XVI, most current ecotheologies cannot significantly contribute to the resolution of ecological crises. Even worse, they deviate from the Biblical view of the ecology, which focuses on evangelism in the age of post-ecology. Among the major vanities of current ecotheologies are: an overemphasis on meditation instead of concrete actions; the failure to address the collective-action problem of the ecology; their

79. Truth or Fiction, "Energy."
80. Washington Post, "Story."
81. For the warning against hypocrites, see Isa 66:3; Matt 6:2,5,16; 7:5; 15:7; 22:18; 23:13–15, 23–29, 51; 24:51; Mark7:6; Luke 6:42; 12:1; 12:56; 13:15.

arguments based on the erroneous scientific and theological assumptions that the "the heavenly kingdom on earth" is renewable; their theological journey into the controversial dessert of pantheism; and by incorporating issues of social, economic and political justice for the sake of political correctness, they make any future ecological program too complex and too costly to implement at local churches.

What exactly does the Bible say about ecology or post-ecology? By analyzing 120 verses or paragraphs which explicitly address issues related to the ecology, section 2 of this chapter does find strong Biblical support for the respect for God's creation of nature and for God's delegation to humans to manage nature. These Biblical verses seem to fit perfectly into most of the current ecotheologies. However, among these verses are also those prophesizing post-ecology, that is, the inevitable total destruction of this world by the Trinitarian God before a new one can be established. Most current ecotheologies simply bypass these Biblical verses.

To address to the vanities of current ecotheologies and to incorporate all Biblical teachings about ecology and post-ecology, section 3 constructs a practical neuro-institutional post-ecotheology for the church. In a nutshell, the church should refocus its mission on evangelism in expectation of the fast coming of the Judgment Day. With regard to local ecology, the church should formulate their ecological programs through a democratic deliberation among church members, following the legal regulations of the local governments, and working with the local communities; no more or no less. Particularly, the church should plan more spiritual and material resources in preparation for the inevitable disastrous ecological crises. Inspired by the Holy Spirit, individual Christians may engage in more radical personal ecological programs than the church's, without being judged by the church.

5.

Capitalism and Post-Ecotheology

In 2004, I took sabbatical leave at the University of California, Berkeley. I was very impressed by the residents in the Bay area, who are well known for their zealous commitment to personal fitness and the ecology. The popularity of vegetarian restaurants in the Bay area certainly served witness to the sincerity of their commitments to both personal fitness and the ecology. One day, my wife and I visited a famous vegetarian restaurant in downtown San Francisco to partake in this physical and spiritual venture, but also to blend into the liberal environment. While awaiting our dishes' arrival, we were amazed by two large-sized people at the next table. With two seven-inch-tall glasses of diet coke, they started their "diet" plan with two nine-inch-diameter salad bowls covered with a thick layer of low-fat fruit yogurt, followed by two large plates of steamed rainbow trout generously covered with low-calorie cheese sauce plus heaped side dishes, and ended their diet plan with a colorful mountain of ice-cream balls made of skim milk. After they cleaned all the plates and drinks, they could barely move out of their table to pay the bill. Neither could we. It was such a "fulfilling" experience both spiritually and physically.

If this story resembles a bit of vanity to us, the ecological economic programs we have adopted in the past fifty years are probably a vanity on an astronomical scale. The fact is that, as much as "the (ecological) wishing is present in me, but the doing of the good is not,"[1] we continue to hurt the ecology and ourselves by indulging in "green" products beyond what the earth and our bodies can sustain. What we need to do to make ecological programs work is to change both institutions and individuals.

1. Rom 7:18.

This chapter evaluates different proposals to change the economic institution of capitalism and economic behaviors of individuals. Section 1 evaluates secular economists' ecological solutions both from the right and the left. Section 2 analyzes theological solutions which build on the rightist and leftist economist proposals. Section 3 constructs a neuro-institutional post-ecotheology as a practical alternative to these ecotheologies.

Vanity of Rightist and Leftist Ecological Solutions

It is beyond the scope of this book and my expertise to systematically examine all ecological solutions proposed by economists. On the one hand, there are just too many mathematical equations with which to deal. On the other hand, as the academic joke goes: "Ten economists enter a conference room to figure out what to do with the economy, they come out with eleven proposals." To reduce the usage of economics jargons and equations, I construct simplified models of rightist and leftist ecological economic theories to reveal their common merits and weaknesses. Some representative works of each school are cited. Many current ecological economic theologies combine these rightist and leftist theories and will be evaluated afterwards.

On the rightist side, a model ecological theory would let the free market adjust itself to the supply and demand of ecological goods/bads, and ecological crises would consequently go away. Government intervention in the market is kept at a minimum except for preventing market failures. When natural resources become scarce, their prices will go up, their demand will go down, and the exploitation of these resources will be reduced. At the same time, as natural resources become scarce, investments in technology to efficiently use natural resources, to recycle natural resources, or to substitute natural resources will go up. Therefore, the rates of exploitation of these resources will go down. The government should not intervene in the market of natural resources or efficient technology because it will distort the market, slow down economic growth, and raise unemployment rates.

How about pollution? Apply the same logic of supply and demand through the market of pollution. Like in the original metaphor the Coase Theorem is developed, the problem of pollution is resolved through bargaining between the polluter and the local community. If the polluter has the property right to pollute, the local community can pay the polluter to reduce its pollution level; if the local community has the property right, the polluter can pay the local community to allow it to pollute to a certain level the local community can tolerate.[2] Instead of paying to the local community, the polluter also has an option to invest in pollution-control technology if the local community has the property right. The assignment of property right is enforced by various pollution-control laws and judicial decisions. As long as the Congress and the courts do their jobs, ecological crises are no more.

The same logic of the free market is also applicable to population control to resolve the Malthusian ecological crisis.[3] As the population grows, the demand for natural resources, goods and services grows as well. Their prices increase accordingly. Fewer people will have the ability to get enough goods and services to survive or to raise children. Therefore, either child-birth rates will decline (as in advanced industrial economies), or more people will die of hunger, malnutrition, illness, civil wars or international wars (as in developing countries) until the supply and demand of these goods and services are once more balanced.

There are several problems associated with this rightist model of ecological theory. First, the free market system cannot prevent the exhaustion of natural resources, nor can they reduce the accumulated amount of ecological damages. Prices will go up when the supply of natural resources go down. However, as long as there is a demand and unless perfect substitutes for natural resources are invented, the market for natural resources will continue to exist until the last unit of natural resources are consumed. Recycling and substitutes of natural resources have not successfully reduced the consumption of natural resources and may, in fact, have produced more hazardous ecological crises (e.g., entropy of recycled materials, biofuel, and nuclear energy). Ecological crises are caused by the total accumulated amount, not by marginal increases, of ecological damages. Rightist ecologists are interested in slowing down the marginal increases of ecological damages, but cannot resolve the simple question of the accumulated net amount of damages.

Secondly, the Coase Theorem states that regardless of whether the polluter or the community holds the property right, the level of pollution remains the same throughout market exchange: either the polluter pays the community to allow it to pollute to a level the market price is right, or the community pays the polluter to reduce pollution to a level the market price is right. They aim not at eliminating pollution altogether but at reducing pollution to a level acceptable to the local community. Since the local community often values current consumption (local job creation, goods and services

2. Coase, "Nature of Firm."
3. Robert, *Essay*.

provided by the polluting firm) and discounts future payment due to damage to health and environment, the pollution problem is not resolved but goes on as usual. Developed in 1937, this Theorem has repeatedly been confirmed by the general failure of pollution-control policies which reassigns property rights from the polluter to the public by imposing various pollution taxes or the carbon-quotas market. What if the pollution level becomes unbearable to the local community? Well, the polluter either invests in the more efficient technology of pollution-control, pays more to the local community for its pollution, or moves to another city in another country where the local community is willing to accept a higher level of pollution in exchange for local job creation and goods and services provided by the polluter. Global pollution is not resolved but goes on as usual, and even expands globally.

Thirdly, the Malthusian ecological crisis has not been alleviated since World War II either by declining population growth in advanced industrial countries or by wars in developing countries. The rapid growth and dissemination of medical technology has reduced infant mortality rates and increased average life expectancies faster than the above rates of population decline.

Fourthly, there are moral controversies with regard to population-control methods such as birth control, abortion, and war. These controversies are not parts of these rightist ecological equations, but will indubitably determine the effectiveness of their programs. And, finally, technological innovation (i.e., green technology) of production efficiency and pollution-control may not come fast enough before the ecology collapses. In fact, many of those companies which produce green technology may be polluting their local community by dumping their chemical wastes into the river and the sea.

The leftist ecological theory would blame the failures of rightist ecological programs on the intrinsic structural contradictions between capitalism and ecological protection. As leftist economist, John Bellamy Foster, correctly argues "the realms of ecology and capitalism are opposed to each other – not in every instance but in their interactions as a whole."[4] What the world needs is not a vanity derived from the above-market solutions pretending that these solutions would resolve ecological crises, but the immediate abolishment of capitalism and replace it with socialism.[5] A model leftist ecological theory would start with critics of two fundamental flaws in rightist ecological theory: market value and production relation.

---

4. Foster, *Ecology Against*, 7.
5. Burkett, *Marxism*.

In terms of market value, capitalist markets deliberately overvalue the capital and undervalue other costs of production, e.g., the labor and pollution. Profits are attributed to the growing productivity of the capital while the productivity of the labor is held constant, and pollution cost is externalized or minimized. Because of the logic of market competition, capitalists have no choice but to reinvest their profits to produce more or better goods and services from the local market to the global market, thus, resulting in fast exploitation of natural resources and ecological crises.

Capitalist values are also hazardous to the ecology because they overvalue material goods, and measure one's welfare by money. Capitalism is an economic system which encourages the consumption or stockpiling of material goods while downplaying human values such as compassion, altruism, identity, belonging, self-realization, and ecological concerns. Even in rare cases where these human values are incorporated into economics equations, they are measured in monetary terms. "There is nothing money can't buy" seems to underpin the operational ethic of capitalism.

In terms of production relation, the capitalists control the tools of production and dominate over labor. Workers are alienated from production relations and have little bargaining power against the capitalists to address their ecological concerns such as wages, pollution-control technology and a healthy environment within factories. The capitalist state is either captured by the capitalists through their representatives in elected offices or is structurally dependent upon the capitalist class for state revenue. Therefore, the capitalist state is nothing but an instrument of the capitalist class to maintain the capitalist mode of production by promoting economic growth and by suppressing the labor.

From the Marxist perspective, green technology and sustainable development are simply vanities created by the capitalist system to pacify the labor and the ecologists, which seem to have worked very well so far. Workers and ecologists buy more eco-friendly products and services, the capitalists produce more eco-friendly products, profits go up, stock prices rise, wages and benefits of workers are raised, and workers buy even more eco-friendly products and services. Economic development is sustained by adopting green technology, but the ecology is not sustained. In the end, "sustainable development [...] is essentially the same thing as sustained economic growth."[6] What about the increased wastes and pollutions associated with expanded production? Well, they are treated outside the capitalist system with minimum care until the

---

6. Foster, *Ecology Against*, 79.

proverbial hell freezes over (or the earth boils). To find ecological solutions within the capitalist system is tantamount to seeking salvation from the devil.

Therefore, the only solution to ecological crises is to abolish the capitalist system which depends structurally on the production and reproduction of damages to the ecology. What is the alternative economic system to capitalism? It is a form of socialism in which workers take control of all tools of production. Collective ownership of the economy and property would be able to set human values, not material goods, as the goals of production. Public management of the economy would be able to re-calibrate the relationship between economic development and ecological concerns. Resources and products are distributed equally among people by communities, workers' associations, and/or the socialist state. But what exactly are the economic institutions of socialism? Marx and Engels did not provide a detailed blueprint. Contemporary Marxism can only provide an ambiguous statement like: "Their vision leaves room for a variety of institutional and cultural developments consistent with its basic principle of sustainable human development based on dis-alienation of the conditions of production."[7]

It is this institutional ambiguity that makes Marxist ecological theory unpopular in both the ecologist and political communities. As laudable as its emphasis on human values and ecological concerns is, however, the burden of proof that socialism is better than capitalism in resolving ecological crises lies in the hands of Marxist ecologists. So far, there is none. The collapse of the Soviet Union and the socialist bloc in 1989 as well as the abandonment of socialism in China after 1979 have proved that socialism fails to be a viable economic system to satisfy basic human needs, not to mention about human development. Furthermore, production inefficiency and ecological damages during the socialist regimes turned out to be much worse than that of their capitalist neighbors during the same timeframe and remains so after they abandoned socialism.

Furthermore, why and how do people, both capitalists and workers, change their capitalist values to human values? Why should human (collectivist) values be more sacred and vital than capitalist (individualist) values? How do they overcome old habits and social pressures? Can the state, education system, and mass media, which have been supported by the capitalist class, suddenly forget about their capitalist values and begin to embrace human values?

---

7. Burkett, *Marxism*, 331.

Finally, the free market, contrary to many rightist and leftist ecologists, does not mean the absence of government intervention in the market. The godfather of the Chicago School of Liberal Economics, Milton Friedman, assigned several vital functions to a government in a free market:

> A government which maintained law and order, defined property rights, served as a means whereby we could modify property rights and other rules of the economic game, adjudicated disputes about the interpretation of the rules, enforced contracts, promoted competition, provided a monetary framework, engaged in activities to counter technical monopolies and to overcome neighborhood effects widely regarded as sufficiently important to justify government intervention, and which supplemented private charity and the private family in protecting the irresponsible, whether madman or child – such a government would clearly have important functions to perform. The consistent liberal is not an anarchist.[8]

The debate between the rightists and leftists seem to be of the degree of governmental intervention in the market. The rightists think that there is always too much governmental intervention, while the leftists think that it is too little. On the ecology, the debates are most heated about redefining the property rights of pollution, preventing neighborhood effects of pollution, and protecting local communities against irresponsible corporations. These debates provide room for negotiation and compromise between the rightist and leftist ecological theories.

Before going next to the compromise between the rightists and leftists, it is necessary to consider another misleading agenda of ecological debates. With his New York Times Best Seller, *Capital in the Twenty-First Century*, economist Thomas Piketty brought social scientists around the world to study the increasing income inequality in the world. The book helped the "Occupy Wall Street" movement quickly spread from the United States to many countries. Many ecologists and ecotheologians discussed in the last chapter and this chapter have also treated it as an important agenda in ecological programs. However, there is little statistical data to support their relationships. Does income inequality cause more ecological crises, and/or vice versa? Logically speaking, neither causal relationship holds, because income inequality is national phenomenon influenced by national financial policies (e.g., progressive income tax, capital tax, inheritance tax, minimum wage), while ecological crises are caused by broader national economic policies (e.g., industrial

---

8. Friedman, *Capitalism and Freedom*, 34.

policies, environmental regulations) and international factors (free trade and ecological treaties). In fact, Piketty's data demonstrates that many of the Western industrial states had substantial income inequality from 1910 to 1940, when global ecological problems were not serious. Then, income inequality declined in all these countries almost by half from 1940 to 1980, when ecologists began to raise the flag of ecological crises. While Anglo-Saxon countries (the United States, Britain, Canada, and Australia) began to diverge from other industrial countries after 1980 in fast deterioration of income inequality, other industrial countries remained relatively the same. Global income inequality widened from 1700 to 1970, but gradually reduced due to faster economic development in Asian and African states, especially in China, which also became the largest polluter in the world.[9] In sum, income inequality may impose a disproportional burden on the poor or developing countries when ecological crises hit. However, it requires an adjustment in national financial policies, not ecological policies. Adding a social justice agenda to any ecological program is more likely to undermine than strengthen it.

Between the rightist and leftist ecological theories, Tim Jackson's book, *Prosperity without Growth: Economics for a Finite Planet*, is selected for its holistic treatment of ecological problems combining both rightist ecological economics and leftist arguments.[10] Much of the current ecological economics deal with specific economic subjects such as green taxes (levied on pollutants, use of petro-energy and thermos-energy), international trade of carbon quotas, limited property rights granted to polluters, subsidies to green technologies, population control, national debts, and impact of income inequality on the ecology. Jackson builds on these rightist ecological economics and espouses sectoral changes and changes in social values as fundamental solutions to ecological crises.

Jackson starts with the assumption that global economic growth has approached its limits due to drastically declining natural resources and collapsing ecosystems caused by reckless industrial production in the "age of irresponsibility," namely, the post-World War Two era. He argues that the age of irresponsibility "is not about casual oversight or individual greed," but a "systematic, sanctioned from the top, and with one clear aim in mind: the continuation and protection of economic growth."[11]

---

9. Piketty, *Capital*, 61, 272, 291, 316–20.
10. Jackson, *Prosperity*.
11. Jackson, *Prosperity*, 31.

He proposes a fundamental change in social values concerning prosperity from an obsession with economic growth, material opulence and consumerism to "bounded capabilities" for flourishing in life, bodily integrity, practical reason, affiliation, play, and control over one's environment.[12]

Concomitant with these changes in social values are institutional changes of capitalism. Jackson first rejects the "decoupling" approach which most rightist economists propose.[13] "Decoupling" aims to reduce or eliminate negative ecological impacts of economic growth through the development of resource-efficient technologies. "Production processes are reconfigured. Goods and services are redesigned. Economic output becomes progressively less dependent on material throughput. In this way, it is hoped, the economy can continue to grow without breaching ecological limits – or running out of resources." The decoupling strategy has not worked so far, Jackson says. What we have observed today is that "far from acting to reduce the throughput of goods, technological progress serves to increase production output by reducing factor costs." So, automobile factories roll out more cars, cellphone companies introduce new powerful models every year, and scholars publish more articles and books by using labor-saving technologies. Investments in de-materialized service sectors, rather than material industrial sectors, have not been able to reduce resource consumption; for example, tourism. When these "green reforms" hit their bottleneck in 2008, the International Monetary Fund, the World Bank, and national governments adopted "green Keynesianism" and "green New Deal" in the hope to create a "green recovery." Based on the poor track-record of the decoupling approach, Jackson suspects that the recovery would only mean a "return to business as usual."[14]

What an effective ecological economics requires, Jackson proposes, is to deal with the consumer's side, not the producer's side. The logic cannot be simpler: if consumers do not increase their spending on goods and services, producers will not produce more. The economy will not collapse but simply stops growing – it is the "zero-growth" of which many ecologists dream. Then, why cannot consumers see and follow this simple logic? It is because consumers embrace consumerism encouraged and protected by materialistic "social shame" (social status determined by the possession of material products), by government policies (e.g., effective subsidies to private transportation rather than public transportation, and waste disposal), by financial institutions

12. Jackson, *Prosperity*, 37–46.
13. For instance, Ayres, "Sustainability Economics," 281-310.
14. Jackson, *Prosperity*, 67, 95, 118.

(cheap consumer loans and credit cards), by the media (lifestyles of the rich and famous, brand names), and by the education system (aiming for high-income professions). "Little wonder that people trying to live more sustainably find themselves in conflict with the social world around them."[15]

Although Jackson acknowledges the sources of consumerism are multiple, he expects a powerful green state to tackle all the above sources. This green state will adopt three sets of ecological policies. First, to establish the limits of growth by setting resource and emission caps (even better, reduction targets), implementing fiscal reform for sustainability, and supporting for ecological transition in developing countries. Secondly, to fix the economic model by developing an ecological macro-economics, investing in jobs, assets and infrastructures, increasing financial and fiscal prudence, and revising national budget accounts. Thirdly, to change the social logic by reducing working hours, tracking systemic inequality, measuring capabilities and flourishing, strengthening social capital, and dismantling the culture of consumerism. With these measures, Jackson concludes that "prosperity without growth is no longer a utopian dream. It is a financial and ecological necessity."[16]

Jackson's ecological program is praiseworthy for its comprehensive coverage and concrete reform policies. In particular, he goes beyond what most ecological economists would do to address the fundamental necessity for changes in social values. However, contrary to what Jackson claims, his ecological program is precisely a utopia for four "impossibilities" of changes: changes in the social value of consumerism, comprehensive changes, the establishment of a Messiah green state, and even these changes are possible, the deadline for changes has been passed. The term "impossibility" is used here for a specific source and purpose: Nobel Laureate economist Kenneth Arrow's Impossibility Theorem which describes a general theorem that vital social values of capitalism and democracy cannot co-exist.[17] These impossibilities of changes, which involve some of Arrow's social values, are explained below.

First, the impossibility of changes in the social value of consumerism. Social values do change, but not easily or quickly. Social values are a system of enduring beliefs about what is good and bad in human interaction. They are passed on from one generation to another. Those social values which are closely related to human survival are particularly difficult to change (e.g., family values); so are those social values which are sanctified by ideology or

---

15. Jackson, *Prosperity*, 198, chapter 9.
16. Jackson, *Prosperity*, chapter 11.
17. Arrow, *Social Choice*.

religion. Consumerism is such a social value. How can we change a social value which is part of human nature?

Secondly, the impossibility of comprehensive changes. Jackson's comprehensive reform program requires a sophisticated and precise planning that human societies have never experimented before. It needs to build up capable new economic institutions and political constituencies to implement these reforms when old economic institutions and political constituencies refuse to give up their vested interests. One example is the financial reform which lies at the core of Jackson's reform program. Its counter-example is that the U.S. financial reform aimed to correct the systemic flaws of banking institutions ended up subsidizing these banking institutions. Even worse, the same groups of banking managers came back to the banking community with the blessing of reform-policymakers who had a similar background in the banking community. As Jackson noted before, it is politics as usual. How can we expect that Jackson's reform program does not end up with this déjà vu? Furthermore, as Arrow's impossibility theorem predicts that fundamental social and political values cannot co-exist, Jackson's comprehensive reform program is likely to contain many contradictory policies. For instance, promoting income equality may also promote consumerism of the lower and middle classes.

Thirdly, the impossibility of a Messiah green state. Jackson's comprehensive reform program amounts to a social revolution similar to that of communist revolutions in Russia (1917) and China (1949) carried out by a totalitarian state. Jackson expects state leaders to be fully committed to the ecology and be competent to carry out these reform policies resolutely. The state is even entrusted to change social values just as the communist regimes did. Can or should such a Messiah green state ever be built? More on the politics of the green state will be elaborated in the next chapter of this book.

Fourthly, the deadline for changes has been passed. Jackson starts his analysis by quoting, among others, the series of *Limits to Growth* by Meadows et al. to warn about the initiation of an ecological breakdown in as early as the year 2020. What Jackson's reform program is missing is that even if all his reform policies are implemented by the global community now, it is already too late to save the world. As discussed before in chapter 1 of this book, Meadows et al. and many ecologists have admitted that ecological deterioration has passed the point of no return in as late as 2002. Any comprehensive reform program will serve only to slow down a little bit the inevitable ecological collapse in the next fifty years or so.

There are other seminal ecological economics works that share both the merits and deficiencies of Jackson's. For instance, in their *Limits to Growth: The 30-Year Update*, Meadows, Randers and Meadows propose a list of seventeen ecological reforms (see below). These seven reforms can be grouped into three categories: seven social value reforms, six economic reforms, and four political reforms. Most Marxist ecologists would not disagree with these social value reforms, while rightist ecological economists would agree with these economic reforms. The four political reforms will be discussed in chapter 6 of this book. After reading these seventeen ecological programs, most readers of this book would wonder whether they are consistent with human natures, individually or institutionally at all, or whether this green state is even more perfect than the New Heaven and New Earth.

> Seventeen Ecological Programs by Meadows, Randers and Meadows (*Limits 30-Year*, 273-274):
>
> 1. Sustainability, efficiency, sufficiency, equity, beauty, and community as the highest social values.
>
> 2. Material sufficiency and security for all. By individual choice as well as communal norms, low birth rates and stable populations.
>
> 3. Work that dignifies people instead of demeaning them.
>
> 4. Leaders who are honest, respectful, intelligent, humble, and more interested in doing their jobs than in keeping their jobs, more interested in serving society than in winning elections.
>
> 5. An economy that is a means, not an end, one that serves the welfare of the environment, rather than vice versa.
>
> 6. Efficient, renewable energy systems.
>
> 7. Efficient, closed-loop materials systems.
>
> 8. Technical design that reduces emissions and waste to a minimum, and social agreement not to produce emissions or waste that technology and nature can"t handle.
>
> 9. Regenerative agriculture.

10. The preservation of ecosystems in their variety, with human cultures living in harmony with those ecosystems.

11. Flexibility, innovation, and intellectual challenge.

12. Greater understanding of whole systems as an essential part of each person's education.

13. Decentralization of economic power, political influence, and scientific expertise.

14. Political structures that permit a balance between short-term and long-term considerations.

15. High-level skills on the part of citizens and governments in the arts of nonviolent conflict resolution.

16. Media that reflect the world's diversity and at the same time unite cultures with relevant, accurate, timely, unbiased, and intelligent information, presented in its historic and whole-system context.

17. Reasons for living and for thinking well of ourselves that do not involve the accumulation of material things.

In sum, both rightist and leftist ecologists are correct in their criticisms of capitalism as the manufacturer of global ecological crises. The rightists suggest reforms within the capitalist system, while the leftists suggest revolution of the capitalist system. Both sets of reforms are doomed to fail if capitalist values are not reformed. But why and how do people change their values? Neither the rightists nor the leftists provide plausible and practical answers because they fail to adequately address the neuro-institutional origins of capitalism, to which the next section now turns.

Vanity of Sustainable Ecotheology

By combining both the rightist and leftist diagnoses, capitalism can be described as a quasi-religious economic system which reproduces itself by constantly stimulating individual human emotional greed, sustaining this emotional greed with liberal economic institutions, and sanctifying both human emotional greed and liberal economic institutions with the sanctified liberal economics. How should the church respond to these defects of capitalism? What kind of economic system, reformed capitalism or socialism, should the church support? Could the church make a difference in ecological outcomes?

Representative of the rightist ecotheology is *Money, Greed, and God: Why Capitalism is the Solution and Not the Problem* written by Jay W. Richards who is one of the leaders of the Acton Institute for the Study of Religion and Liberty which has been one of the leading voices of rightist theology in the United States. The main purpose of this book, as well as other works published by the Acton Institute, is to provide theological justifications of liberal capitalism against socialism or the welfare state. He started his analysis with the rationale of the micro-foundation of capitalist: self-interest. He argues that most critics of capitalism wrongly attribute greed as the micro-foundation of capitalism. According to Adam Smith, the founding father of the theory of the free market, self-interest is the micro-foundation of capitalism. Although self-interest is an imperfect moral status, it is a realistic description of human behaviors in capitalism. "Capitalism doesn't need greed. At the same time, it can channel greed, which is all to the good." Furthermore, capitalism imposes certain morals on economic actors, such as obedience to the law, hardworking, cooperation, stable families, self-sacrifice, saving, and entrepreneurship. Capitalism also enables people to engage in charity, both domestically and internationally. As regards ecological crises, Richards argues that, first, there are no ecological crises. Resources will not be exhausted; even if they will, new resources will always be invented through the free market. The scientific data about global warming is still debatable; even if it is a fact, global warming is bad news for tropical places but good for cold places. Even if we reduce carbon dioxide emissions, which will drastically reduce economic growth and severely hurt Third-World economies, we will not make a significant difference in global warming. What we need to solve all the problems of poverty, economic injustice and ecological crises (if they exist) are to promote a freer market with fewer state intervention, and a stable family system with religious devotion. Richards even provides a spiritual criticism of the environmental movement which "has now become the last line of defense in the left's attempt to stem the tide of global capitalism. Like communism, the environmental movement provides an all-encompassing vision of reality. Unlike communism, it has the benefits of a gratifying nature spirituality."[18]

---

18. Richards, *Money*, 86–116, 169–71, 1981, 1986–95, 2003, 2110-63, 2979-3208.

Many rightist ecological theorists have been frustrated with the lack of progress in ecological movements and, therefore, proposed a holy alliance between the green (ecological movement) and religion in the hope that religion can provide the necessary spiritual and institutional power to change social values, economic institutions, and government policies, as recommended by Meadows et al. above. Thanks to Lynn White, who was the first ecologist to blame ecological crises on Christianity, Christian theologians began to take up the responsibility to construct ecotheologies. The majority of ecotheologians have worked on the same assumption that consumerism is changeable, capitalism is reformable, and the ecology can be sustainable if, and only if, the church (or along with other religions) is fully engaged in ecological movements. It is also on the subject of values change that most ecotheologians feel comfortable and confident to provide religious solutions to ecological crises.

Then again, can global consumerism indeed be changed by Christianity or a coalition of religions? Consumerism commenced in primitive gatherer-hunter societies where the supply of food was volatile. Humans consumed as much as possible before the next meal became available in a day or two or longer. In agricultural societies, the supply of food was relatively more stable but still subject to the whim of natural disasters. Therefore, humans hoarded food in various forms and acquired agricultural land to improve their chances of survival. When monetary instruments were developed, ownership of these instruments and their derived goods and services improved their owners and their owners' offspring's survival chances. The initiation of Industrial Revolution dramatically improved the chances of human survival by increasing agricultural productivity and medical innovation. However, soon human greed propelled the reproduction of capitalism which in turn fueled all kinds of human greed. Designer clothing, shoes, watches, luxury automobiles, portable phones, exotic foods, fancy houses, and international tourism were no longer about human survival and happiness only, but also greed. These goods and services transformed into symbols of social status in daily conversation, schools and news media. The proliferation of new financial instruments since the 1980s, such as credit cards, easy loans, stocks, and futures, added gasoline to the fire of already run-away consumerism by encouraging "consumption now and pay later." In sum, consumerism as a social value originated in human nature and had been shaped by various economic institutions from primitive gatherer-hunter economy to contemporary financial capitalism. Therefore, to change the social value of consumerism, it is necessary to modify the economic institutions which mold consumerism in the hope that an alternative economic institution may produce ecological social values. Can the church offer such an alternative economic institution?

There are two prominent Christian views of ecological economic institutions: agricultural economy or socialist economy. In his book, *The Garden of God*, Pope Benedict XVI tackles the institutional foundation of consumerism and suggests a return to the agricultural economy, not only for the sake of feeding the poor but also for cultivating sacred ecological social values. "In Christian tradition," he says, "agricultural labor takes on a deeper meaning, both because of the effort and hardship that it involves and also because it offers a privileged experience of God's presence and his love for his creatures. Christ himself uses agricultural images to speak of the Kingdom, thereby showing a great respect for this form of labor." Furthermore, "the rural family needs to regain its rightful place at the heart of the social order . . . Investment in the agricultural sector has to allow the family to assume its proper place and function, avoiding the damaging consequences of hedonism and materialism that can place marriage and family life at risk." With respect to the direct relationship between ecology and agricultural section, he advocates that "a strategic revitalization of agriculture is crucial. Indeed, the process of industrialization has often overshadowed the agricultural sector, which . . . lost importance with notable consequences, even at the cultural level. It seems to me that it is time to re-evaluate agriculture, not in a nostalgic sense but as an indispensable resource for the future . . . We should promote personal responsibility along with a social dimension of rural activities based on the undying values of hospitality, solidarity, and sharing the toil of labor."[19]

The "return to agriculture" approach has several merits. First, it is consistent with the creation ecotheology discussed in chapter 4 of this book. Secondly, it brings humans back to the rural area to re-build their direct contact with an appreciation of nature. Thirdly, it helps to resolve the most urgent problem of hunger in post-ecology. Fourthly, it may help to form an inter-religious ecological alliance because all the major religions originated in agricultural societies and developed their core ethics in the agricultural context.

Nevertheless, the "return to agriculture" approach suffers from several drawbacks. First, can human societies turn back their clock on economic development? Can humans de-memorize the pleasures associated with industrialization and urbanization? What scale of resources and institutions are needed to re-locate capitalists, workers and services from urban industrial areas to the countryside? Even if these answers are affirmative, secondly, industrialization

19. Pope, *Garden*, 142–43, 198–99; see also, 153–55, 174–76, 201–8.

and financialization have transformed agricultural technology, organization and social relations in the rural area in the past fifty years. Farmers use more efficient farming tools to replace workers, many of whom are seasonal migrant workers anyway. Large agricultural companies have bought out small farmers due to their superiority in technology, capital and marketing. Is this the agricultural sector to which we want to return? Can a jump-started traditional agricultural sector provide more and cheaper food than this already industrialized and financialized agricultural sector? Thirdly, agriculture is not necessarily more ecological. The intensive use of pesticides and chemical fertilizers, the adoption of the single-crop plantation system, the budding production of genetically engineered food, the invasion of agricultural land into forests, and the wastes generated by domesticated animals, all significantly contribute to ecological crises. Will the "return to agriculture" reduce these problems or exacerbate them? The most controversial case of the global "sustainable" (what it calls itself) agricultural conglomerate Monsanto seems to point to the direction of the latter.

The other recommended approach by ecotheologians is a religious socialist economy different from the Marxian economy. It is built on one possible Christian tradition: the collective communes of the early apostolic churches. Immediately after Jesus' Ascension, the apostolic church at Jerusalem adopted a religious commune system for a while in which "all those who had believed were together, and had all things in common; and they began selling their property and possessions, and were sharing them with all, as anyone might have need."[20] The Greek morphology of "selling" (ἐπίπρασκον; *epipraskon*) and "sharing" (διεμέριζον; *diemerizon*) are iterative imperfects which mean that the apostolic church conducted these behaviors for a time. Similarly, "the congregation of those who believed were of one heart and soul; and not one of them claimed that anything belonging to him was his own; but all things were common property to them . . . For there was not a needy person among them, for all who were owners of land or houses would sell them and bring the proceeds of the sales, and lay them at the apostles' feet; and they would be distributed to each, as any had need."[21] At its initial stage, the apostles were so adamant about enforcing this commune system that when a couple, Ananias and Sapphira, lied about their devotion to the commune system, they were cursed to death by Apostle Peter. David L. Mealand argues that the phrase of "not one of them claimed that anything belonging to him was his own; but all

20. Acts 2: 44–45.
21. Acts 4: 32, 34–35.

things were common property to them" in Acts 4:32 was probably strongly influenced by the utopian philosophies in the Greek literature of the time. Some Jewish communities also might have practiced this form of community life.[22]

However, for how long and how far did this commune system last in the early Christian churches? Probably not long, as a "great fear came upon the whole church, and upon all who heard of these things."[23] In the rest of Acts or other parts of the NT, there was no more mention of this commune system. Outside Jerusalem, there was little evidence that Christian churches adopted this commune system.[24] Soon afterwards, donations to the church were made largely voluntary, and there was no strong enforcement of this norm as in the case of Ananias and Sapphira. The first episode that signaled the ending of the commune system happened during the rule of Claudius Caesar (41-54 AD) when there was a famine in Judea. The newly-formed gentile church in Antioch heard about this and donated to the church in Judea. The donation was neither compulsory nor collective, but "in the proportion that any of the disciples had means, each of them determined to send a contribution for the relief of the brethren living in Judea."[25] In short, it is a problematic argument that the commune system is a Christian model for an economic system.[26]

In fact, as sociologist Max Weber (1864–1920) explained well, it was Protestantism that unintentionally justified and promoted capitalism in the first place. Martin Luther and John Calvin developed the concept of "calling" to encourage fulfilment of Christian duties to God. This "calling" was not a new theology before the sixteenth century. However, one thing was "unquestionably new: the valuation of the fulfilment of duty in worldly affairs as the highest form which the moral activity of the individual could assume. This it was which inevitably gave every-day worldly activity a religious significance, and which first created the conception of a calling in this sense."[27] Accordingly, capitalists would fulfil their calling by increasing their capital, strict avoidance of all spontaneous enjoyment of life, and conform to capitalistic rules of action. Workers would fulfil their calling by working hard and obedience to the capitalist boss. "The differentiation of mean into the classes and occupations established through historical development became ... a direct result of the

22. Mealand, "Community."
23. Acts 5: 1–11.
24. Bock, *Acts*, 152-152, 222-228.
25. Acts 11: 25–30.
26. Bock, *Acts*; Mealand, "Community."
27. Weber, *Protestant*, 40.

divine will. The perseverance of the individual in the place and within the limits which God had assigned to him was a religious duty." Both capitalists and workers should obey the public law because it was a secular equivalence to the Old Testament.[28] Even the last element of Puritan frugality which contemporary ecotheologians consider as beneficial to ecology was removed from the Christian ethical catechism and replaced by the "inalienable right of the pursuit of happiness" coined in the American Declaration of Independence. The "pursuit of happiness" was further augmented by the Prosperity Gospel in the 1980s, which treated increase of personal wealth as a direct sign of God's blessing and reward to the rich people's generous donation to the church, or better, to the pastors.[29] A capitalist market, thus, is fully legitimized outside and within the church.

Similar theological and practical controversies occur in John B. Cobb's critique of capitalism. He correctly identifies "economism" (capitalism) as the dominant religion of the twentieth and twenty-first centuries, whose "destructive consequences . . . will be irreversible ruin for the planet." Economism has taken solid control over the economy, democracy, academia, the Federal Reserve Bank, and even the church leadership. What, then, is the alternative? Cobb calls for resistance by organizing para-church organizations. "The best answer I can come up with is that we can resist by identifying fundamental alternatives to the system to which we have become accustomed and spreading interest in these alternatives as far as possible . . . When another collapse occurs, public anger might be mobilized in support of radical needed change."[30] But it might be too late and too feeble an attempt to save the ecology by then. This is the so-called "Giddens' Paradox": people do not take ecological actions until they see ecological crises, by which time it is already too late. The Giddens' Paradox will be discussed in more details in the next chapter.

Following Cobb's leftist critique of capitalism, theologians Philip Clayton and Justin Heinzekehr reshape the deterministic, universalistic, collective Marxism into a locally adaptive "Organic Marxism" as an alternative to capitalism in dealing with ecological crises. Their policy guidelines include: (1) national interests are no longer the only defining context for government decision making; (2) to address the reality that power now falls in the hands of an ever smaller number of people, who control more and more of the world's wealth; and (3) from each according to his ability, to each according to his

28. Weber, *Protestant*, 106, 108–110.

29. Jones and Woodbridge, *Health*.

30. Cobb, *Theological*, 227–33. See also his classic works: Cobb, *Common Good*.

need. Translated into concrete policies, Organic Marxism proposes to replace GDP growth with other social welfare indicators, sustainable agriculture, green manufacturing, sustainable management (e.g., share ownership), and a socialist banking system. If these policy guidelines and concrete policies look politically naïve to the readers, they do not escape Clayton and Heinzekehr's academic radar either. They realize from historical facts that capitalists are not likely to "freely agree to support a socialist system" prescribed above. So, the incentive for reform should come from outside the capitalist system, namely, "the coming environmental catastrophe will provide the needed catalyst." Either the "the global crisis will bring out the more noble side of those in power," or the masses will rise against them.[31] Again, this last hope will be destroyed by the Giddens' Paradox: it might be too late and too feeble an attempt to save the ecology.

Despite its efforts to raise Marxism from the dead, Organic Marxism reveals the same strengths and weaknesses as the dead leftist ecotheology discussed before. It provides a convincing description of the structural imperatives of capitalism to produce and reproduce ecological crises. If we paraphrase Lenin's argument in *Imperialism the Highest Stage of Capitalism*,[32] that global capitalism will only collapse after it reaches its highest stage, then, Organic Marxism is correct in arguing that global capitalism leads to global ecological crises which, in turn, will lead to the rapid collapse of global capitalism. Nevertheless, Organic Marxism is betting on the same utopian rational assumptions about the workers, the capitalists and politicians to forgo self-interests for the sake of the ecology. More surprisingly, written by two Christian theologians, Organic Marxism builds few of its arguments based on the Bible, relying more so on Marxism and Daoism.[33] Christianity, when mentioned in the book, is a collaborator with the capitalists to destroy the ecology.[34] Furthermore, like the American leftists who eulogized the Soviet Union in the 1950s, Clayton and Heinzekehr eulogized the Chinese government for her accomplished promotion of an "ecological civilization,"[35] despite the fact that, so far, most of these

---

31. Clayton and Heinzekehr, *Organic Marxism*, 6–8, 212–221, 230–231.

32. Lenin, *Imperialism*.

33. Clayton and Heinzekehr, *Organic Marxism*, 13, 80, 159, 164, 167, 185, 198–99, 232–33. Clayton and Heinzekehr seem to ignore the fact that Chinese Daoism was always associated with ecologically devastating revolutionary wars in traditional China. See Lee, "Daoist Tribulation."

34. Clayton and Heinzekehr, *Organic Marxism*, 44, 198, 232.

35. Clayton and Heinzekehr, *Organic Marxism*, 10–12, 76–80.

"green programs" and "green industries" continue to exacerbate ecological degradations much faster than they save energy and the ecology.

Finally, even if we follow the reform solutions proposed by the rightist ecotheology or the revolutionary solutions proposed by the leftist ecotheology with utmost sincerity and devotion, it is already too late to halt the incoming ecological collapse. It took three hundred years for capitalism to develop to its current scale and complexity. How long will it take to reform all the agricultural, industrial, and financial institutions to the sustainable level? It took seventy years for communism to develop to its full scale in 1989, and only to find out that it could never possibly work. The former Soviet countries and China transformed instead to capitalism, rapidly contributing since to global ecological crises. How long will it take, if ever possible, to reform Christian values associated with capitalism? How long will it take to ask Christians to give up their jobs in pollution-related sectors (by a broad definition, all sectors are polluting industries)? How long will Christian capitalists survive the capitalist market if they strictly follow ecological principles of doing business? How long will it last for those priests and pastors who dare their lay-believers, or even themselves, to live their lives according to strict ecological principles (no purchase of new clothing, shoes, and home appliances; buy only at second-hand markets; repair broken home appliances; or enjoy leisure facilities only within the parameter of the city)?

In sum, as long as the church is embedded in the complex institution of capitalism, rightist sustainable ecotheology is probably as utopian as leftist sustainable ecotheology. What, then, is a practical, alternative ecotheology?

Capitalism and Post-Ecotheology

Similar to the opening statements in section 3 of the last chapter, a neuro-institutional post-ecotheology of capitalism develops its concrete actions based on two inter-related simple principles at the individual and collective levels. At the individual level, the church should take only those ecological actions which do not substantially reduce the overall happiness of her congregation members. At the collective level, local churches should take only those ecological actions which do not substantially reduce their overall happiness and only when these ecological actions receive a consensus within the local community. Both principles emphasize tolerance and compromise toward different ecological positions among individual Christians and between the church and the local community. An ecological action which substantially reduces individual or collective happiness is not likely to garner persistent support.

A post-ecotheology starts with the assumption, as its name reveals, that the ecology has passed the point of no return. There is no need for repentance and radical ecological actions. However, there is a need for accommodation of social-ecological norms and preparation for ecological doomsday.

The economic components of the post-ecotheology begin with the neuro-institutional theology of human nature as it relates to the economic institution. That is, humans conduct market exchanges for survival purposes as well as for greed to benefit themselves as individuals, families, communities, states, and in a global economic community. The Bible encourages believers to engage in responsible and fair market relationships for their short-term and long-term survival needs. However, the Bible does condemn greed/coveting. The Tenth Commandment says, "You shall not covet your neighbor's house; you shall not covet your neighbor's wife or his male servant or his female servant or his ox or his donkey or anything that belongs to your neighbor." Psalmists rebut the greedy man: "For the wicked boasts of his heart's desire, and the greedy man curses and spurns the LORD." Jesus admonishes immoral behaviors of "fornications, thefts, murders, adulteries, deeds of coveting and wickedness." "Beware, and be on your guard against every form of greed; for not even when one has an abundance does his life consist of his possessions." Apostle Paul re-iterated Jesus' admonition against greed/coveting, "for this you know with certainty, that no immoral or impure person or covetous man, who is an idolater, has an inheritance in the kingdom of Christ and God." "Free from the love of money . . . For the love of money is a root of all sorts of evil, and some by longing for it have wandered away from the faith, and pierced themselves with many a pang."[36]

While the Bible condemns greed and coveting, it does not forbid believers to accumulate wealth in general; it was the excessive wealth acquired by greed and injustice that is condemned. In the OT, Job was an incredibly wealthy man. He lost his wealth, not because of his greed but because Satan challenged God to do so. In the end, he received more sheep, camels, oxen, and donkeys than before as a reward for his tenacious religious commitment to God.[37] When Jesus says, "No one can serve two masters; for either he will hate the one and love the other, or he will hold to one and despise the

---

36. Exod 20:17; Ps 10:3; Mark7:21–22; Luke 12:15; 1Tim 3:3; 6:10; Eph 5:5.

37. Job's wealth in Job 1:3 compared to 42: 13–14.

other. You cannot serve God and mammon,"[38] He was probably speaking of excessive wealth based on greed and without concomitant religious devotion. So is His remarks on wealthy people entering God's kingdom, "it is easier for a camel to go through the eye of a needle, than for a rich man to enter the kingdom of God."[39] Apostle Paul exhorts Christians to follow his attitude toward poverty or wealth: "I know how to get along with humble means, and I also know how to live in prosperity; in any and every circumstance I have learned the secret of being filled and going hungry, both of having abundance and suffering need."[40] During his second evangelical mission, Paul stayed in the house of Lydia who was a seller of purple fabrics, which was a lucrative business.[41] In the often-neglected passage in chapter 16 of the Epistle to the Romans, Paul mentions a number of close co-workers who were probably rich people: Phoebe, who "has been a helper of many;" the married couple of Prisca and Aquila, who were in the lucrative tent business and opened their house for worship; and Erastus, who was the city treasurer.[42] It is not a shame to live in either poverty or prosperity. What matters is whether Christians live a righteous life and fulfill their evangelical duties.

The rightist ecotheologians are correct by arguing that capitalism is better equipped than socialism to satisfy human needs. However, the leftist ecotheologians are quick to point out that capitalism has developed way beyond the realm of the need and gone deep into the inferno of greed. However, greed is not a necessary or sufficient condition for capitalism. Greed existed in hunter-gatherer societies, agricultural societies, and in capitalist societies because it is a characteristic of human nature; it is an original sin. It is debatable whether humans are greedier in capitalism than in hunter-gatherer societies or agricultural societies.

Greed, as discussed in chapter 2 of this book, is a social-psychological concept and is always a relative concept. On the one hand, rich people can be greedy, but so too can poor people. On the other hand, most individuals who are greedy probably do not think they are greedy until someone else tell them so. To those people living in poverty and have only one meal a day, a middle-class professional eating a dinner buffet once a week is greedy. To those middle-class professionals, a Wall-Street trader taking his clients to

38. Matt 6:24; Luke 16:13.
39. Matt 19:24; Mark10:25; Luke 18:25.
40. Phil 4:12.
41. Acts 16:14; Bock, *Acts*, 534.
42. Rom 16:1–5, 23.

five-star Michelin restaurants once a week is sinfully greedy. However, this Wall-Street trader probably does not think himself greedy at all because one of his clients regularly hires a chef from a five-star Michelin restaurant to prepare his daily meals. Was Pope Benedict greedy when he wore the red Prada shoes and traveled in first class? I was once invited to a vegetarian banquet hosted by a Chinese Buddhist abbot, who managed a chain of temples around the world in a very capitalist way. The first course was a salad decorated with a real gold flake. It is not necessary to mention the luxury that accompanied the other eleven courses served on gold-plated plates or bowls. Is this abbot greedy or sinfully greedy in the eyes of a Tibetan monk?

This is not to justify capitalism by the excuse of "everybody does that," or "greed is a relative term, you are just jealous." There are practical rules of thumb to make "inter-subjective objective" criteria of greed. (1) Personal criteria. Do I spend more money than I earn? Do I work too hard to hurt my health and my family? (2) Social criteria. The lifestyle of a middle-class professional is probably a good reference point to balance personal consumption habits and social standards.

Therefore, the debate about the virtues and vices of capitalism is probably considered to be wrong-headed by both the rightist and leftist ecotheologians. Capitalism itself is one of the man-made economic institutions that facilitate the production of goods and services for the survival and happiness (and/or greed) of humans in a particular economic context. There is nothing intrinsic, morally right or wrong with capitalism as it is with the hunter-gather economy, agricultural economy, industrial economy, or financial economy. The production of goods and services is an economic issue internally determined by economic contexts, such as natural resources, technology, capital, management, demand, and supply.

If there is anything significantly sinful with capitalism, it is its tremendous power to magnify the quantity and variety of the production of goods and services. Our emotional brain is constantly bombarded, or tempted, by the sheer quantity and new variety of goods and services. New products and services, through the omnipresent and omnipotent advertisement agents, consume all our senses' attention on a daily basis: sight, sound, smell, taste and touch. Our rational brain and God brain could hardly catch up to the speed of our emotional brain's responses to these attractive signals. Capitalism makes people healthier, happier and greedier. No longer is the sky not even the limit for human emotional desires, but the sky is moving ever higher via the reproduction and global expansion of capitalism. However, is this really the fault of capitalism, a powerful machine to efficiently produce large amount and variety of goods and services? Or is it we humans, the agents of capitalism, who are at fault? Do we, by instinct, shift the blame, as Adam and Eve did, from ourselves to others?

What is morally right or wrong about any economic institution is basically a social and political controversy attached externally to the economic institution, particularly, the distribution side of goods and services. Capitalism can be morally right and wrong, depending on how the production and distribution of capitalism is regulated. Capitalism is not intrinsically demonic, as leftist theologians would argue, nor is it intrinsically angelic, as rightist theologians would argue. Capitalism is like an airplane. It brings people faster from one city to another. It can be a virtuous instrument as it produces extra pleasures for tourists, new business opportunities for business people, and additional emotional bondages for family members who live afar. Yet, it can also be demonic if the airplane becomes a strategic nuclear bomber, or hijacked by terrorists, or falls into the hands of a drunken pilot. Besides, most travelers never like the idea of the division of seats and services into first class, business class, and economy class, except for those who can afford the first and business classes.

Therefore, from a Christian view, the debate should be about how to regulate capitalism instead of replacing it with an entirely different economic institution, agricultural or socialist, which may generate more demonic than virtuous consequences. The focus, then, shifts from endless debates about the nature of capitalism to concrete religious and political reforms with regard to the ecology. Political reforms will be dealt with in the next chapter. Religious reforms related to capitalism are discussed in the chapter following political reforms.

As the neuro-institutional theology discussed in chapters 2 and 3 of this book implies, the church is best suited to encourage ecological behaviors through suppressing desires, sanctifying the ecology, and conducting rational ecological planning. In terms of religious reforms, the church can promote ecological reforms on local capitalism in several ways. On the consumption side, the church can promote a self-paced frugal lifestyle with reference to the church's middle-class. The pastors should take the lead by taking the salary of the average income of their congregation members, while the wealthy elders and deacons should avoid wearing expensive jewelry on Sunday worship if most members are much poorer. This promotion is consistent with the Bible's balanced teaching on enjoying life and living in frugality. The church may, through collective discussion and decision, promote ecological programs to recycle products and hold garage sales to reduce demands for material goods.

On the production side of capitalism, pending on the composition of congregation members and the nature of specific industries, the church may encourage them to transfer their jobs from polluting industries to less-polluting industries (since no industry is entirely free from polluting the environment). If there are few alternative jobs available, the church may encourage them to help the company to improve efficiency, their pollution-control technology and management structures. Christian capitalists and workers should reserve as much time as possible for church activities and family members. By keeping constant the work hours, the pollution associated with production can also be held constant. Whichever job (polluting or non-polluting, capitalist or worker) Christians have, they need to work as hard as their average competitors do, not much more nor much less, to survive in the capitalist market, which is improbable to disappear until the arrival of doomsday.

On the distribution side of capitalism, the church should encourage tithe, charity, and donation of inheritance to support the poor and the above ecological programs within and outside the community. Christian capitalists should provide larger shares of profits than their average competitors to their workers.

However, even if these religious reforms are possible, the church should have a clear teaching to believers that capitalism or socialism will not matter to Christians on doomsdays. Unless interpreted spiritually in its entirety, the book of Revelation describes what will actually happen to Christians and their relationships to economic system (capitalism or socialism) during the Judgment days: Christians will be excluded from the market and, then, the global market will be destroyed by Jesus. In his letter to the church in Smyrna, Apostle John knew about the church's suffering from "extreme poverty." [43] What could be the causes of this extreme poverty? Colin. J. Hemer proposed four possible explanations: the gentile and Jewish mobs robbed Christian properties, Smyrna Christians were poor to start with, Smyrna Christians were generous in charity, and Smyrna Christians were forced out of jobs by the hostile gentiles and Jews.[44] As compared to the other six churches in Revelation, the second and the third explanations are less plausible because Christians in the main cities were doing comparatively better at that time and because charity was not specifically implied in the letter to the Smyrna church. The

43. Rev 2:9.
44. Hemer, *Letters*, 68.

first and the fourth explanations are both directly related to the economic persecution by the gentiles and Jews at that time and in the days of Judgment. Most theologians would also explain the poverty in Smyrna church and in Pergamum church in terms their refusal to join local guilds which regularly held religious rituals.[45] Either way, Christians were and will be excluded from the market. During the Judgment days, another beast will come up from under the earth. "He causes all, the small and the great, and the rich and the poor, and the free men and the slaves, to be given a mark on their right hand, or on their forehead, and he provides that no one should be able to buy or to sell, except the one who has the mark, either the name of the beast or the number of his name."[46] This economic sanction will be more comprehensive and compulsory than the Roman Empire's; Christians will be totally excluded from the market.[47]

While the Christians will be excluded from the market, the global market, in the end, will be destroyed in its entirety by Jesus Christ. The beast from the earth will reign the whole world through its world government in Babylon, which will be the political, economic and religious capital of the world.[48] After the whole world is devastated by the natural and supernatural disasters of the seven seals, seven trumpets and seven bowls, Jesus will now deal with Babylon. The seventh bowl will first hit Babylon with a mega-earthquake; the city is split into three parts. Fire, probably set by its political allies, burns the city to the ground. All the trade within the city and between the city and the rest of the world is stopped. Finally, the city sinks into the ocean "and will not be found any longer."[49] If world capitalism (or world socialism) lasts to the Judgment Days, it will be destroyed before Jesus' Second Coming, because it is a fair judgment in revenge of the evil empire's economic oppression against Christians described above.[50] Again, it is not the intrinsic vices of capitalism the book of Revelation aims at, because capitalism was not yet born. It is the immoral distribution of goods and services based on sinful natures of humans that the book of Revelation condemns.

When Apostle John wrote the Revelation, neither a world capitalism nor a world socialism had existed before his time. It was a global agricultural

45. Beale, *Book of Revelation*, 239-264.
46. Rev 13: 11, 16–17.
47. Osborne, *Revelation*, 518.
48. Rev 17.
49. Rev 17:15; 18:1–23.
50. Osborne, *Revelation*, 631–660.

economy with active commerce. It is not likely that he would have either a preference for capitalism or socialism. For the same reason, the Bible probably does not have a clear preference for capitalism or socialism, no matter it is an improved, equitable, and/or efficient economic institution. It does not matter how much human efforts are invested into improving existing economic institutions. In the end, all will be unrighteous and devious in the eyes of God and will be exterminated.

So, what should Christians do to capitalism (or socialism) for the sake of the ecology? First, business as usual. "Submit yourselves for the LORD's sake to every human institution, whether to a king as the one in authority, or to governors as sent by him for the punishment of evildoers and the praise of those who do right."[51] The economic institution is only one of the human institutions Christians should submit. Christian workers do not need to reduce their working hours unless their employers ask them to. Christian capitalists do not need to scale down their production levels unless the market demands go down. Both the workers and capitalists continue to buy new clothing, shoes, home appliances, and get out of town for tourism, as their income permits. "So I commended pleasure, for there is nothing good for a man under the sun except to eat and to drink and to be merry, and this will stand by him in his toils throughout the days of his life which God has given him under the sun."[52]

Secondly, business not as usual. If the church collectively decides to promote a slightly more frugal lifestyle, submit yourselves to this ecological economic program. For instance, the church may hold more frequent garage sales, classes for home appliance repairs, and tourism in groups. If the church pushes even further and make you extremely uncomfortable, move to another church that does not. If the church is not an active participant in ecological programs, join a local ecological movement and spend your extra time and energy there, instead of picking on the pastor and deacons

Thirdly, save for the raining days. On the Judgment Days, Christians will need spiritual, physical and material strengths to live through natural and supernatural disasters. Although they will not suffer directly from these disasters, apostates and unbelievers will attack Christians in revenge of God's judgments on them.

Moreover, those Christians who live in the future world capital, which may refer to any metropolitan area, will need some money to move out of the capital and survive the rest of the days before Jesus' Second Coming. An

51. 1Pet 2:13–14.
52. Eccl 8:15.

angel cries out when Babylon breaks into three pieces, "come out of her, my people, that you may not participate in her sins and that you may not receive of her plagues."[53] So, in addition to business as usual, business not as usual, Christians need to save for the raining days. Individual Christians need to do so, just as the church also needs to do so by putting some of the tithes into a savings account to cope with the growing natural and supernatural disasters affecting the global economy and the local church.

Summary

The consensus among most ecologists is that capitalism is the major villain to be blamed for ecological crises. So, if we can successfully reform capitalism, ecological crises will come no more. But how do we reform capitalism? Both rightist and leftist economists have proposed their version of reforms. However, the rightist ecological proposals are flawed because by itself the free market cannot discontinue the increase of ecological damages; the re-assignment of property rights (e.g., carbon-quota trade) does not change the original amount of pollution, and may ironically further encourage pollution; population control is not an integrated part of their proposals; and the innovation of cost-effective green technology may not come fast enough before the ecology collapses. The leftist ecological theories accurately point out the above flaws of the rightist proposals. However, they fail, amongst others, on one pivotal challenge: What is the alternative? Most socialist countries have either transformed themselves into capitalist countries or remain a poverty-stricken hermit country like the North Korea. Furthermore, evidence from these former socialist countries shows that they probably caused more severe ecological problems than capitalist countries did. Finally, both the rightist and the leftist proposals require a change of capitalist values (e.g., capitalist competition, consumerism, and blind faith in technology) long-held by individuals since the eighteenth century. But neither rightist nor leftist proposals provide convincing arguments and methods to do so within their rational economic ideology. The church could provide a complementary solution to both.

Rightist ecotheologians and leftist ecotheologians build their ecotheologies on the rightist and leftist economic theories respectively. However, they suffer from the same weaknesses as the rightist and leftist economic theories do. Even worse, by adding the spiritual and organizational power to ecological

53. Rev 18:4.

programs, the church may exacerbate theological controversies within the church and ecological crises outside the church. Besides, all markets, socialist or capitalist, will be exterminated by Jesus Christ on the arrival of doomsday. The church does not have a vital stake in the maintenance or reform of capitalism.

A neuro-institutional post-ecotheology of the church starts with the assumptions that there is no need to drastically reform capitalism, which has been the most efficient way to satisfy the human needs of survival and happiness. What needs to be changed is the greed of humans, magnified by capitalist values and institutions. While the government can pass laws to regulate capitalism, the church may employ spiritual and social means to discourage human greed on the part of both producers and consumers. In particular, the church needs to pay increasing attention to the distribution of goods and services to the disadvantaged people. However, the church should perform these ecological programs only through democratic deliberation among church members without significantly distracting believers from their Christian duty of evangelism in the age of post-ecology.

6.

Democracy and Post-Ecotheology

SINCE THE PUBLICATION OF the first volume of the *Limits to Growth* series in 1972, there has been a significant growth of ecological awareness at the grassroots level around the world. However, the growing ecological awareness has not been able to halt back or to prevent a global ecological meltdown in the coming decades. The previous chapter reveals that although leftist and rightist ecologists disagree on whether capitalism is the foremost culprit, both sides agree that the current capitalist system needs to be regulated by the state. But what kind of a state, i.e., authoritarian or democratic? While some leftists and rightists propose "green authoritarianism" to replace or strictly regulate capitalism, other leftists and rightists prefer "deliberative democracy" to reform the current capitalism dominated by big corporations.

The first and second sections of this chapter evaluate the proposals of green authoritarianism and deliberative democracy. The third section introduces Anthony Giddens' "Third-Way" political ecology, which not only aims to mediate between the authoritarian and liberal political ecologies but also takes a holistic approach to address the issue from the local community level up to the global level. Following the debates in the first three sections, the fourth section provides a theological link between these secular political ecotheories and political ecotheologies by exploring the hermenutic politics of the "kingdom of God on earth." The fifth section develops a neuro-institutional post-ecotheology with regard to the proper relationships between the state and church in post-ecology. The final section summarizes the arguments of this chapter.

Vanity of Green/Red Authoritarianism

The first contemporary scholar to initiate the political debate about the ecology is probably Garrett Hardin, a biologist who published his seminal article in *Science*,[1] the same journal as Lynn White for his controversial article on Christianity and the ecology. Hardin's article is entitled "The Tragedy of the Commons" which has been borrowed by most ecologists as an epitome of all ecological problems.

The Tragedy of the Commons is an allegory about a group of herdsmen who raise their cattle in a common pasture. Each "rational" herdsman calculates the utility (personal gain) and cost (less grass for all herdsmen) of adding another cow or bull to his herd and concludes that

> the only sensible course for him to pursue is to add another animal to his herd. And another; and another . . . But this is the conclusion reached by each and every rational herdsman sharing a commons. Therein is the tragedy. Each man is locked into a system that compels him to increase his herd without limit – in a world that is limited. Ruin is the destination toward which all men rush, each pursuing his own best interest in a society that believes in the freedom of the commons. Freedom in a commons brings ruin to all.[2]

Hardin applies the Tragedy of the Commons to the cases of population growth and pollution and suggests that under the current free market system protected by the liberal democracy there is "no technical solution" but "requires a fundamental extension in morality." His appeal to morality is not an appeal to human conscience, which would likely lead to schizophrenia oscillating between personal rationality and collective morality, but a political system which uses coercion to enforce morality and responsibility. Although Hardin does not specifically use the word "authoritarianism" to describe his ideal political system, he supports a political system that allows "mutual coercion mutually agreed upon by the majority of the people affected" to restrict the human rights of the "freedom to breed (children)" and to impose heavy taxes on the property rights to pollute, including tourism. "Only so," Hardin says, "can we put an end to this aspect of the tragedy of the commons."[3] In another article, he reiterates his arguments with yet another allegory of the lifeboat: the ecology is like a lifeboat carrying already too many people in it

---

1. Hardin, "The Tragedy," 1243–48.
2. Hardin, "The Tragedy," 1244.
3. Hardin, "The Tragedy," 1246-1248.

while some within the lifeboat continue to give birth to children. Probably, in anticipation of liberal challenges to his coercion argument, Hardin tones down his earlier political proposal but insists that "only under a strong and farsighted sovereign – which theoretically could be the people themselves, democratically organized – can a population equilibrate at some set point below the carrying capacity."[4]

Building on Hardin's "strong and farsighted sovereign," leftist economic ecologist Robert L. Heilbroner contributes to green/red authoritarianism by arguing for a political system that "blends a religious orientation with a military discipline." Heilbroner also starts with the concern over the incoming ecological collapse caused by the exponential growth of population and industrial pollution. Like Hardin, Heilbroner finds cause and solution to ecological collapse in human nature. Two possibilities exist: first, humans are selfish, myopic and inert until they actually see the ecological collapse. Then, we rely on human nature's capabilities to change and adapt. However, this is probably too slow and too late for ecological collapse. To mobilize human ecological actions before ecological collapse arrives, Heilbroner suggests exploiting the human nature of "hunger for political authority and the fantasy of political identification" at the time of crises. Only nation-states with centralized governments that blend "a religious orientation with a military discipline" would be capable of saving the human societies. When the third edition of Heilbroner's book was published in 1991, his ideal ecological state was the rising China.[5]

As Heilbroner correctly identifies the common root of all authoritarian polities, the green/red authoritarianism appeals to the most dynamic and fundamental human nature – the survival instinct discussed in chapter 2 of this book. The urgency and totality of ecological collapse justify an emotional response of "drastic times require drastic measures." Heilbroner, furthermore, tries to add a religious dosage to magnify the power of green/red authoritarianism.

Philip Clayton and Justin Heinzekehr develop a political ecotheology of Organic Marxism similar to Heilbroner's green/red authoritarianism. Instead of liberal individual freedom, they propose freedom for the community. Instead of the liberal "blue" rights of the property rights for the wealthy, they propose "red and green rights" of employment, health care, education, participation in community culture, as well as animal and nonhuman rights.

4. Hardin, "Living Lifeboat," 41.

5. Heilbroner, *An Inquiry*, 8, 131-132, 146-147, 176-177.

Instead of the liberal democracy or European social democracy which is always at the service of the market/capitalists, they propose a government ruled by the people supplemented by autonomous community governments; that is, a "community of communities" (Daly and Cobb's term) instead of sovereign states. Clayton and Heinzekehr urge nations to set up this type of government and/or community of communities in preparation for a window of opportunity to occur between the time initial ecological crises force human beings to take collective actions and the time the devastating ecological crises become unstoppable. In response to the initial wave of ecological crises, either those in power "will bring out the more noble side of (them)," or the masses "will rise up against this treatment (by those in power)." The "community of communities" will thus replace capitalist states. Which country comes closest to their model of green/red state? Again, the People's Republic of China.[6]

Despite its short-term appeal, green/red authoritarianism contains both normative and empirical drawbacks which render it another vanity in resolving ecological crises. Normatively speaking, first, should human survival trump other human values, in particular, human rights and democracy? Supporters of green authoritarianism would say yes because without human existence there are no human rights to speak off. However, supporters of liberal democracy would argue that human existence is meaningless without human rights. What is good about a political "animal farm" where the authoritarian ecological leader Napoleon dictates what and whether other animals can eat, do, play, and stay alive?[7]

Secondly, by what criteria do we select the "best" ecological leader who has the "best" knowledge about ecology and the "best" personalities to implement the "best" ecological policy? How do we make sure this authoritarian leader does not abuse his absolute power for personal gains and consistently implement the "best" ecological policy?

Thirdly, all democratic constitutions empower their political leaders to declare martial law, suspend habeas corpses, and take strong actions in times of domestic crises or foreign wars. How much more political power does a green authoritarian ruler need to cope with ecological crises?

Finally, Clayton and Heinzekehr do not seek their green Messiah in the contemporary system of capitalism and democracy. They place their hope on a window of opportunity between the time an initial ecological crisis forces

---

6. Clayton and Heinzekehr, *Organic Marxism*, 101-116, 122-130, 230-231; Daly and Cobb, *Ecological Economics*.

7. Orwell, *Nineteen*.

human beings to take collective actions and the time the devastating ecological crises become unstoppable, to expand their "community of communities." During this window of opportunity, either those in power will repent, or the masses will replace those in power with a "community of communities." This argument has little foundation in political psychology.[8] In crisis situations, it is more likely that those in power will deepen their exploitation of the weak while the masses will turn into mobs, as evidenced by the increasing number of "failed states" in recent decades.[9]

Empirically speaking, authoritarian states tend to generate more ecological disasters than democratic states. Heilbroner cited the "Rising China" to support his green authoritarianism when he published his work in the early 1990s. Ten years later (2006), the Chinese government published, for the first time, it's green GDP growth rate which showed that it reached 10 percent for the past decade. That means, all the fast economic growth, which averaged around 10 percent, in the 1990s required the same amount of future resources and investment to clean up the pollution produced during the same decade.[10] It took another 10 years to pass before the authoritarian Chinese government began to "reconsider" the adoption of green GDP as a guide to their ecological programs. This most powerful authoritarian government has yet to prove itself to be a green government for a sustained period of time at the national level while so many human rights have been suppressed. In general, local party secretaries and public officials still prioritize GDP growth rates over ecological protection, if not for corruption's sake. Environmental protection agencies at the local level are understaffed and do not have much say in local economic development programs. The court, nongovernmental organizations, and mass media are under tight control by the local political leadership, unless there is a factional struggle within the leadership. Thus, it will take generations to change the economic behaviors of the 1.4 billion Chinese people. Evidenced by the worsening smog in metropolitan Beijing, Tianjin, Shanghai, and Shenzhen, one can hardly see light at the end of the ecological tunnel in China.

In 2012 and 2013, Yunnan University of Finance and Economics in the Yunnan Providence of southwest China and the National Chengchi University in Taiwan co-sponsored two conferences to study "Water Governance and

---

8. Huddy, Leonie, et al., *Political Psychology*.

9. Rotberg, *When*; Olivier, "Fragile."

10. The initial green GDP figure was more than 10 percent, but the Chinese government decided to publish the 10 percent figure in response to the strong protest from local governments which took economic development as their priority. Wee, "China."

Sustainable Development" in China, in which I participated. They covered not only cases related to water governance (e.g., irrigation system, polluted lakes, international rivers, hydraulic electricity, ecological refugees, and urban water supply) but also forest development, green cities, and university towns. About seventy papers were delivered. Most papers documented the ecological programs promoted by the central and local governments. However, few programs reported any success. On the contrary, in the name of "green economic development" most programs simply exacerbated ecological crises, human suffering, social injustice, and corruption in the localities.[11]

For the first time in decades, residents in Beijing finally saw blue sky almost every day in the winter of 2017. The clean air returned to Beijing only, not other metropolitans, because the central government had ordered the cement companies, steel companies, and coal mines in nearby provinces to close down for three months in the winter. However, other metropolitan areas, such as Shanghai and Shenzhen continued to suffer from health-threatening smog. After all, President Xi Jinping and members of the Politburo live in Beijing, not in Shanghai and Shenzhen. Although Xi Jinping has made much stronger commitments to ecological programs than his predecessors, the effects of their implementation remain to be seen.

Another empirical problem with green/red authoritarianism is that even if it works in authoritarian countries, consolidated democratic countries are not likely to go back to authoritarianism. Democratic values and institutions can be improved but cannot be un-learned. These democratic values and institutions have become the sacred cores of what Robert Bellah calls a "civil religion." A civil religion, in the American context, is "a set of [democratic] beliefs, symbols, and rituals . . . It reaffirms, among other things, the religious legitimation of the lightest political authority."[12] To the citizens of consolidated democracies, authoritarianism is tantamount to the devil. Most democratic citizens, Christian or not, probably would agree with the Biblical verse: "do not fear those who kill the body, but are unable to kill the soul; but rather fear Him who is able to destroy both soul and body in hell."[13]

11. Yang, *Research*; Wang, *Proceeding*.
12. Bellah, "Civil Religion."
13. Matt 10:28.

Vanity of Deliberative Democracy

The term "deliberative democracy" was coined by political scientist Joseph M. Bessette to describe a supplementary institution to the representative democracy. About the same time, German political philosopher Jürgen Habermas develops his counterpart of deliberative democracy, called the "theory of communicative action."[14] Deliberative democracy is a form of direct democracy in which citizens personally engage in informed and rational deliberation among different opinions and interests related to public policy. It is an institutional supplement to representative democracy because elected officials do not accurately represent their constituents and are not accountable to their constituents until the next election. When properly designed, deliberative democracy is conducive to rational and balanced solutions to public policy debates, rather than being manipulated by special interests and political parties at the expense of common citizens. Deliberative democracy works best when its institutional designs include accurate information, substantive balance and diversity among all perspectives, all participants sincerely consider the merits of all arguments, and the final decision gives equal consideration to the merits of all arguments.[15] It is worth noting that although the term "deliberative democracy" was coined by him, Joseph Bessette was not very confident about whether it would work in reality because it "is likely to be influenced profoundly by slick advertising campaigns, the most immoderate voices on each side of the controversy, and the passions of the moment."[16]

Addressing the same issue of the "Tragedy of the Commons," political scientist and Nobel Laureate in Economics, Elinor Ostrom, offers a democratic alternative to green authoritarianism: deliberative democracy. Like other ecologists, Ostrom identifies the root of ecological disasters as an institutional problem of free rider, no matter the metaphor is the tragedy of the commons, the prisoner's dilemma, or the public goods (together Ostrom names them "common pool resources" or CPR). She distrusts both the state institution and the market institution to resolve ecological problems. Rather, between the state and the market, there are a variety of institutions capable of resolving these free-rider problems. These institutions need to meet the following criteria:[17]

---

14. Bessette, "Deliberative Democracy," 102–16. See Habermas, *Theory Communicative*.
15. Fishkin, *When*, 160.
16. Bessette, "Deliberative Democracy," 115.
17. Ostrom, *Governing*, 1, 6, 90.

1. Clearly defined boundaries. Individuals or household who have rights to withdraw resource units from the CPR must be clearly defined, as must the boundaries of the CPR itself.

2. Congruence between appropriation and provision rules and local conditions. Appropriation rules restricting time, place, technology, and/or quantity of resource units are related to local conditions and provision rules requiring labor, material, and/or money.

3. Collective-choice arrangements. Most individuals affected by the operational rules can participate in modifying the operational rules.

4. Monitoring. Monitors, who actively audit CPR conditions and appropriator behavior, are accountable to the appropriators or are the appropriators.

5. Graduated sanctions. Appropriators who violate operational rules are likely to be assessed graduated sanctions . . . by other appropriators, by officials accountable to these appropriators, or by both.

6. Conflict-resolution mechanisms. Appropriators and their officials have rapid access to low-cost local arenas to resolve conflicts among appropriators or between appropriators and officials.

7. Minimal recognition of rights to organize. The rights of appropriators to devise their own institutions are not challenged by external governmental authorities.

8. Nested enterprises. Appropriation, provision, monitoring, enforcement, conflict resolution, and governance activities are organized in multiple layers of nested enterprises.

Ostrom's CPR institutions work against the free market by all their criteria, while green authoritarianism cannot meet its criteria #3 (collective-choice arrangements), #4 (monitors are accountable to the appropriators or are the appropriators), and #7 (minimal recognition of rights to organize).

Applying the above institutional analytical framework, Ostrom and her research team studied fourteen cases of CPR around the world. These cases support her argument: in those six cases which meet the above institutional criteria performed well in resolving CPR problems, while those eight cases which lacked at least one of the above institutional criteria turned out to be fragile or prone to failure. Why did one CPR community differ from other CPR communities in their institutional designs as well as their results in success or failure? Ostrom cites five possible variables: the total number of decision makers, the number of participants minimally necessary to achieve the collective benefit, the discount rate in use, similarities of interests, and the presence of participants with substantial leadership or other assets.[18]

However, the very last qualifications of Ostrom's CPR institutions spell the limits of her institutional solution and make this type of deliberative democracy another vanity in resolving ecological crises. All her cases involve participants in relatively small communities; the largest involves about 15,000 participants.[19] Apparently, the size of the community directly or indirectly affects all her qualifications of CPR institutions. Directly, it puts a practical limit on the total number of decision-makers and the number of participants in any meaningful deliberation process. Opinion leaders, representatives, experts and lawyers are likely to dominate the deliberation process when the size of the community becomes large and when the total deliberation time is limited. Indirectly, a consensus on the discount rate in use among a large number of decision-makers and participants is difficult to reach. Furthermore, similarities of interests among a large group are difficult to assume, and the presence of participants with substantial leadership or other assets may be easier to find in large communities but may ironically undermine other conditions of deliberative democracy.

If these coordination and monitoring problems are difficult to resolve at the community level, then how much more difficult would it be when most of the CPR problems cut across communities, provinces, and countries? Moreover, how long will it take to build-up these institutions, if they can indeed ever be built? Has not the most optimistic ecological "point of no return" been passed at the beginning of the twenty-first century? What will happen to these successful CPR institutions when the global ecological crises hit on these communities? Can participants conduct rational deliberation under crisis situations when someone in the big crowd cries "fire"?

Ostrom did mention one possible variable which may change the odds against the large size of community: the norms, although she prefers to dwell on the rational aspect of CPR institutions. "Shared norms that reduce the cost of monitoring and sanctioning activities can be viewed as social capital

---

18. Ostrom, *Governing*, 180, 188.
19. Ostrom, *Governing*, 182.

to be utilized in solving CPR problems."[20] But who provides the norms in a local community? In particular, who provides the sanctification of ecological norms in a local community? If polluters hold maximization of profits as their sacrosanct norm and if some residents of the community hold maximization of material compensation provided by polluters as their supreme norm of the land, as neoclassical economics would assume, deliberative democracy is not likely to reach the goal of "sustainable development." Equipped with a vast amount of resources (money, technicians, public-relations personnel, friendly politicians, and lawyers), national and global polluters would certainly develop "divide and rule" strategies, promote the norms of economic growth over the ecology, intimidate ecological activists, and manipulate the procedures of deliberative democracy in their favor. The fact that deliberative democracy is designed to function at local communities dramatically tips the bargaining power toward the favor of national and global polluters, who can simply bribe the whole community and force ecological activists to leave the community through a manipulated deliberative democracy.

A similar research project with similar theoretical and empirical problems is the "co-management project" by Canadian geologists Derek Armitage, Fikret Berkes, and Nancy Doubleday. In order to construct an effective institution of co-management, participants need to consider at least seven sets of factors: complex systems thinking; adaptive capacity and resilience; institutional design for adaptive co-management; partnership and power-sharing; conditions of adaptive co-management success and failure; learning, knowledge use, and social capital; and policy implications.[21] If a church is not busy enough to proclaim the gospel and wishes to spend her spare time on ecological CPR institutions or "co-management," she should at least know in advance the politically and administratively complex situation she is getting into.

Acknowledging the weaknesses of liberal deliberative democracy, political philosopher Robyn Eckersley proposes "the green democratic state" to jump start liberal deliberative democracy with a green, critical, reflexive approach to the state. She argues that liberal deliberative democracy has trouble overcoming the anarchic character of the system of sovereign states, the capitalist state's promotion of capitalist accumulation over ecological concerns, and the resulting democratic deficits of the liberal democratic state. These obstacles enable the capitalists to circumvent real ecological programs by promoting

---

20. Ostrom, *Governing*, 36.
21. Armitage et al., *Adaptive*, 6-10.

"ecological modernization" which promotes cost minimization strategies for industry and reduction of the rate of ecological deterioration, instead of deep structural transformation of the economy and reduction of aggregate levels of environmental degradations. However, she finds hope in the rise of environmental multilateralism, the emergence of green competitive strategies of corporations and the state, and the emergence of environmental advocacy within the civil society and the administrative state. Based on deliberative democracy's principles of "unconstrained dialogue," "inclusiveness," and 'social learning," she proposes an eleven-clause "charter of citizens" environmental rights and responsibilities as part of the standard list of civil and political rights" to institutionalize these principles. Together with this "green constitution," the green civil society will be able to work in close collaboration with the green state to ensure that the green democratic state sincerely implements genuine ecological programs instead of cosmetic ecological modernization.[22]

The problem with Eckersley's green democratic state or the green liberal deliberative state, in general, is their strong assumption about human ecological rationality and the homogeneity of this ecological rationality across social classes and the states. The theoretical and empirical realities are that it simply does not exist. As discussed in chapter 2 of this book, if such a homogeneous ecological rationality were to exist, there must be the prior existence of a homogeneous ecological emotion because "rationality is often a slave of emotion." Furthermore, if deliberative democracy were to work, major religions are critical supplements to it. On the one hand, major religions could sanctify ecological norms and demonize excessive material gains and desires. On the other hand, major religions could mobilize the resources of their local, national and global religious networks to counter-balance those of national and global polluters. The presumptions of equal representation and rational deliberation of deliberative democracy would thus be preserved.

To strengthen the liberal deliberative state, many ecological philosophers evaluate various ecotheories of promoting "ecologism" in green lifestyle, local institutions of communitarianism, direct action, fiscal incentives and ecological citizenship.[23] But who can perform these complicated tasks of inspiration, coordination, monitoring, reward and punishment? It is not scholars, not theologians, not local or central governments, not non-governmental organizations, nor the United Nations. All of these task requirements seem to point to religious organizations. Sociologist Chris Baker suggests that religious

---

22. Eckersley, *Green State*, 14–15, 70–79, 115–38, 243–46.
23. Dobson, *Green*, 119–46.

organizations are equipped with "spiritual capital" to deal effectively with sustainable development even in a postsecular age. They "drive and engage progressive social capital and civic participation from both religious and non-religious sources and actors within the context of postsecular public sphere."[24]

Similarly, without the active involvement of religious organizations, global ecological institutions are not likely to achieve the goal of sustainable development. The next section discusses an exemplary work on global ecological institutions by Anthony Giddens.

Vanity of Global Ecological Institutions

Political sociologist Anthony Giddens' book, *The Politics of Climate Change*, starts with an ecological paradox (he appropriately names it "Giddens' Paradox") confounding all ecologists: "since the danger posed by global warming aren't tangible, immediate or visible in the course of day-to-day life, many will sit on their hands and do nothing of a concrete nature about them. Yet waiting until such dangers become visible and acute – in the shape of catastrophes that are irrefutably the result of climate change – before being stirred to serious action will be too late."[25]

How to avoid the Giddens' Paradox? Since the paradox is created by the common people "in the course of day-to-day life," we cannot expect a solution forthcoming of the common people as they lack incentives and coordination capabilities to deal with global ecological crises. Instead, local governments, the states, and international communities of the states should take the initiatives and implement ecological programs with the help of ecological NGOs at every level of government. Giddens prescribes nine tasks for an ecological state (or "ensuring state"), "within the context of democratic rights and freedoms,"

1. The state must help us to think ahead.

2. Climate change and energy risks must be managed in the context of other risks faced by contemporary societies.

3. The state must promote political and economic convergence, as the main driving forces of climate change and energy policy.

---

24. Baker, "Sustainable Governance," 195–96. But the two cases he examined are related to charity and local development, not directly related to ecology or evangelism.

25. Giddens, *Politics*, 2.

4. The state must make interventions into markets to institutionalize "the polluter pays" principle.

5. The state must act to counter business interests which seek to block climate change initiatives.

6. The state must keep climate change at the top of the political agenda.

7. An appropriate economic and fiscal framework must be developed for moving towards a low-carbon economy.

8. The state must prepare to adapt to the consequences of climate change.

9. Local, regional, national and international aspects of climate change policy must be integrated.[26]

This ecological state is neither green authoritarianism nor deliberative democracy, but a state of "radicalism of the center," which includes the reform of the state to enhance interdepartmental coordination, the formation of cross-party consensus, the establishment of stronger monitoring agency, and the setting of the state itself as an exemplar of ecological actions. In addition, the radicalism of the center also includes regular participation of citizen groups, communities, NGOs, and even business groups in the decision and implementation of ecological programs.[27] This "radicalism of the center" is an extension of Giddens' earlier famous idea of the "Third-Way Radical Center."[28]

Few ecologists would disagree with the ecological tasks Giddens' "ensuring state" should perform. However, the "Giddens' Paradox" is itself a paradox and a vanity in the sense that the state, especially a democratic state, is deeply embedded among the people who created the paradox in the first place. How can a state initiate and implement the above ecological tasks if most of its citizens are determined to "sit on their hands and do nothing of a concrete nature about them . . . waiting until such dangers become visible and acute"? This paradox of the "Giddens' Paradox" is universal from the local government to the state and up to the international communities of states, democratic or authoritarian.

26. Giddens, *Politics*, 94-97.
27. Giddens, *Politics*, 116-128.
28. Giddens, *Third Way*, 70-78.

Besides, in the early 1990s when international communities of the states began to take concrete actions to address ecological crises, international relations scholars immediately warned about the inherent structural weakness of such efforts. Indeed, the early 1990s might be the best time for global ecological cooperation to have a real and effective impact on the ecology. In 1989, the Soviet bloc broke down, China reconfirmed her determination to capitalist reforms after a somber internal ideological struggle, and the United States poised as the only superpower in the world. These gave rise to the global optimism of the triumph of capitalist democracy: *The End of History and the Last Man* (1992).[29] The Single European Act was passed in 1987 and contributed to the Maastricht Treaty and issuing of Euro in 1993. Twenty years after the establishment of the United Nations Conference on the Human Environment (1972), the United Nations Conference on Environment and Development embarked on ambitious global programs to address the ecological crises, along with the help of numerous ecological NGOs.

International relations scholars welcomed this global cooperation but also cautioned against unwarranted optimism. After all, the nature of the international political community is anarchy in which national interests in economic development and security prevail over global ecological interests. A research team of international scholars observed:

> Divergences of environmental interests as defined by states themselves make the achievement of unanimity among the parties responsible and directly affected by an environmental problem a political and diplomatic challenge. One of the primary problems of global environmental politics is the ability of one or more states to block or weaken multilateral agreements and how to overcome such blockage. For a regime to be formed, veto states and coalitions must be persuaded to abandon their opposition to a proposed regime or at least compromise with states supporting it.[30]

Another research team working on successful cases of international cooperation on the ecology pointed out the importance of three sets of variables: increasing governmental concern, enhancing the contractual environment, and increasing national capacity (together these are called 3Cs). However, they reminded the readers that "environmental politics is replete with symbolic action, aimed at pacifying aroused publics and injured neighbors without imposing severe costs on domestic industrial or agricultural interests. Politics

---

29. Fukuyama, *End*.
30. Porter and Brown, *Global Environmental Politics*, 32.

within international institutions are also often highly symbolic: governments can vote one way and act another."[31] The above 3Cs were conspicuously present in the early 1990s but probably no more in the 2010s: there are increased governmental concerns of economic development above the ecology due to global economic slowdown; the global contractual environment is overshadowed by military tensions between Russia and Europe, China and Japan, and by radical Islamists everywhere. Moreover, national capacity has declined drastically in those "failed states" in Africa, Middle East, and South America.

The initial achievements and subsequent failures of the 1997 Kyoto Protocol exposed this structural weakness of international cooperation on the ecology. The withdrawal of the United States of America in 2017 from the 2015 Paris Climate Accord, which contains no country-specific targets nor effective enforcement clauses, is yet another proof of international capitalism's triumph over the global ecology. Climate change is certainly not a "hoax" as American President Donald Trump referred to it. However, international climate agreements have become the emperor's new clothes at the international scale: everyone thinks they are beautiful and it is "politically correct" to think so, but they have little impact on the ecology, either positively or negatively. In the end, the capitalists have successfully manufactured global ecological programs, not by reducing their items, but by adding additional items. They clandestinely modified the agenda from the ecology (e.g., United Nations Conference on the Human Environment, 1972), to the ecology and development (e.g., United Nations Conference on Environment and Development, 1992), and then to the ecology, development and society (e.g., UNECE Convention on Access to Information, Public Participation in Decision-making and Access to Justice in Environmental Matters, 1998), making any ecological program too big, too complex to be implemented and keeping it as an emperor's new clothes.

Therefore, the solution to Giddens' Paradox must come from outside the paradox, not from within. This external focus is where the church once more comes in. As discussed above, the church is able to resolve the paradox by changing the motivation, calculation, and action of common citizens and business people through sanctifying ecological values and demonizing anti-ecological behaviors. The church also helps to strengthen the "radical centers" through its religious institutional networks from the local community level up to the international community level. The church is a critical and integral part of any effective solution to global ecological crises.

31. Haas et al., *Institutions for Earth*, x, 18-23.

If the church is a critical and integral part of any effective solution to global ecological crises, this book probably should end here and humans on earth will live happily ever after. Unfortunately, this book will argue that the church should not and cannot be a critical part of any effective ecological solution, and, therefore, humans on earth will have to face the incoming ecological catastrophes. Current ecotheologies are built upon a millennium political theology of the Kingdom of God on Earth. The next section will argue that this political theology does not have a sound basis in the Bible nor the ante-Nicene church history, and has been proven a vanity in the Christian history.

Vanity of the Kingdom of God on Earth

Tarnished by their fundamentalist images in opposing evolution theory, abortion, divorce, and homosexual marriage in the postwar era, many pastors, deacons and elders finally find the ecology a "politically correct" issue to deal with and by which to justify their active participation in local and national politics. After exposing the weaknesses of relying on the corporation, government, and university to protect the ecology, theologian Max Oelschlaeger argues that the church is probably the only institutional Savior to save the earth:

> The local church is a point of initiation for shaping voter preferences that lead to public policies addressing ecocrisis. The church is where individuals, caught up in the flow of their lives, in their joys and sorrows, can begin to grapple with the complexities of social existence. The church, in other words, is the natural home for dialogue that centers on creation, our place in the Creation, and our obligations to creation. The church is a place for conversation, where the faithful tell and retell stories that are emotionally evocative, psychologically persuasive, and ethically charged . . . It is the church, in its function as a public church, that will help make environmentalism a reality.[32]

Although the American constitutional principle of the separation of church and state (or its French cousin of *laïcité*; the principle of secularization) has been a common sense in democratic societies for more than two hundred years (one hundred years for the *laïcité* law in 1905), Christian theologians and pastors in old and new democracies have never hesitated to cross the "wall of separation" in order to establish "the heavenly kingdom (or kingdom of God)" on earth. So wrote Thomas Jefferson in 1802:

32. Oelschlaeger, *Caring*, 192–98, 213.

Believing with you that religion is a matter which lies solely between Man and his God, that ... the legitimate powers of government reach actions only, and not opinions, I contemplate with sovereign reverence that act of the whole American people which declared that their legislature should "make no law respecting an establishment of religion, or prohibiting the free exercise thereof," thus building a wall of separation between church and State.[33]

By comparison, the political theology of the heavenly kingdom on earth has a much longer history than the separation of state and church. It began in the first Council of Nicaea (325 AD) in which Christian bishops in the Roman Empire responded to Emperor Constantine's (272-337) call for a meeting to settle religious disputes among them. When some bishops (Arius and his followers) refused to accept the majority view of the Trinitarian theology, the-yet-to-be-Christian Emperor Constantine endorsed the Council's decision to banish them into exile. To most bishops and theologians at the time, the kingdom of God formally descended upon earth in 380 when Emperor Theodosius (379-392) issued the Edict of Thessalonica and proclaimed Nicene Christianity the state religion of the Roman Empire. The Roman Empire was no longer the Great Whore in the book of Revelation but the New Heaven and New Earth. Nor was Rome the city of the Great Babylon but the city of New Jerusalem.[34]

However, the perpetual peace of this "kingdom of God on earth" did not last long because after Theodosius' death, the Empire was no longer united and the barbarians sacked Rome in 410. Roman pagans blamed the sack of Rome on the Christian religion which offended Roman gods and due to its status as the state religion banning all other pagan religions. Envisaging this theological embarrassment and in fear of persecution by pagan officials, St. Augustine constructed the first theology of the separation of state and church, *The City of God*, which argued that both the state (City of Man) and the church (City of God) are equal but separate servants to God.[35] The state should not interfere with or persecute the church. On the contrary, the state should actively assist the church to persecute the heresies and pagans who blasphemed God and brought the furious judgment on Rome through the barbarians. By modern criteria of the separation of state and church, Augustine's theology of "two cities" is a one-sided separation. It served only to defend the church from

---

33. Jefferson, "Wall."
34. Schaff, *History*, chapter 1; Pagels, *Revelations*.
35. Augustine, *City*.

the arbitrary interference of the secular state, but not to keep the state from the influence of the church. The state was supposed to be a Christian state to manage secular affairs according to the guidance of the church in the kingdom of God on earth.

This Augustinian theology of separation of state and church continued to rule the European societies during the Middle Age when the Roman Church had the power to anoint feudal lords and to interfere with their succession. The more the church interfered with secular affairs, the weaker the Roman Empire seemed to be. The balance of power between the state and the church finally tilted toward the other side during Renaissance when some theologians became disgusted with the corruption of the Roman Church and its arbitrary interference in secular politics resulting in constant wars among feudal lords. Dante (1265-1321) picked up Augustine's political theology of "two cities" but employed it in a defensive way for any prince who would unify the empire again. He provided detailed Biblical justification and historical evidence of the Roman Empire that "imperial authority derives directly from the summit of all being, that is from God," and "the empire had all its authority at a time when the church did not exist or had no influence; therefore the church is not the cause of the empire's power."[36]

When Martin Luther and John Calvin initiated the Reformation, they challenged the corrupt rule of the Pope, but not the Augustine's idea of the kingdom of God on earth. In his "Twenty-Seven Articles Respecting The Reformation Of The Christian Estate," Luther criticized the Pope's corruption as being an abuse of God's kingdom on earth in favor of a new (German) kingdom on earth: "God has used the Pope's wickedness to give the German nation this empire and to raise up a new Roman empire, that exists now, after the fall of the old empire."[37] In his opening statement addressed to the King of the French for his *Institutes of the Christian Religion*, John Calvin addressed the King's title as "HIS MOST CHRISTIAN MAJESTY, THE MOST MIGHTY AND ILLUSTRIOUS MONARCH, FRANCIS." He reminded the king of his duty of maintaining the kingdom of God on earth: "Your duty, most serene Prince, is, not to shut either your ears or mind against a cause involving such mighty interests as these: how the glory of God is to be maintained on the earth inviolate, how the truth of God is to preserve its dignity, how the kingdom of Christ is to continue amongst us compact and secure." And the "characteristic of a true sovereign is, to acknowledge that, in

36. Dante, *Monarchy*, 86–87.
37. Luther, *Martin*, 615.

the administration of his kingdom, he is a minister of God. He who does not make his reign subservient to the divine glory, acts the part not of a king, but a robber."[38]

Political philosopher and theologian Thomas Hobbes (1588-1679) alleviated the power of the prince even higher than Dante did. In an ideal "Christian Commonwealth" (i.e., the kingdom of God on earth), not only do Christian kings derive their power and authority directly from God and had irretrievable absolute power from and over the people, they are "the supreme pastors of their people" and the heads of the church in their own dominions. Both "state and Church are the same men."[39] It is not clear how much influence Henry the VIII's (1491-1547) establishment of the Church of England had on Thomas Hobbes' *Leviathan*, but Hobbes apparently bestowed upon European kings and queens in the ferment nationalist period from the seventeenth to the twentieth centuries a solid religious legitimacy against the church (Catholic or Protestant) and against the people. All the European nationalist modernity programs were propelled by a religious fever to establish a kingdom of God on earth, starting from individual states, to Europe, and finally, to the world – The Christendom.

Although there was a democratic genre of the kingdom of God on earth, as promoted first by John Locke (1632-1704), expanded by Thomas Paine (1737-1809; a Deist) before the American Revolution, deepened by theologians of the Social Gospel in the early twentieth century in both Europe and in America, radicalized by the Liberation Theology in the 1970s in Latin America, and fundamentalized by the Christian Rights since the 1980s around the world, they share with their authoritarian Christian counterparts the same ultimate goal of the establishment of the kingdom of God on earth.[40]

The above summary of the history of the separation of state and church is intended to demonstrate that major Christian theologians since the Council of Nicaea never whole-heartily embrace the modern sense of the separation of state and church. The political theology of the kingdom of God on earth has been the consistently dominant theological tradition for over almost two thousand years and is still thriving, despite its diversities between and within the authoritarian and democratic schools of political theology. However, does

---

38. Calvin, *Institutes*, 4–5.

39. Hobbes, *Leviathan*, 355-360.

40. Locke, *Two*; Paine, *Right*; for Social Gospel, see Niebuhr, *Moral Man*; for Liberation Theology, see Gutiérrez, *Theology*; for an improved version of Christian Rights, see Sider, *Just*.

this political theology hold true in the Bible? Did God, Jesus, the apostles, and the ante-Nicene church fathers ever endorse such a political theology? Did the kingdom of God actually refer to the Godly kingdoms on earth or to modern Christian states? Should any ecotheology build up the theology of the kingdom of God on earth? The answers to all these questions are: Probably not.

First, based on relevant Bible verses and the Biblical history that the kingdom of God either referred to the heavenly kingdom yet to come, or to the religious community of Yahweh believers, or Christian believers on earth, almost never was there a secular political community of Judo-Christian believers. When Abraham first received the calling from God to leave his tribe in Haran and go to Palestine, the Yahweh belief was his family religion, not a state religion. God promised Abraham that he would become a great "nation" (גוֹי; *goi*), which was to be a faith community, not a secular kingdom (מַמְלָכָה; *mamlakah*).[41] Moses led roughly two million Israelis out of Egypt to return to Palestine. During the process, he established not only the priestly institution of the Yahweh belief but also an administrative/judicial institution of leaders of thousands, of hundreds, of fifties and of tens.[42] Was the Yahweh belief a state religion or the kingdom of God? Not yet. Using a modern term, it was only a "mega church" with a complicated church hierarchy. It remained a faith community. The first attempt to transform the kingdom of God from a faith community into a religious state occurred toward the end of the rule of Judge Samuel, when the Israelis requested the establishment of a secular kingdom institution alongside the religious hierarchy. God reluctantly gave permission and directed Samuel to select a king for the Israelis with a permanent curse casted upon the secular kingdom institution: all of you will become slaves to the king and "you will cry out in that day because of your king whom you have chosen for yourselves, but the LORD will not answer you in that day."[43] Although God did bless some kings for their devotion to the faith and promised them a long-lasting kingship for their descendants,[44] the kingship was conditioned on their belief and, therefore the kingdom was meant to be a religious kingdom of God, not a secular kingdom. The political connotation of this blessing would be no more or no less than a blessing on a Christian chairwoman of a big family-owned multinational company. If she prayed and read the Bible every day, went to church every week, submitted her tithe every

---

41. Gen 12:2; Holladay, *Concise*.
42. Exod 18.
43. 1Sam 8:11–18.
44. 1Kgs 9:5, 16:2; 2Kgs 9:3.

month, and gave generously to charity, God would equally bless her with a long-lasting ownership for her descendants. This very point was evidenced by the fact that when the secular kingdoms in the south and north no longer held fast on their Yahweh belief, God sent barbarians to destroy them.

Afterwards, the Israelis lost the protection of a secular kingdom but regained the personal protection of God, resulting in the long-lasting revival of the Jewish faith. In the minds of the major Jewish leaders during the Second Temple period, they probably had a consensus not to establish a kingdom of God on earth, i.e., a Jewish state independent from the Babylonian and Persian empires. It would be tantamount to an ethnic suicide, given the several attempts by hostile ethnic groups to implicate the Israelis in the empires.[45] Some Jewish leaders, such as the Maccabees and the Zealots, tried to restore the Israeli kingdom of God but all failed for lack of majority support from the Jewish faith community.

How to survive as a minority religious community was, even more so, a daily concern for Jesus Christ and His disciples because they faced double political pressures from the Jewish faith community and the polytheist Roman Empire. Before Jesus began His ministry, Satan tempted Jesus three times. The third temptation was the same political temptation faced by many religious leaders: do you want to become both a religious and a political leader? Jesus resolutely rejected the temptation.[46] Jesus did not deny His role as the king of the Israelis. However, His "kingdom was not of this world," and the "Israelis" referred not to the ethnic Israelis but to all who believe in the Trinitarian God. The kingdom of God which Jesus urged His disciples to establish was a faith community, not the kingdom of God on earth; and He was the king of this kingdom of God in heaven, which is not of this secular world.[47] It was the Jews who framed Jesus and His disciples as revolutionaries. It was doubtful that Jesus and His disciples would welcome such a political label at the time.

In the NT, the terms of "kingdom of heaven," "kingdom of God," "kingdom of the Father," "kingdom of Christ," "kingdom of the Son," or "the Lord's kingdom" are used interchangeably to refer to the Christian faith community in this world (the church) or in the heaven. Never once do they imply a secular kingdom, even if it is a Christian kingdom. Are there kingdoms in the New Heaven and New Earth? Yes and no. Yes, there is only one universal kingdom, the kingdom of God; but, no, there is no secular kingdom beyond

---

45. Ezra, Neh, Est.
46. Matt 4: 1–11.
47. John 18:36; Matt 28:16-20; Mark16:15-18; Luke 24: 46-48; Acts 1:8.

that. There are "nations" (τὰ ἔθνη; *ta ethnei*; ethnic communities) and even "kings" (οἱ βασιλεῖς; *hoi basileis*; here better translated into "rulers" as their counterparts in the faith community of Moses) who will govern these ethnic communities. In the book of Revelation, the secular kingdom was the Roman Empire which was the evil empire, the Great Whore, and the Babylonians. The apostles were busy escaping the snarl and persecution of the Roman Empire. It was beyond their most vivid imagination to establish a Christian Roman Empire.

Similarly, the ante-Nicene church fathers could hardly expect the Roman Empire would one day become their kingdom of God on earth. On his way to Rome to become a martyr, Ignatius of Antioch (35-108; disciple of John the Apostle), wrote an epistle to the Romans: "Allow me to become food for the *wild beasts*, through whose instrumentality it will be granted me to attain to God."[48] There was no doubt among the apostles, early church fathers, and church leaders that the term "wild beasts" referred to the Roman Empire. Irenaeus of Lyons (130-202), in his *Against Heresies*, cited the prophecies from Apostle John and Prophet Daniel about the dissolution of the Roman Empire, which would be followed by the total destruction of the world and coming of the kingdom of Christ, not a Christian Roman Empire.[49] Justin Martyr (100-165), in his First Apology Addressed to Roman Emperor Antoninus Pius, made the last plea to the Emperor before he became a martyr: "For we forewarn you, that you shall not escape the coming judgment of God, if you continue in your injustice; and we ourselves will invite you to do that which is pleasing to God."[50] He was not trying to convert the Emperor to a Christian, but rather, only to do what is pleasing to God.

Secondly, even if some radical nationalists in the Bible and Christian history wanted to establish a kingdom of God on earth, they never succeeded. The religious/political dilemma they face is how to do deal with the pagans within the state boundary and with God's people living in other states. If pagans continue to exist within the state boundary and if some believers in God continue to live in other states, then it cannot be called a kingdom of God on earth. To establish a kingdom of God on earth, the political leader is forced to conduct an ethnic cleansing at home and take possession of nearby or far away states. This, however, will be very costly both militarily and politically; and by modern human rights standards, it is a crime against humanity. However, if

48. Schaff, *History*.
49. Schaff, *History*, Irenaeus, *Against Heresies*, Book V, chapter 26, L. 270042.
50. Schaff, *History*, Justin, *The First Apology*, chapters 1-2, L. 399813.

the political leader allows pagans to live within the state boundary and pays no attention to God's people living in other states, then his kingdom of God on earth cannot be called the kingdom of God on earth. God may not bless this earthly kingdom.

I call this dilemma the *Solomon's Dilemma* because he was the first Judo-Christian Emperor to face this religious/political dilemma. Upon the completion of the holy temple, Solomon prayed to God and asked for His blessing on this kingdom of God on earth.[51] God answered his prayer but set up a condition for His blessing: "But if you or your sons shall indeed turn away from following Me, and shall not keep My commandments and My statutes which I have set before you and shall go and serve other gods and worship them, then I will cut off Israel from the land which I have given them, and the house which I have consecrated for My name, I will cast out of My sight. So Israel will become a proverb and a byword among all peoples."[52]

With his wisdom, Solomon probably interpreted God's warning politically to solve the religious/political dilemma: I will keep the Yahweh belief intact among God's people while allowing the pagans to worship their gods within this kingdom of God on earth. In this way, the pagans are happy, I can make peace with the neighboring states, and God will be happy too. However, this is not the way God sees it. If it is supposed to be a kingdom of God on earth, there should be one and only one God within the territory. Throughout the Chronicles, the authors repeatedly complained about "the high places were not taken away" within the South and North Kingdoms. These pagan beliefs led Solomon to turn his "heart away after their gods" and finally provoked God to exile the Israelis.

The Catholic emperors and nobles of the Holy Roman Empire (962-1806) were not able to solve the Solomon's Dilemma either. Under pressure from the Popes, they conducted incessant wars against domestic heresies (including Protestant states during the Thirty Years' War from 1618 to 1648) and more than a dozen Crusades to save their "brothers and sisters" in the Byzantine Empire (330-1453) from the hands of Muslims. Broadly speaking, both attempts failed miserably.

The zeal for the kingdom of God on earth took on different shapes and sizes in the modern era. France (the Napoleon Empire) and Germany (First and Second World Wars) each temporarily established a European kingdom of God on earth. Later on, they cooperated in the establishment of the

---

51. 1Kgs 8: 22–66.
52. 1Kgs 9: 6–7.

European Union. The invasion of Western imperialism in Asia, Latin America and Africa was justified by the "Whiteman's Burden" to establish a global Christendom. *Pax Britannica* of the nineteenth century and *Pax Americana* since the second half of the twentieth century expanded God's kingdom on earth. These cases all went through the Solomon's Dilemma at the grave cost of suppressing domestic religious/political heresies and of foreign wars against the pagans. The secular kingdom of God on earth has been proven a vanity.

In fact, the church shifted its attention from purely religious issues to social/political issues and resulted in the liberal and conservative theological debates only in the nineteenth century. Church historian J.F. Maclear collected 186 important public documents issued by various states and the church (Catholic, Protestant, and some Jewish) from 1606 to 1990 to address church-state relationships.[53] Based on their major concerns, I divide them into six categories: religious (religious doctrines, organizations, personnel, tolerance or about state church status), political (church loyalty to the state or the state incorporates the church), social (religious education in public school, racial discrimination, economic inequality), religious/political, political/social, and social/religious issues. Cross-referenced to their publication years, I find that in the seventeenth century, among the subtotal of 21 documents, 19 focus exclusively on religious issues. In the eighteenth century, among the subtotal of 26 documents, 22 deal with religious issues only. Then, in the nineteenth century, among the subtotal of 83 documents, only 39 documents focus exclusively on religious issues while 23 focus mainly on political issues, 12 focus on social issues, and 9 focus on religious/political issues. In the twentieth century, the ratio of focus tilts even further away from purely religious issues: among the subtotal of 75 documents, only 25 exclusively deal with religious issues, another 25 deal with political issues, 12 deal with social issues, and the rest of 13 documents deal with combined issues.[54] The theologies of the kingdom of God on earth seemed to get their momentum only in the nineteenth century, not a long history ago.

Furthermore, in the postwar era, the political theology of the kingdom of God on earth has had a more corrosive effect on the authentic kingdom of God (i.e., the church) than any other period in Christian history, and is partially responsible for the rapid decline or degeneration of the church in Western Christian countries. In response to a series of social/political issues,

---

53. Maclear, *Church*.

54. Kuo, *Checks*, 259, 289–304. Since some documents fit into more than two categories, the total number of categorized cases is 205, instead of 186 of the original collection.

such as gender equality, abortion, divorce, homosexuality, creationism, racism, income inequality, immigration and ecology, the conservative church fail to adapt their conservative theology to the political tastes of younger generations. They, the younger generations, wonder why the church shows little sympathy for the weak and the suppressed people related to the above social/political issues, and why the church always seems on the side of the abusive male chauvinists, big capitalists, white supremacists, and anti-science bigots. The conservative church's crusade to put creationism into the curriculum of biology hits a brick wall in the mind of the younger generation who grew up in an education system emphasizing science and mathematics. Frustrated by the arrogance of church leaders, who painstakingly cling to the idea of a conservative kingdom of God on earth, the younger generations within the church join the exodus to the secular world, while those outside the church are intimidated by the bondages and suppressions alluded to by the conservative theology. Without the recruitment of the younger generation, conservative churches soon decline in a generation or two after World War II.

The liberal church is able to keep or attract some of younger generation by developing the liberal theology in full accommodation to the needs of the weak and the suppressed in the name of God's unconditional love. Their idea of a kingdom of God on earth is one which puts little or no condition on divorce, abortion, and homosexual behavior, while it promotes equality in gender, sexuality, income, race and immigration. Liberal churches often build their social/political agenda on the liberal theology which challenges the inerrancy of the Bible, the theology of Trinity, the literal interpretation of the Bible, and the applicability of Mosaic laws to modern society. Many of the lay leaders and pastors in these liberal churches are themselves gays, lesbians, bisexuals or remarried (instead of born-again) Christians. In the eyes of the conservative church, these are tantamount to the total degeneration of Christianity as described in the book of Revelation. Confused by the acrimonious debate within and between conservative and liberal churches, many of the younger generations either become atheist, deist, agnostics, or find refugee status in Asian religions or other spiritual movements like the New Age, which focus their religious activities on issues "not of this world."

Therefore, an ecotheology should not build upon the political theology of the kingdom of God on earth, either its leftist or rightist version, because both started on the wrong footing with regard to the Bible and the early church history. If the leftist and the rightist theologians cannot reach a consensus on other social/political issues, how can we expect them to derive a theological consensus on the ecology which seems to suck in all other social/political issues into this global issue?

The next section will argue that a better ecotheology to get out of the confusing mud-sling debates between the rightist and leftist theologies is to build on the Jeffersonian separation of state and church principle as implied in the Bible and early church history. The next section explains this argument.

Democracy and Post-Ecotheology

Similar to the opening statements in section 3 of the last chapter, a neuro-institutional post-ecotheology of democracy develops its concrete actions based on two inter-related, simple principles at the individual and collective levels. At the individual level, the church should take only those ecological actions which do not substantially reduce the overall happiness of her congregation members. At the collective level, local churches should take only those ecological actions which do not substantially reduce their overall happiness and only when these ecological actions receive a consensus within the church and between the church and the local community. Within the ecological policy parameters set by the democratic government, both principles emphasize tolerance and compromise toward different ecological positions among individual Christians as well as between the church and the local community. An ecological action which substantially reduces individual or collective happiness is not likely to garner persistent support.

A neuro-institutional post-ecotheology of the state consists of three major arguments. First, the Bible and the early church fathers prescribe the separation of state and church, which prohibits the church from taking a proactive role in the state's ecological projects. Secondly, the church's fundamental freedom of religion, and hence its choice of ecological programs, is better protected by a democratic regime than an authoritarian regime. Following these two arguments, finally, the church better prepares itself with an ecological program that prioritizes the Great Commission and disaster relief with a reactive ecological program.

First, the Bible and the early church fathers prescribe the separation of state and church, which prohibits the church from taking a proactive role in the state's ecological projects. Based on Biblical verses and early church fathers, the last section has rejected the conservative and liberal theologies of the kingdom of God on earth. Instead, the Bible and early church fathers seem to propose the separation of church and state.

In the Bible, the separation of state and church took its rudimentary form when Moses set up the priestly system within the faith community so that Moses himself and his officials of tens, hundreds, and thousands could pay more attention to military and secular affairs.[55] The separation was not meant to be an impenetrable one in the sense that each takes care of only its own affairs. Rather, there was some overlap in their division of labor so that the administrative branch would support the priestly works, while the priests would provide religious advice on administrative works. However, there was a clear division of personnel and most work, until rare occasions occurred that required the guidance or assistance from the other side. Any breach of this separation of church and state would invite punishment from God.

For instance, King Saul did not wait for Prophet Samuel to arrive and presented burnt offerings before a war. When Samuel found out that Solomon took over his priestly work, he told Solomon that God had chosen another king.[56] When Israeli King Jeroboam set up a golden calf for the Israelis to worship and instituted a separate priestly system to administer religious rituals, a man of God set a curse on him and dried up his hands.[57] Similar punishments were laid on King Joash of Juda and Israeli King Uzziah when they violated the priestly system.[58]

Many other teachings in the OT also support the separation of state and church. "You shall not curse God, nor curse a ruler of your people." "Fear the LORD and the king; do not associate with those who are given to change." "Keep the command of the king because of the oath before God." "If the ruler's temper rises against you, do not abandon your position, because composure allays great offenses." And, "in your bedchamber do not curse a king."[59]

In the NT, Jesus proclaimed: "Then render to Caesar the things that are Caesar's; and to God the things that are God's."[60] Paul advised the Romans not to resist secular authorities even when they were not Christians. He urged Timothy to pray "for kings and all who are in authority." He asked Titus to remind church members "to be subject to rulers, to authorities, to be obedient, to be ready for every good deed." Moreover, Peter wrote to Christians

---

55. Exod 28–29.
56. 1Sam 13:8–14.
57. 1Kgs 12–13.
58. 2Chr 24: 20–25; 26: 16–20.
59. Exod 22:28; Prov24: 21–22; Eccl 8: 2–5; 10: 4, 20.
60. Matt 22: 15–22; similar verses in Mark12: 13–17, Luke 20: 20–26.

living in Asia Minor: "submit yourselves for the LORD's sake to every human institution, whether to a king as the one in authority."⁶¹

There were many occasions in the Bible when the secular administrative system or the priestly system deviated from the religious doctrines, the leaders of the two systems were given a blessing by God to temporarily intervene in the other's jurisdiction. King David was blessed for setting up the job descriptions for the priests and the Levites. King Solomon provided further instructions to the priests and Levites. When the priestly system became corrupt, King Hezekiah and King Josiah revived the ritual and quality of the Yahweh belief.⁶²

When the kings deviated from religious or moral norms, the prophets would severely criticize the kings, even at the risk of their lives. Prophet Nathan did not hesitate to curse King David for his affair with Bathsheba, and Prophet Gad cursed King David for conducting a census of his people. Many prophets gave specific military advice to the kings. Additionally, Priest Jehoiada even went so far to stage a coup d'état against Queen Athaliah and closely supervised the new king Jehoash until he was fit for the political leadership position.⁶³

However, these verses, which show checks and balances between the political leaders and the religious leaders, are not applicable to those in modern states. As noted before, these verses refer to the relationships between the clergy and the administrators within the same religious community, not between Yahweh religious leaders and pagan political leaders. It is in the exile and the NT periods that we find cases of separation of the state and church in the modern sense.

There are at least thirteen cases or verses in the exile period which seemed to follow the checks and balances patterns during the period of the kingdoms.⁶⁴ The significant difference, however, is that all these thirteen cases or verses dealt with one and only one issue: the religious freedom of the Israelis. Daniel and his friends resisted the king's orders to participate in pagan rituals, but they did not request that the pagan kings give up their religions nor to behave according to the Mosaic laws, except where the kings violated the Jewish

---

61. Rom 13: 1–7; 1Tim 2:1–3; Tit 3:1; 1Pet 2:13–17.

62. 2Kgs 22, 23; 1Chr 17; 2Chr 8: 14–15; 2Chr 29, 30.

63. 2Sam 12; 2Sa 24; 1Kgs 12: 20–24; 1Kgs 20: 13–30; 2Kgs 3; 2Kgs 11–12; 2Kgs 18; 2Chr 20: 13–25.

64. Ezra 1; Ezra 5–6; Ezra 7; Neh 13: 4–14; Dan 1: 8–16; Dan 2: 37; Dan 3; Dan 4: 25–27; Dan 5: 13–29; Dan 6: 6–24; Zech 2: 1–4; and the entire book of Esther.

faith. The pagan kings of Persia subsidized the Jews to return to Jerusalem and rebuilt their temple. Scribe Ezra and Magistrate Nehemiah thanked the kings' patronage but did not request the pagan kings to give up their religions nor to behave according to the Mosaic laws. When Queen Esther took revenge on the ethnic enemy of the Israelis, she made no effort to convert the Persian king Ahasuerus to Judaism.

In the NT, John the Baptist criticized Herod the tetrarch for marrying his sister-in-law. However, it was because Herod chose to follow some Mosaic laws and violated it. When Jesus heard about John the Baptist's death, He "withdrew from there in a boat, to a lonely place by Himself," instead of criticizing Herod. Jesus made no effort to criticize or to convert any Roman official, except for the centurion who came to Him.[65] John the Baptist also told some tax-gatherers and soldiers, who came to him to be baptized, how to behave according to Mosaic laws.[66] These tax-gatherers and soldiers were very likely Jews taking the low administrative positions of the Roman government.

After he had risen from death, Jesus spoke to His disciples of the things concerning the kingdom of God over a period of forty days. Some disciples probably still could not tell of which kingdom Jesus had been referring, so they asked: "Lord, is it at this time You are restoring the kingdom to Israel?" Jesus clarified to them for the last time that He was not interested in, and it was not even His or the disciples' business, to restore the secular Kingdom of Israel. Instead, He called his disciples to "be My witnesses both in Jerusalem, and in all Judea and Samaria, and even to the remotest part of the earth." Having said this, He immediately ascended to heaven, leaving no doubt in His disciples' mind that He did not want to spend even a second on their secular interest.[67] His kingdom, after all, was not of this world but will replace all the secular kingdoms after His Parousia.

Similarly, the separation of state and church (in the sense of religious freedom) was probably the only concern of early church fathers when the Roman Empire showed no signs of turning herself from the Great Whore to a kingdom of God on earth. Ignatius of Antioch, confronting Emperor Ignatius face to face, defended his freedom of religion. He explained that Christians refused to worship Roman gods by offering sacrifices to the idols because Christians worship only Jesus; other gods were just demons. In his debates with Roman officials, Justin Martyr defended Christianity by the high

---

65. Matt 14: 13; Matt 8: 5–13; John 18: 36.
66. Luke 3: 12–14.
67. Acts 1: 6–9.

moral standards that the righteous God set for His believers as compared to the lust, incest, adultery, sodomy and murder often associated with Roman and Greek gods and their believers. If these believers of Roman and Greek gods were not persecuted, why were Christians persecuted for being "holy men" and being resistant to worshipping these gods?[68] The attitudes of these ante-Nicene fathers toward church-state relations were very different from those of post-Nicene fathers like Lactantius (250-325), who was an advisor to Emperor Constantine, praised the Emperor for taking his advice to persecute Roman polytheism: "And we now commence this work under the auspices of your name, O mighty Emperor Constantine, who were the first of the Roman princes to repudiate errors, and to acknowledge and honor the majesty of the one and only true God."[69] From then on, the political theology of the Bible and the ante-Nicene church fathers became distorted by the excessive entanglement of the state and church.

Therefore, if we follow the distorted political theology of the post-Nicene era, the modern church would have no choice but to take the lead on ecological programs in order to establish a kingdom of God on earth. However, if we accept the principle of church-state separation promoted by the Bible and the ante-Nicene church fathers, the modern church would only follow, instead of lead, whatever ecological programs the political authorities decide.

Given the principle of church-state separation, should Christians prefer democracy over authoritarianism as an instrument to design and execute ecological programs? The following sections offer a conditional positive answer to this question.

Secondly, the church's fundamental freedom of religion, and hence its choice of ecological programs, is better protected by a democratic regime than an authoritarian one. The Bible and the ante-Nicene church fathers did not develop a theological preference for democracy. They did not comment on the Athenian democracy which began around the fifth century BC and was destroyed by the Macedonian Empire in 338 BC. Plato (428?-348? BC) witnessed the operation of the first "democracy" in the world, Athenian democracy, but did not like it; his mentor Socrates was sentenced to death by the Athenian democracy. Instead, Plato preferred a polity led by philosophical

---

68. "The Martyrdom of Ignatius," "The Second Apology of St. Justin Martyr Addressed to the Roman Senate," "The Martyrdom of Justin" (Schaff, *History,* 269360–269379; 399861-400011; 403637- 403724.

69. "Divine Institutes," Book I, Schaff, *History,* 403758.

kings, probably as his career dream.[70] Aristotle (384-322 BC) developed a category of different constitutions: monarchy, aristocracy (based on merits) and timocracy (based on the landed class) as well as their degenerated deviations of tyranny, oligarchy and democracy (based on average citizens, excluding women and slaves). He regarded monarchy as the best constitution while democracy as "the least bad of the deviations," which was not much of a compliment to democracy.[71] Besides, he witnessed the fall of Athenian democracy at the hands of the Macedonian Empire whose monarch, Alexander the Great (356-323 BC), became one of his students. Therefore, by the time Jesus and the apostles grew up under the influence of the Roman culture, monarchy was probably the preferred choice, if there was indeed a choice, of the intellectuals.

However, the structure of religious communities of the OT and the NT seems to contain some elements of modern democracy. The Mosaic laws laid down the foundations of the rule of law and rule by law in the Jewish community. There were checks and balances among the political (or administrative) leaders, priests and prophets, similar to their counterparts of administration, judiciary and legislature in a modern democracy. The persistence of priests and prophets with different interpretations of the Bible also implied that there was a considerable tolerance of freedom of speech in both OT and NT religious communities. The freedom of speech in the Bible is sanctified by the power of the Holy Spirit Who may dwell upon any believer.[72] Finally, some political/administrative or religious leaders of the religious communities were elected by the believers.[73] According to Philip Schaff, the early church of apostles established a new leadership position "bishop" (ἐπίσκοπος; *episkopos*; episcope, supervisor, superintendent),[74] in addition to apostle, presbyter (πρεσβύτερος; *presbuteros*; elder) and deacon (διάκονος; *diakonos*). At the beginning, the positions of bishop and presbyter were interchangeable; in some churches, the position was called presbyter; in others, bishop. Gradually, bishops were

---

70. Plato, *Republic*.

71. Aristotle's definition of "timocracy" is close the contemporary democracy, while his "democracy" is close to anarchy. Aristotle, *Complete Works of Aristotle*, 1834, 2030-2066.

72. Prominent cases of inspiration by the Holy Spirit: Samson (Jud 14:6); King Solomon (1Sam 10:10); King David (1Sam 16:13); Elisha (2Kgs 2:15); Virgin Mary (Matt 1:18); Elizabeth (Luke 1:41); Simeon (Luke 2:25); the apostles on Pentecostal (Acts 2:4); Paul (Gal 2:8); John in Revelation (Rev 1:10).

73. Elected Israeli tribal heads (Deut 1:13); elected tribal representatives to distribute land (Jos 18:4); elected the twelfth apostle (Acts 1:23–25); elected deacons (Acts 6:3–5); elected elders (Acts 14:23).

74. Schaff, *History*, 6856–7113; Acts 20:28; Phi 1:1; 1Tim 3: 1–7; Tit 1:7.

separated from presbyters and got more power than presbyters. Ranked only behind apostles, bishops were the highest leaders among co-workers in a local church or churches (one bishop might lead more than one church). Some bishops might have been appointed by the apostles, but others seemed to have been elected by local churches. After the twelve apostles (plus Paul) passed away, bishops became the successors to the apostles in spiritual authority and administrative power. Usually, a bishop was chosen from presbyters who were in turn chosen from amongst the deacons. Some bishops might be promoted directly from deacons. In fact, in the writings of the ante-Nicene fathers, many churches had strong reservation about the spiritual authority or administrative (in particular, financial) power of the bishop. Some local churches even fired their bishops against the wishes of the church fathers (e.g., Clement of Rome, Ignatius of Antioch).[75] Regrettably, all of these democratic elements within the religious communities were either explained away or dismissed in favor of a monarchical form of church polity by the post-Nicene church. It is worth noting that the book of Revelation does not mention the position of bishop but only of presbyter in the heavenly court.

Therefore, the modern church does not need to follow the state's ecological programs on the premise that the state is or is not a democracy, which was probably not a favorable constitutional choice by Jesus or the apostles. In particular, a church in an authoritarian state should not engage in democratic movements for any reason (including the ecology), other than religious freedom. It is satisfactory if church members are democratic activists in response to God's calling, and the church should bless and comfort these church members in their suffering just like they would average believers. When pastors, priests, elders, deacons, and other co-workers decide to engage in democratic movement, they should immediately resign from their church positions to shield the church from the political interference of the state.

Nevertheless, given the democratic elements of the Bible, the history of the early church, and the history of better protection of religious freedom by democracies, the church could endorse democratic values and institutions by incorporating them into church teachings and organization. As political scientist Alfred Stepan argues, religion and democracy are complementary to each other when both develop democratic norms and institutions of "twin tolerations" to allow each "the minimal boundaries of freedom of action"

---

75. Schaff, *History*, 172011–172066, 172387–172391; Clement of Rome, First Epistle; 268884–268909, 268996–269014; Ignatius of Antioch, Epistle to the Ephesians, Epistle to the Magnesians.

vis-à-vis the other.⁷⁶ Ecological programs are complicated, sometimes mutually contradictory, and their adjustment costs may be unevenly distributed among church members. A democratic church is best suited to address these problems of collective decision and implementation to keep the church united from the local level, regional level, national level, up to the international level. The beneficial political byproduct of a democratic church is the increase of democrats and a sanctification of their participation in democratic movements, which may contribute to the long-term democratization of authoritarian states as well as to the consolidation of democratic states.

Thirdly, when following the state's ecological programs, the church should prioritize the Great Commission, local community needs, and disaster relief, while avoiding any program which may cause a significant delay of the Great Commission, substantial disharmony among church members or between the church and the local community. The church's primary calling is the Great Commission, and no ecological reason could justify itself if it undermines this calling. That does not mean that the Great Commission and ecological programs are necessarily in conflict. The church could merge the Great Commission into most ecological programs by introducing God's creation and Jesus' Parousia as related to the ecology. In particular, the reality of incoming ecological crises could provide a strong stimulus to humans' God brain and seek salvation immediately in a church. The church should also prioritize local community needs by participating in ecological programs designed by the state. Some communities may be sensitive or vulnerable to national ecological programs, for instance, anti-pollution regulations in industrial districts. After reaching a consensus internally, the church should negotiate with the state about the content of these regulations, the timetable of implementation, and complementary subsidies to help community members adjust their lives. Finally, the church could help the local community and the state to develop a program in preparation for disaster reliefs, that is, to help growing number of ecological victims of pollution, heat, storm, flooding, earthquake, pandemic and wars (terrorism), which are horribly described in the book of Revelation.

At the same time, the church should avoid involvement in any controversial ecological program designed by the state that might cause substantial disharmony among church members or between the church and the local community. Many Biblical verses encourage believers to seek peace with the heathens unless they threaten the religious freedom of the former. "Depart from evil, and do good; seek peace, and pursue it." "Counselors of peace have

---

76. Stepan, "Religion."

joy." "Judge with truth and judgment for peace in your gates." "Blessed are the peacemakers, for they shall be called sons of God." "Have salt in yourselves, and be at peace with one another." If possible, so far as it depends on you, be at peace with all men." "So then let us pursue the things which make for peace and the building up of one another." "God has called us to peace." "Pursue peace with all men." "Let him seek peace and pursue it."[77]

As discussed before, theologians of Social Gospel and Fundamentalist Evangelism seem to bypass these Biblical verses of "seeking peace" when they confront the social/political issues of feminism, abortion, divorce, homosexual marriage, economic inequality, immigrant, and evolution theory in the postwar era. These issues divided the church and society as well as causing internal divisions within the church, resulting in either a fast decline or degeneration of the church. The issue of ecology has generated similar divisions between the church and the society (thanks to Lynn White's effort to blame ecological crises on Christianity) as well as within the church (industrialists and their workers versus ecological activists). Few churches actually seek peace between the pros and the cons. That is not to say that the church should not adhere to Biblical teachings on these moral/political issues. Nevertheless, there is considerable room for accommodating oppositional views based on different verses in the Bible. Furthermore, even on issues like homosexuality, where the Bible has a rather clear standpoint, the church could be better off by insisting the moral code within one's own church while not imposing this Christian morality on the heathens through secular laws. On ecological issues, it means that the church should consult with the majority of church members and the local community before it takes on concrete ecological programs. If the local community disagrees with the church's ecological program, the church can still implement its own program without hurting the local community in any way. If the local community opposes national ecological programs, the church should not join the state to force the local community to accept these programs. It is not the business of the church to get involved in politics.

Lastly, admittedly there is growing consensus over the need to take ecological actions in society as well as within the church. However, the church is better off taking on the simplest and least controversial parts of national ecological programs, such as garbage recycling, energy-saving in the household, and cleaning neighborhood parks and beaches. Biofuel, nuclear power and alternative powers, "energy-saving" technologies, and "green" buildings

---

77. Ps 34:14; Prov 12:20; Zech 8:16; Matt 5:9; Mark 9:50; Rom 12:18; 14:19; 1Co 7:15; Heb 12:14; 1Pet 3:11.

or cities are among those most complicated and controversial issues within ecological movements themselves. The church would lose its credibility and harmony when it quickly endorses one such program only to find out that the "green" program generates much more ecological or human sacrifice in a few years. For instance, the biofuel program in the Amazon River imposed a heavy cost on the ecology by causing the burning down of rainforest to cultivate sugar cane. Likewise, corn fields in Third World countries are turned into sugar cane farms, creating a shortage-crisis of this invaluable staple food of the poor. The worst hoax a church can perpetrate is to tell its members that if we implement all these ecological programs now, we can still save the earth. What will happen to the church if Jesus comes to destroy the earth next year? Do Christians tell Jesus: "We do not need You! We can save the kingdom of God on earth by ourselves. Go home!"? In sum, there is no universal prescription for ecological actions, only localized and even personalized ecological prescriptions for individual Christians as long as they feel "safe and happy" (as discussed in chapter 2 of this book) and spiritually prepare for the Parousia.

Summary

Both the rightist and the leftist ecologists agree that capitalism needs reform to save the ecology, and that the state has the power and responsibility to perform this reform of capitalism. However, they disagree on what kind of state is best suited to perform these ecological duties. Some political ecologists recommend green/red authoritarianism. However, it suffers from both normative and empirical flaws. Normatively speaking, should human survival trump other human values such as human rights and democracy? By what criteria do we select the "best" ecological leader with the "best" knowledge about the ecology and the "best" personalities to implement the "best" ecological policy? Beyond the power to declare martial law in democratic constitutions, what other exorbitant political power does a green authoritarian ruler need to cope with ecological crises? Empirically speaking, authoritarian states tend to generate more ecological disasters than democratic states. Even if green/red authoritarianism works in authoritarian countries, consolidated democratic countries are not likely to go back to authoritarianism over the issue of ecology.

Other political ecologists recommend deliberative democracy to reduce the political side-effects of red/green authoritarianism and have successfully implemented this political institution to resolve ecological problems.

However, most of these successful cases are in small communities with homogeneous norms and robust community organizations to facilitate the deliberation process and enforce simple ecological programs. It cannot work in large communities with conflicting norms, weak community organizations and complex ecological programs, which is the very root of global ecological crises. The church may provide homogeneous norms and strong community organizations to facilitate the deliberation process and enforce ecological programs, but only under certain favorable conditions within and outside the church.

Anthony Giddens extends the deliberative democracy to the global level to resolve the "Giddens' Paradox" which says that we are not willing to take ecological actions when we do not see ecological catastrophes, but it will be too late to take ecological actions when we actually see them. However, Giddens' solution to the Giddens' Paradox is itself a paradox and vanity because the democratic state is deeply embedded among the people who created the paradox in the first place. All the global ecological programs made from the deliberative process have failed, including the most recent withdrawal of the United States from the 2015 Paris Climate Accord. The church may provide a critical supplement to Giddens' solution to the paradox by sanctifying ecological values and demonizing anti-ecological behaviors, and through its religious institutional networks from the local community to the international community. But is it Biblical for the church to do so?

The theological arguments in favor of the church's active participation in ecological programs are based on the millennium political theology of the "kingdom of God on earth" which merges the church and the state into one in this world. It is therefore the duty of the church to help the state to save the ecology to ensure that the kingdom of God on earth is everlasting. However, relevant Bible verses and the Biblical history clearly demonstrate that the kingdom of God either refers to the heavenly kingdom yet to come or to the religious community of Yahweh believers or Christian believers on earth, almost never a secular state composed of Judo-Christian believers on earth. Even if some radical nationalists in the Bible and Christian history wanted to establish a kingdom of God on earth, they never succeeded. And, finally, in the postwar era, the political theology of the kingdom of God on earth has a more corrosive effect on the authentic kingdom of God (i.e., the church) than in any other period in Christian history, and is partially responsible for the rapid decline or degeneration of the church in Western Christian countries.

Instead, this chapter constructs a neuro-institutional post-ecotheology of the state, which contains three major arguments. First, the Bible and the early church fathers prescribe the separation of state and church, which prohibits the church from taking a proactive role in the state's ecological projects. Secondly, the church's fundamental freedom of religion, and hence its choice of ecological programs, is better protected by a democratic regime than an authoritarian one. Following these two arguments, finally, the church better prepares itself, through democratic consultation within and outside the church, with an ecological program which prioritizes the Great Commission and disaster relief with a reactive ecological program.

7.

Conclusion: Too Little to Save and Too Many to Save

> God, give us grace to accept with serenity
> the things that cannot be changed,
> Courage to change the things
> which should be changed,
> and the Wisdom to distinguish
> the one from the other. (Reinhold Niebuhr, 1892-1971)

THIS BOOK STARTED WITH several general ecotheological and empirical puzzles faced by most Christians, and even more so to me as a converted Chinese Christian social scientist. Why do most of the current ecotheologies make the assumption that we can save the ecology, while scientific evidence and the book of Revelation seem to suggest that the ecology is not savable? Why do these ecotheologies propose solutions and programs which are inconsistent with the theories and findings of social sciences, and hence would be impossible to implement, or if implemented, would be ineffective or even counter-productive? Why do many proponents of ecological programs themselves fail to live the ecologically friendly life they proposed? Why do some of them eulogize Chinese religions and the Chinese government as their ideal ecological models when empirical evidence demonstrates the contrary? Should the church actively support radical ecological programs regardless of different opinions among church members or between the church and the local community? How much energy and time should the church spend on ecological programs instead of on evangelism?

With the available ingredients sampled from current ecotheologies, we could prudently construct a politically and religiously correct ecotheology.

Conclusion: Too Little to Save and Too Many to Save

Spiritual ecotheologies would begin with the most popular recipe of the "meditation theology" which urges Christians to meditate on the holiness of God's creation of the universe and God's ultimate revelation to renew the universe, thereby Christians become committed to ecological actions. Economic ecotheologies would add a mix of rightist or leftist procedures, which are equally popular recipes, to promote the virtues or suppress the evils of capitalism in an effort to avoid ecological crises when we still have time to do so. The promotion or suppression of capitalism requires political actions. Thus, political ecotheologies would add the final icing on the theological cake, following the recipes of green authoritarianism or deliberative democracy; the latter being the more popular choice. Baked for one to three years in an air-conditioned ivory tower, there comes another politically and religiously correct ecotheology in the overcrowded book market.

However, if Christians do take seriously the large amount of scientific evidence and the literal meanings of the book of Revelation (as chapter 1 of this book reveals), all the above recipes become vanities in the sense of the Ecclesiastes. Among their other weaknesses, they are all insufficient to address the collective action problems of ecological crises, the hypocrisy of "green technology" and "green consumption," and the practical problems of green authoritarianism or deliberative democracy. Even if these problems can be worked out in the long run (say, a hundred or two hundred years), scientific evidence and the book of Revelation together predict the coming of global ecological collapse in the next generation or two. The church needs to calibrate the above theologies to the short-term and desperate needs of crisis management. Above all, the church needs to re-prioritize their missions from active social, economic and political engagements associated with the ecology to their original intent or "first love" – the Great Commission, which is also the last warning to the churches in the book of Revelation.

This book reconstructs the above ecotheologies from a different theoretical foundation – that of neurotheology. Chapter 2 of this book introduces the latest scientific understanding of human nature, i.e., the complex system of interactions among rationality, emotion and religious thinking. A practical ecological program should build on not just human rationality, as most ecological programs do, but on all three components of human nature and their interactions. In particular, rationality is often the slave of emotion, but spirituality may regulate both rationality and emotion. If religions had caused ecological problems, they are also a necessary component of the solutions. Chapter 3 matches the neurotheology to most chapters of the Bible and concludes that the Bible urges its readers to live a balanced and mutually-enforced life of rationality, emotion and religious thinking, with the last being most pivotal of all. Thus, human relationships with God and the Great Commission should be ranked first in individual and collective ecological programs of the church in post-ecology.

Examined against this neuro-institutional post-ecotheology, chapters 4 to 6 sequentially expose the vanities of the popular meditation ecotheology, rightist and leftist economic ecotheologies, as well as green authoritarianism and deliberative democracy. Chapter 4 begins with an evaluation of Chinese ecotheories to dispel the myth that Daoism and Buddhism are somehow more ecological than Christianity. However, many Christian ecotheologies do share the weaknesses of Chinese ecotheories. Among the vanities of the popular meditation ecotheology, chapter 4 points out their overemphasis on meditation as opposed to concrete actions; the failure to address the collective-action problem; the erroneous scientific and theological assumptions that the "the heavenly kingdom on earth" is renewable; the controversy of pantheism; and that they make any future ecological program too complex and too costly to implement by local churches. Chapter 5 criticizes both rightist and leftist ecological proposals as well as those ecotheologies built on these economic ecotheories. Apart from respective flaws, both the rightist and the leftist proposals require a change of capitalist values long-held by individuals since the eighteenth century. However, neither rightist nor leftist proposals provide convincing arguments and methods to do so within their rational economic ideology. The church could provide a complementary solution to both. However, rightist and leftist ecotheologies suffer from the same weaknesses as the rightist and leftist economic theories do. Even worse, by adding the spiritual and organizational power to ecological programs, the church may exacerbate theological controversies within the church and ecological crises outside the church. Chapter 6 evaluates the political dimension of ecotheologies. Most of them are based on the millennium political theology of the "kingdom of God on earth" which merges the church and the state into one in this world. It is therefore the duty of the church to help the state to save the ecology in order to make the kingdom of God on earth everlasting. However, relevant Bible verses and the Biblical history clearly demonstrate that the kingdom of God either refers to the heavenly kingdom yet to come or to the religious community of Yahweh believers or Christian believers on earth, almost never a secular state composed of Judo-Christian believers on earth. The Bible and the early church fathers prescribe the separation of state and church, which prohibits

Conclusion: Too Little to Save and Too Many to Save

the church from taking a proactive role in the state's ecological projects. The church should choose an ecological program that prioritizes the Great Commission and disaster relief with a reactive ecological program.

In addition to criticisms of current ecotheologies, chapters 4 to 6 also propose moderate and practical ecological programs that redirect the church's attention to the incoming crisis management and the even more urgent Great Commission before the arrival of the Doomsdays. In the teachings and sermons, the holiness of God's creation should be addressed, but only in light of the total destruction of the universe by the Trinitarian God Himself prior to the descendance of the New Heaven and New Earth from above. Through collective negotiation and decision making, all done in consultation with community criteria, the church should develop moderate ecological programs that take into consideration both collective interests and individual preferences. The church does not need to take initiatives in community ecological programs but only respond to the existing programs agreed upon by most of the community and promulgated by the state. Any radical ecological program which threatens the livelihood of church members, causes great inconvenience to church routines, and severely divides (within and among) the churches should be rejected. The wealthier members of the churches should donate to the church more than their fair shares in preparation for crisis management, while the average members should work as hard as their counterparts in the free market, also in preparation for crisis management. Christians living in authoritarian regimes should follow the regime's ecological programs no matter how far or how little they deviate from international standards. Within these regimes, the churches should not engage in democratic revolutions for the sake of the ecology, unless their freedom of religion is at stake. However, the church in democratic countries should internalize democratic values and behaviors in both her theologies and organizational structures so that the decisions and burdens of ecological adjustments are appropriately distributed and reflects the majority will of the church. Above all, every ecological program should be an integral part of the church's Great Commission and should not impede the latter.

Will these moderate and practical ecological programs "extinguish the dimly burning wick" and kill off the last chance of saving the ecology?[1] For one thing, as many ecologists have consistently argued since the 1960s, it is already too late to save the ecology even if there arises an authoritarian world government to implement all the ecological programs they recommended.

---

1. Isa 42:3; Matt 12:20.

For another, should the last chance of saving the ecology ever occur, these moderate and practical programs would prepare Christians to efficiently and peacefully cope with Revelation disasters and the reconstruction of the ecology, more so than most existing programs the majority of which are theologically controversial, impractical in implementation, and politically divisive both within the church and between the church and the community.

In the end, the church and each Christian should reflect upon themselves in the age of the post-ecology: There is only so much one can do to save the world in such a short time, if it is indeed savable at all. However, there are so many souls one can save in such a short time, and they are worth saving by all means.

APPENDIX 3.1

Neurotheology in the Bible

God Brain (GB), Emotional Brain (EB), Rational Brain (RB)

Neurotheology Types	Bible Chapters	Criteria
GB	Gen 1 (God's creation)	Emphasis on Trinitarian God's transcendence, omnipotence, omnipresence and glory, usually of, by, and for Himself.
	Job 1–42 (God is above human rationality and emotion)	
	Pss 8, 29, 65, 90, 93, 96, 97, 104, 113, 114, 117, 135, 145–150	
	Eccl 1–12 (human rationality and emotion are vanity; fear God)	
	Jonah 1–4 (God is above Jonah's rationality and emotion)	
	John 1:1–34 (Transcendence of Jesus)	
	Heb 1–10 (Transcendence of Jesus)	
	NT verses (Transcendence of Spirit)	
GB + EB	Gen 1–2 (God and human), 9 (God blessed Noah), 12–18, 20–35 (God blessed Abraham, Isaac, Jacob), 37–50 (God blessed Joseph)	Emphasis on God's emotional relationship with His believer. God provides protection, grace, and blessings to satisfy human emotion, while the believer is urged to love, praise, talk and sing to God to please God.
	Exod 1–12 (God blessed Moses); 13–19, 21–25 (God blessed Israeli exodus)	
	Num 11, 20–24, 31 (God blessed Israelis in the wilderness)	

Appendix 3.1

	Deut 12–20 (Religious rituals)	
	Josh 1–24 (God blessed Israeli occupation of Palestine)	
	Ruth 1–4	
	1Sam 16–30 (God blessed David)	
	2Sam 1–10 (God blessed David)	
	Esth 1–10 (Through Esther, God protected Israelis from genocide)	
	Ps 2, 3, 5–7, 13, 16, 20–24, 27, 28, 30, 35, 40–49, 54–57, 59–64, 66–71, 77, 79, 80, 84, 87, 88, 91, 92, 95, 100, 102, 105, 108–110, 115, 116, 118, 120–129, 133, 134, 136, 138–144	
	Obad (God will judge Edom and promise Israeli revival)	
	Matt 8–9 (Jesus healed the sick)	
	Mark 1–3 (Jesus healed and blessed)	
	Luke 4, 6, 7 (Jesus healed the sick)	
	Rev 8–9, 16–20 (Jesus and God unleashes judgments but spares believers)	
	Rev 21–22 (Believers in New Heaven and New Earth)	
	Gen 28–35 (God blessed Jacob)	God's love over justice and human rationality
	Exod 5, 11–21, 31–34 (God blessed Israeli exodus)	
	Ps 32, 38, 51, 85, 86, 103, 130	
	Song 1–8 (God forgives Israeli religious adultery)	
	Lam 1–5 (Jeremiah pleaded God to ease Israeli sufferings, despite their sins)	
	Hab 1–3 (God judged Chaldeans and saved sinful Judah)	
	Zech 1–14 (God removed Israeli sins and promised Messiah arrival)	
	Matt 1; Luke 1–2 (Birth of Jesus)	
	Matt 4; Mark 1; Luke 4 (Jesus' choice of death over worldly values)	
	Matt 26–28; Mark 14–16; Luke 22–24; Joh 12–21 (Crucifixion of Jesus and Great Commandment)	

	Acts 1–28 (Apostles, Paul and Christians persecuted by both Jews and Romans but guided by the Spirit)	
GB + RB	Gen 3–4 (Original sin), 19 (Sodom)	Emphasis on God's laws and judgment
	Exod 20–40 (Moses laws and golden calf)	
	Lev 1–27 (Moses laws)	
	Num 1–19, 25–30, 35, 36 (Moses laws and Israeli rebellions)	
	Deut 21–33 (Moses laws)	
	2Sam 11–20 (God judged David)	
	1Kgs 3–10 (Solomon's rise and fall)	
	2Chr 1–9 (Solomon's rise and fall)	
	Ezra 3–10 (Ezra rebuilt Temple and restored Moses law)	
	Neh 1–13 (Nehemiah rebuilt Jerusalem walls and promulgated Moses law)	
	Pss 1, 14, 15, 19, 36, 37, 50, 52, 53, 58, 72–76, 81–83, 101, 111, 112, 119, 132, 137	
	Prov 1–31 (Moral codes and pragmatism)	
	Ezek 1–48 (God judged Israelis and nations; restored Temple and law)	
	2Thess 2 (Jesus will judge heresies)	
	1Tim 1 (God will judge heresies)	
	1Tim 2–6 (Church governance)	
	2Tim 2–4 (Church governance)	
	Titus 1–3 (Church governance)	
	Phlm (Church governance)	
	Jas 1–5 (Church governance)	
	1Pet 2–3 (Social moral codes)	
	1Pet 4 (God's judgment)	
	2Pet 2–3 (Judgment of Parousia)	
	1John 1–5 (Church governance)	
	2John (Church governance)	
	3John (Church governance)	
	Rev 1–20 (Last judgment)	

APPENDIX 3.1

	Gen 22 (Abraham sacrifice Isaac)	Controlling desires
	Prov 4–7 (Warnings against sexual desires)	
	Dan 1, 3–6 (God protected law-biding Daniel in hard choices)	
	Hag 1–2 (Temple and law are more important than personal needs)	
	Matt 4:1–11; Luke 4:1–13 (Temptations of Jesus: survival, pride, politics)	
	Mark 11–14 (Jesus proclaimed rules, judgments, doomsday)	
	Rom 1–3 (Paul proclaimed judgment on the desires of nations, of Jews, of human); 7 (Paul explained how God controlled his emotion)	
	1Cor 1–15 (Paul's teaching for controlling desires, marriage, idolatry, rituals, and spiritual pride)	
	Eph 4–6 (Paul's teaching for controlling desires, marriage, and family life)	
	Col 2–3 (Paul's teaching for controlling desires and family life)	
	1Thess 4–5 (Paul's teaching for controlling desires and church life)	
GB + EB + RB	Gen 6–9 (Noah)	All three elements are emphasized; connections among three brains are strengthened.
	Deut 1–30 (Moses recounted God's blessings and judgments), 32 (Song of Moses)	
	Judg 1–21 (Cycles of God's blessing and judgment of Israelis)	
	1Sam 1–8 (Judge Samuel); 9–15, 31 (God blessed and judged Saul)	
	1Kgs 1–22 (God blessed and judged kings)	
	2Kgs 1–25 (God blessed and judged kings)	
	2Chr 10–36 (God blessed and judged kings)	
	Pss 9–12, 17, 18, 25, 26, 31, 33, 34, 78, 89, 94, 98, 99, 106, 107	
	I Sam 1–66 (Triune God judged Israelis and nations but passion over repented Israelis)	

	Jer 1–52 (God judged Israelis and nations but grace to repented Israelis)
	Hos 1–14 (God judged adulterous Israelis but promised grace to repentance)
	Joe 1–3 (God punished Israelis with locusts but promised grace)
	Amos 1–9 (God judged Israelis and nations but promised Israeli revival)
	Mic 1–7 (God judged Judah and Israel but promised Messiah peace)
	Zeph 1–3 (God judged Judah and nations but promised Jewish revival)
	Mal 1–4 (Malachi reprimanded priests and Israelis but promised grace)
	Matt 5–7; 10–16; 17–25 (Jesus healed and proclaimed Beatitudes, rules, and blessings)
	Luke 4–21 (Jesus healed and proclaimed Beatitudes, rules, and blessings)
	John 4–21 (Jesus healed and proclaimed rules and blessings)
	Rom 3–15 (Righteousness by faith)
	Gal 3–6 (Righteousness by faith)
	Phil 1–4 (Righteousness by faith)

Notes: Most Biblical chapters include stimulation and education of all three brains, forging circuits among all. These categories are subjectively relative emphases. The number of chapters of GB + EB is the largest, followed by GB + EB + RB, then by GB + RB. The importance of GB + EB is shown particularly in its prevalence over RB. GB + EB + RB are usually long chapters.

APPENDIX 4.1

Ecology and Post-Ecology in the Bible

Verse Number	Verse Content or Gist of Verses	Note
Gen 1:1–21	God created nature, "God saw that it was good"	GNL
Gen 6:7–7:24	God destroyed all lives on land except those in the ark	GNL
Gen 8:1–14, 21–22	God restored the nature after the flood	GNL
Gen 9:10–16	God's covenant with all animals	GNL
Gen 14:19	Blessed be Abram of God Most High, Possessor of heaven and earth	GNL
Exod 7–10, 12	God exercised His supernatural power through ten plaques	GNL
Deut 10:14	Behold, to the LORD your God belong heaven and the highest heavens, the earth and all that is in it.	GNL
2Kgs 19:15	O LORD, the God of Israel, who are enthroned *above* the cherubim, You are the God, You alone, of all the kingdoms of the earth. You have made heaven and earth.	GNL
1Chr 16:26	For all the gods of the peoples are idols, but the LORD made the heavens.	GNL

1Chr 29:16	"O LORD our God, all this abundance that we have provided to build You a house for Your holy name, it is from Your hand, and all is Yours.	GNL
2Chr 2:12	Blessed be the LORD, the God of Israel, who has made heaven and earth	GNL
Neh 9:6	You alone are the LORD. You have made the heavens, The heaven of heavens with all their host, The earth and all that is on it, The seas and all that is in them. You give life to all of them and the heavenly host bows down before You.	GNL
Job 9:8	Who alone stretches out the heavens and tramples down the waves of the sea	GNL
Job 12:10	In whose hand is the life of every living thing, and the breath of all mankind?	GNL
Job 36:26–37:22	God created natural law to govern the nature	GNL
Job 38:4–39:30	God created natural law to govern the nature	GNL
Ps 8:3	When I consider Your heavens, the work of Your fingers, the moon and the stars, which You have ordained	GNL
Ps 24:1–2	The earth is the LORD's, and all it contains, the world, and those who dwell in it. For He has founded it upon the seas And established it upon the rivers.	GNL
Ps 33:6	By the word of the LORD the heavens were made, and by the breath of His mouth all their host.	GNL
Ps 50:10	For every beast of the forest is Mine, the cattle on a thousand hills.	GNL
Ps 50:12	If I were hungry I would not tell you, for the world is Mine, and all it contains.	GNL

APPENDIX 4.1

Ps 89:11–12	The heavens are Yours, the earth also is Yours; the world and all it contains, You have founded them. The north and the south, You have created them.	GNL
Ps 90:2	Before the mountains were born Or You gave birth to the earth and the world, even from everlasting to everlasting, You are God.	GNL
Ps 95:5	The sea is His, for it was He who made it, And His hands formed the dry land.	GNL
Ps 96:5	For all the gods of the peoples are idols, but the LORD made the heavens.	GNL
Ps 100:3	Know that the LORD Himself is God; it is He who has made us, and not we ourselves; *We are* His people and the sheep of His pasture.	GNL
Ps 102:25	Of old You founded the earth, and the heavens are the work of Your hands.	GNL
Ps 102:26	Even they will perish, but You endure; and all of them will wear out like a garment; Like clothing You will change them and they will be changed.	GNL
Ps 104:2, 5	Covering Yourself with light as with a cloak, Stretching out heaven like a *tent* curtain… He established the earth upon its foundations, So that it will not totter forever and ever.	GNL
Ps 104:10–14	He sends forth springs in the valleys; they flow between the mountains; they give drink to every beast of the field; the wild donkeys quench their thirst. Beside them the birds of the heavens dwell; they lift up *their* voices among the branches. He waters the mountains from His upper chambers. The earth is satisfied with the fruit of His works. He causes the grass to grow for the cattle, and vegetation for the labor of man, so that he may bring forth food from the earth,	GNL

Ps 104:24, 30	O LORD, how many are Your works! In wisdom You have made them all; The earth is full of Your possessions… You send forth Your Spirit, they are created; And You renew the face of the ground.	GNL
Ps 115:15	May you be blessed of the LORD, Maker of heaven and earth.	GNL
Ps 121:2	My help *comes* from the LORD, Who made heaven and earth.	GNL
Ps 124:8	Our help is in the name of the LORD, Who made heaven and earth.	GNL
Ps 146:6	Who made heaven and earth, the sea and all that is in them; Who keeps faith forever;	GNL
Ps 147: 4,8–9,16–18	God made natural law to govern the nature	GNL
Ps 148:5	Let them praise the name of the LORD, for He commanded and they were created.	GNL
Prov 3:19	The LORD by wisdom founded the earth, By understanding He established the heavens.	GNL
Prov 16:4	The LORD has made everything for its own purpose, Even the wicked for the day of evil.	GNL
1Sam 34:4	And all the host of heaven will wear away, and the sky will be rolled up like a scroll; all their hosts will also wither away as a leaf withers from the vine, or as *one* withers from the fig tree.	GNL
1Sam 37:16	O LORD of hosts, the God of Israel, who is enthroned *above* the cherubim, You are the God, You alone, of all the kingdoms of the earth. You have made heaven and earth.	GNL
1Sam 40:22	It is He who sits above the circle of the earth, And its inhabitants are like grasshoppers, Who stretches out the heavens like a curtain and spreads them out like a tent to dwell in.	GNL

Appendix 4.1

1Sam 40:28	The Everlasting God, the LORD, the Creator of the ends of the earth does not become weary or tired.	GNL
1Sam 42:5	Thus says God the LORD, Who created the heavens and stretched them out, Who spread out the earth and its offspring, Who gives breath to the people on it and spirit to those who walk in it,	GNL
1Sam 44:24	I, the LORD, am the maker of all things, Stretching out the heavens by myself And spreading out the earth all alone	GNL
1Sam 45:12	It is I who made the earth, and created man upon it. I stretched out the heavens with My hands and I ordained all their host.	GNL
1Sam 45:18	For thus says the LORD, who created the heavens (He is the God who formed the earth and made it, He established it *and* did not create it a waste place, *but* formed it to be inhabited), "I am the LORD, and there is none else.	GNL
1Sam 48:13	Surely My hand founded the earth, And My right hand spread out the heavens; When I call to them, they stand together.	GNL
1Sam 51:6	For the sky will vanish like smoke, and the earth will wear out like a garment and its inhabitants will die in like manner; but My salvation will be forever, and My righteousness will not wane.	GNL
1Sam 51:13	That you have forgotten the LORD your Maker, Who stretched out the heavens and laid the foundations of the earth,	GNL
Jer 10:12	*It is* He who made the earth by his power, Who established the world by his wisdom; And by his understanding he has stretched out the heavens.	GNL
Jer 27:5	I have made the earth, the men and the beasts which are on the face of the earth by My great power and by My outstretched arm, and I will give it to the one who is pleasing in My sight.	GNL

Jer 32:17	Ah Lord GOD! Behold, You have made the heavens and the earth by Your great power and by Your outstretched arm! Nothing is too difficult for You,	GNL
Jer 51:15	"It is he who made the earth by his power, who established the world by his wisdom, and by his understanding stretched out the heavens.	GNL
Ezek 47:9	It will come about that every living creature which swarms in every place where the river goes, will live. And there will be very many fish, for these waters go there and *the others* become fresh; so everything will live where the river goes.	GNL
Dan 7:14	And to Him was given dominion, Glory and a kingdom, That all the peoples, nations and *men of every* language Might serve Him. His dominion is an everlasting dominion Which will not pass away; And His kingdom is one Which will not be destroyed.	GNL, Messiah
Joel 1:15	Alas for the day! For the day of the LORD is near, and it will come as destruction from the Almighty.	GNL
Mic 1:4	The mountains will melt under Him and the valleys will be split, like wax before the fire, like water poured down a steep place.	GNL
Nah 1:5	Mountains quake because of Him and the hills dissolve; Indeed the earth is upheaved by His presence, the world and all the inhabitants in it.	GNL
Zech 12:1	The burden of the word of the LORD concerning Israel. *Thus* declares the LORD who stretches out the heavens, lays the foundation of the earth, and forms the spirit of man within him,	GNL
Matt 5:18	For truly I say to you, until heaven and earth pass away, not the smallest letter or stroke shall pass from the Law until all is accomplished.	GNL

Appendix 4.1

Matt 6:26–34	God manages nature and human needs	GNL
Matt 10:29–30	Are not two sparrows sold for a cent? And *yet* not one of them will fall to the ground apart from your Father. But the very hairs of your head are all numbered.	GNL
Matt 24:35, 37	Heaven and earth will pass away, but My words will not pass away… For the coming of the Son of Man will be just like the days of Noah.	GNL
Matt 28:18	And Jesus came up and spoke to them, saying, "All authority has been given to Me in heaven and on earth.	GNL, Jesus
Mark 13	Total destruction of the world on doomsday	GNL
Luke 17:26–27	And just as it happened in the days of Noah, so it will be also in the days of the Son of Man: they were eating, they were drinking, they were marrying, they were being given in marriage, until the day that Noah entered the ark, and the flood came and destroyed them all.	GNL, Jesus
John 1:1–2	In the beginning was the Word, and the Word was with God, and the Word was God. He was in the beginning with God.	GNL, Jesus
John 3:35	The Father loves the Son and has given all things into His hand.	GNL
John 13:3	*Jesus*, knowing that the Father had given all things into His hands, and that He had come forth from God and was going back to God	GNL
Acts 4:24	O Lord, it is You who made the heaven and the earth and the sea, and all that is in them	GNL
Acts 7:50	Was it not my hand which made all these things?	GNL
Acts 14:15	you should turn from these vain things to a living God, Who made the heaven and the earth and the sea and all that is in them	GNL

Acts 17:24–26	The God Who made the world and all things in it, since He is LORD of heaven and earth, does not dwell in temples made with hands; . . . He Himself gives to all *people* life and breath and all things; and He made from one *man* every nation of mankind to live on all the face of the earth, having determined *their* appointed times and the boundaries of their habitation.	GNL
Acts 17:29	Being then the children of God, we ought not to think that the divine nature is like gold or silver or stone, an image formed by the art and thought of man.	GNL
Rom 1:20	For since the creation of the world His invisible attributes, His eternal power and divine nature, have been clearly seen, being understood through what has been made, so that they are without excuse.	GNL
Rom 8:21	that the creation itself also will be set free from its slavery to corruption into the freedom of the glory of the children of God.	GNL
Rom 11:36	For from Him and through Him and to Him are all things. To Him *be* the glory forever. Amen.	GNL
1Cor 8:6	yet for us there is *but* one God, the Father, from whom are all things and we *exist* for Him; and one LORD, Jesus Christ, by whom are all things, and we *exist* through Him.	GNL, Jesus
1Cor 15:27	for He has put all things in subjection under His feet. But when He says, "All things are put in subjection," it is evident that He is excepted who put all things in subjection to Him.	GNL, Jesus
Eph 3:9	to bring to light what is the administration of the mystery which for ages has been hidden in God who created all things.	GNL
Col 1:16–20	God created the nature, secular authorities, and the church	GNL

Appendix 4.1

Heb 1:2–3	in these last days has spoken to us in His Son, Whom He appointed heir of all things, through Whom also He made the world. And He is the radiance of His glory and the exacts representation of His nature, and upholds all things by the word of His power.	GNL, Jesus
Heb 1:10	You, LORD, in the beginning laid the foundation of the earth, and the heavens are the works of your hands	GNL
Heb 3:4	For every house is built by someone, but the builder of all things is God.	GNL
Heb 11:3	By faith we understand that the worlds were prepared by the word of God, so that what is seen was not made out of things which are visible.	GNL
2Pet 2:5	and (God) did not spare the ancient world, but preserved Noah, a preacher of righteousness, with seven others, when He brought a flood upon the world of the ungodly	GNL
2Pet 3:5	by the word of God *the* heavens existed long ago and *the* earth was formed out of water and by water,	GNL
2Pet 3:7	But by his word the present heavens and earth are being reserved for fire, kept for the day of judgment and destruction of ungodly men.	GNL
2Pet 3:10	But the day of the LORD will come like a thief, in which the heavens will pass away with a roar and the elements will be destroyed with intense heat, and the earth and its works will be burned up.	GNL
2Pet 3:12	looking for and hastening the coming of the day of God, because of which the heavens will be destroyed by burning, and the elements will melt with intense heat!	GNL

Rev 4:11	Worthy are You, our LORD and our God, to receive glory and honor and power; for You created all things, and because of Your will they existed, and were created.	GNL
Rev 6:14	The sky was split apart like a scroll when it is rolled up, and every mountain and island were moved out of their places.	GNL
Rev 10:6	and swore by Him who lives forever and ever, Who created heaven and the things in it, and the earth and the things in it, and the sea and the things in it, that there will be delay no longer,	GNL
Rev 14:7	Fear God, and give him glory, because the hour of His judgment has come; worship Him who made the heaven and the earth and sea and springs of waters	GNL
Rev 6,8,9,16–20	Jesus will destroy the nature and punish non-believers and demons	GNL
Rev 21–22	God will create New Heaven and New Earth	GNL
Gen 1:28	God said to them, "Be fruitful and multiply, and fill the earth, and subdue it; and rule over the fish of the sea and over the birds of the sky and over every living thing that moves on the earth.	HMN
Gen 6:19–7:16	Noah brought animals into the ark	HMN
Gen 8:17	Bring out with you every living thing of all flesh that is with you, birds and animals and every creeping thing that creeps on the earth, that they may breed abundantly on the earth, and be fruitful and multiply on the earth.	HMN

Appendix 4.1

Gen 9:1, 7	And God blessed Noah and his sons and said to them, "Be fruitful and multiply, and fill the earth . . . As for you, be fruitful and multiply; populate the earth abundantly and multiply in it.	HMN
Gen 9:2–3	"The fear of you and the terror of you will be on every beast of the earth and on every bird of the sky; with everything that creeps on the ground, and all the fish of the sea, into your hand they are given.	HMN
Gen 41:14–56	Joseph prepared food before famine	HMN
Exod 20:10	but the seventh day is a sabbath of the LORD your God; *in it* you shall not do any work, you or your son or your daughter, your male or your female servant or your cattle or your sojourner who stays with you.	HMN and social justice
Exod 23:10–11	You shall sow your land for six years and gather in its yield, but *on* the seventh year you shall let it rest and lie fallow, so that the needy of your people may eat; and whatever they leave the beast of the field may eat. You are to do the same with your vineyard *and* your olive grove.	HMN and social justice
Exod 23:12	Six days you are to do your work, but on the seventh day you shall cease *from labor* so that your ox and your donkey may rest, and the son of your female slave, as well as your stranger, may refresh themselves.	HMN
Exod 31:12–17	Observe the Sabbath	HMN
Lev 19:9–10	Now when you reap the harvest of your land, you shall not reap to the very corners of your field, nor shall you gather the gleanings of your harvest. Nor shall you glean your vineyard, nor shall you gather the fallen fruit of your vineyard; you shall leave them for the needy and for the stranger. I am the LORD your God.	HMN and social justice

Lev 23:22	When you reap the harvest of your land, moreover, you shall not reap to the very corners of your field nor gather the gleaning of your harvest; you are to leave them for the needy and the alien. I am the LORD your God.	HMN and social justice
Lev 24:19–20	When you reap your harvest in your field and have forgotten a sheaf in the field, you shall not go back to get it; it shall be for the alien, for the orphan, and for the widow, in order that the LORD your God may bless you in all the work of your hands. When you beat your olive tree, you shall not go over the boughs again; it shall be for the alien, for the orphan, and for the widow.	HMN and social justice
Lev 25:7	Even your cattle and the animals that are in your land shall have all its crops to eat.	HMN
Lev 26:35	All the days of *its* desolation it will observe the rest whiChr it did not observe on your Sabbaths, while you were living on it.	HMN
Deut 5:14	but the seventh day is a sabbath of the LORD your God; *in it* you shall not do any work, you or your son or your daughter or your male servant or your female servant or your ox or your donkey or any of your cattle or your sojourner who stays with you, so that your male servant and your female servant may rest as well as you.	HMN and social justice
Deut 20:19	When you besiege a city a long time, to make war against it in order to capture it, you shall not destroy its trees by swinging an axe against them; for you may eat from them, and you shall not cut them down. For is the tree of the field a man, that it should be besieged by you?	HMN
Ps 8:6	You make him to rule over the works of Your hands; You have put all things under his feet,	HMN

Heb 2:7–8	You have made him for a little while lower than the angels; you have crowned him with glory and honor, and have appointed him over the works of your hands. You have put all things in subjection under his feet." For in subjecting all things to him, He left nothing that is not subject to him. But now we do not yet see all things subjected to him.	HMN
Jas 3:7	For every species of beasts and birds, of reptiles and creatures of the sea, is tamed and has been tamed by the human race.	HMN

Notes: God created nature and natural law (GNL), involving GB and EB. God delegates humans to manage the nature (HMN), involving GB and RB.

Bibliography

Albright, Carol, and James Ashbrook. *Were God Lives in the Human Brain*. Naperville, IL: Sourcebooks, 2001.
Allison, Dale C Jr. *Constructing Jesus: Memory, Imagination, and History*. Grand Rapids, MI: Baker Academic, 2010.
Alper, Matthew. *"God" Part of the Brain: A Scientific Interpretation of Human Spirituality and God*. Naperville, IL: Sourcebooks, 2008.
Aristotle. The Complete Works of Aristotle. The revised oxford translation, ed. Jonathan Barnes, Vol. Two. Princeton, NJ: Princeton University Press, 1984.
Armitage, Derek, et al., eds. *Adaptive Co–Management: Collaboration, Learning, and Multi-level Governance*. Vancouver, Canada: UBC Press, 2007.
Arrow, Kenneth J. *Social Choice and Individual Values*. 2nd ed. New Haven, CT: Yale University Press, 1963.
Ashbrook, James B. "Neurotheology: The Working Brain and the Work of Theology. *Zygon* 3 (1984) 331–350.
Augustine, Saint. *Confessions*. New York: Oxford University Press, 1991.
———. *The City of God*. New York: The Modern Library, 1993.
———. *Thomas Aquinas: Selected Writings*. New York: Penguin, 1998.
Aune, David E. *Revelation*. Nashville, TN: Thomas Nelson, 1998.
Au Sable Institute. "Au Sable Institute Forum Statement." *Evangelical Review of Theology*, 2 (1993) 122–133.
Ayres, Robert. "Sustainability Economics: Where do We Stand." *Ecological Economics* 67 (2008) 281–310.
Baker, Chris. "Sustainable Governance in a Postsecular Public Sphere: Re–Assessing the Role of Religion as a Cosmopolitan Policy Actor in a Diverse and Globalized Age." *Sustainable Development* 24 (2016) 190–198.
Bardi, Ugo. *The Limits to Growth Revisited*. New York: Springer, 2011.
Barker, David C and David H. Bearce. "End–Times Theology, the Shadow of the Future, and Public Resistance to Addressing Global Climate Change." *Political Research Quarterly*, 2 (2012) 267–279.
Barker, Philip and Jeff Chang. *Basic Family Therapy*. 6th ed. Hoboken, NJ: Wiley–Blackwell, 2013.
Barnhill, David Landis and Roger S. Gottlieb, eds. *Deep Ecology and World Religions: New Essays on Sacred Grounds*. Albany, NY: State University of New York Press, 2001.
Barrett, Justin L. *Cognitive Science, Religion, and Theology: From Human Minds to Divine Minds*. West Conshohocken, PA: Templeton, 2011.

Barrett, Matthew and Ardel B. Caneday, eds. *Four Views on the Historical Adam*. Zondervan, 2013.

Bauckham, Richard. *Living with Other Creatures: Green Exegesis and Theology*. Waco, TX: Baylor University Press, 2011.

Bauer, Walter, and Frederick William Danker (BDAG). *A Greek–English Lexicon of the New Testament and Other Early Christian Literature*. 3rd ed. Chicago, IL: University of Chicago Press. Built in *BibleWorks*, 2001.

BBC, "Superbugs to kill more than cancer by 2050." 11 (December 2014). http://www.bbc.com/news/health-30416844.

Beale, G.K. *The Book of Revelation: A Commentary on the Greek Text*. Grand Rapids, MI: Eerdmans, 1999.

Beauregard, Mario and Denyse O"Leary. *The Spiritual Brain: A Neuroscientist's Case for the Existence of the Soul*. New York: HarperCollins, 2007.

Beisner, E. Calvin. *Where Garden Meets Wilderness: Evangelical Entry into the Environmental Debate*. Grand Rapids, MI: Acton Institute for the Study of Religion and Liberty, 1997.

Bellah, Robert N. "Civil Religion in America." *Daedalus* 96(1): 1–21; reprinted in *Daedalus*, 4 (1967). http://www.jstor.org/stable/20028013.

Berry, R.J, ed. *Environmental Stewardship: Critical Perspectives*. NY: T.&T. Clark, 2006.

Berry, Thomas. *The Dream of the Earth*. San Francisco, CA: Sierra Club, 1988.

Bessette, Joseph. "Deliberative Democracy: The Majority Principle in Republican Government." In *How Democratic is the Constitution?*, edited by Robert A. Goldwin and William A. Schambra, 102–116. Washington, DC: AEI, 1980.

Bi, Jinfeng. "Theory and Practice on Buddhist Ecological Philosophy." *Studies in Dialectics of Nature*, 5 (2013) 122–126. 畢晉鋒。2013。「佛教生態哲學的理論與實踐」。自然辯證法研究，29卷5期，122–126頁。

Bock, Darrell. *Acts: Baker Exegetical Commentary on the New Testament*. Grand Rapids, MI: Baker Academic, 2007.

Boehm, Christopher. *Moral Origins: The Evolution of Virtue, Altruism, and Shame*. New York: Basic, 2012.

Boswell, John. *Christianity, Social Tolerance, and Homosexuality*. Chicago: University of Chicago Press, 1980.

Bratton, Susan Power. *Christianity, Wilderness, and Wildlife: The Original Desert Solitaire*. Scranton, PA: University of Scranton Press, 1993.

Britton, W.B., and RR Bootzin. "Near-Death Experiences and the Temporal Lobe." *Psychology and Science* 15 (2004) 254–258.

Brunner, Daniel L, et al. *Introducing Evangelical Ecotheology: Foundations in Scripture, Theology, History, and Praxis*. Grand Rapids, MI: Baker Academic, 2014.

Buddhist Compassion Relief Tzu Chi Foundation. *From the Years of Bamboo Tubes to International NGO: The History of Tzu Chi Denomination*. Taipei, TAIWAN: Buddhist Compassion Relief Tzu Chi Foundation, 2011.

Burkett, Paul. *Marxism and Ecological Economics: Toward a Red and Green Political Economy*. Chicago, IL: Haymarket, 2006.

Butkus, Russell A, and Steven A. Kolmes. *Environmental Science and Theology in Dialogue*. Maryknoll, NY: Orbis, 2011.

Callicott, J. Baird, and James McRae. *Environmental Philosophy in Asian Traditions of Thought*. Albany, NY: State University of New York Press, 2014.

Calvin, John. *Institutes of the Christian Religion*. Trans. Henry Beveridge. Grand Rapids, MI: WM. B. Eerdmans, 1989.

Carr, Alan. *Positive Psychology: The Science of Happiness and Human Strengths.* 2nd ed. New York: Routledge, 2011.

Case-Winters, Anna. "The End? Christian Eschatology and the End of the World." *Interpretation: A Journal of Bible and Theology* 1 (2016) 61–74.

Cassel, J. David. "Stewardship: Experiencing and Expressing God's Nurturing Love." *American Baptist Quarterly* 1 (1998) 26–40.

Chardin, Pierre Teilhard de. *The Phenomenon of Man.* Trans. Bernard Wall, NY: Harper & Row, 1959.

Chen, Hongbing. "Buddhist Ecological Philosophy Research in Context of Western Environmental Philosophy." *Nangjing Linye Daxue Xuebao* 3 (2015) 29–35.陳紅冰。2015。「西方環境哲學背景下的佛教生態哲學研究」。南京林業大學學報，3期，29–35頁。

———. "On Taoist Ecological Thoughts and Culture." *Nangjing Linye Daxue Xuebao*, 1: 29–35. 陳紅冰。2017。「試論道家道教生態思想文化」。南京林業大學學報，1期，29–35頁。

Chryssavgis, John, and Bruce V. Foltz. *Toward an Ecology of Transfiguration: Orthodox Christian Perspectives on Environment, Nature, and Creation (Orthodox Christianity and Contemporary Thought).* New York: Fordham University Press, 2013.

Clayton, Philip, and Justin Heinzekehr. *Organic Marxism: An Alternative to Capitalism and Ecological Catastrophe.* Claremont, CA: Process Century, 2014.

Coase, R.H. 1937. The Nature of the Firm. *Economica*, 4(16): 386–405.

Cobb, John B Jr. *Is It Too Late? A Theology of Ecology.* Revised ed. Denton, TX: Environmental Ethics, 1972/1995.

———. *For The Common Good: Redirecting the Economy toward Community, the Environment, and a Sustainable Future.* 2nd ed. Beacon, 1994.

———. *Sustaining the Common Good.* The Pilgrim,1994.

———. *Theological Reminiscences.* Anoka, MN: Process Century, 2014.

Coleman, Mark. *Awake in the Wild: Mindfulness in Nature as a Path of Self-Discovery.* Maui, HI: Inner Ocean, 2006.

Cole-Turner, Ronald. *The New Genesis: Theology and the Genetic Revolution.* Louisville, KY: Westminster John Knox, 1993.

———. *Transhumanism and Transcendence: Christian Hope in an Age of Technological Enhancement.* Washington, DC: Georgetown University Press, 2011.

Cook, Michael. *A Brief History of the Human Race.* New York: W.W. Norton, 2003.

Daly, Herman E. and Joshua Farley. *Ecological Economics: Principles and Applications.* 2nd ed. Island, 2010.

Dante. *Monarchy.* Trans. Prue Shaw. New York: Cambridge University Press, 1996.

Davis, James C. *The Human Story: Our History, from the Stone Age to Today.* New York: HarperCollins, 2004.

Dawkins, Richard. *The God Delusion.* 2nd ed. New York: Houghton Mifflin Harcourt, 2008.

Deane-Drummond, Celia. *A Primer in Ecotheology: Theology for a Fragile Earth.* Eugene, OR: Cascade, 2017.

DeWitt, Calvin B. *Caring for Creation: Responsible Stewardship of God's Handiwork.* Grand Rapids, MI: Baker, 1998.

Diamond, Jared. *Guns, Germs, and Steel: The Fates of Human Societies.* New York: W.W. Norton & Company, 1999.

Dobson, Andrew. *Green Political Thought.* 4th ed. New York: Routledge, 2007.

Dupuis, Jacques. *Toward a Christian Theology of Religious Pluralism*. Maryknoll, NY: Orbis, 1997.
Dyk, Peet J. Van. "'Responsible Stewardship' – The Root of All Evil in Eco-Theology?" *OTE* 24/2 (2011) 523-535.
Earth Overshoot Day, www.overshhotday.org.
Eckersley, Robyn. *The Green State: Rethinking Democracy and Sovereignty*. Cambridge, MA: The MIT Press, 2004.
EcoWatch, "Global Fish Stocks Depleted to 'Alarming' Levels." https://www.ecowatch.com/one-third-of-commercial-fish-stocks-fished-at-unsustainable-levels-1910593830.html.
Edwards, Andrés R. *Thriving Beyond Sustainability: Pathways to a Resilient Society*. Gabriola Island, BC, Canada: New Society, 2010.
Fingelkurts, Alexander A., and Andrew A. Fingelkurts. "Is Our Brain Hardwired to Produce God, or Is Our Brain Hardwired to Perceive God? A Systematic Review on the Role of the Brain in Mediating Religious Experience." *Cognitive Process* 10 (2009) 293–326.
Fishkin, James S. *When the People Speak: Deliberative Democracy & Public Consultation*. New York: Oxford University Press, 2009.
Foster, John Bellamy. *Ecology Against Capitalism*. New York: Monthly Review, 2002.
Fox, Matthew. *Creation Spirituality: Liberating Gifts for the Peoples of the Earth*. San Francisco, CA: Harper & Row, 1991.
Freud, Sigmund. *Totem and Taboo*. Trans by James Strachey. New York: Norton, 1919/1952.
Friedman, Milton. *Capitalism and Freedom*. 2nd ed. Chicago: University of Chicago Press, 1982.
Fukuyama, Francis. *The End of History and the Last Man*. New York: Free, 1992.
Gagnon, Robert A.J. *The Bible and Homosexual Practice: Texts and Hermeneutics*. Nashville, TN: Abingdon, 2001.
Gardner, Gerald T. and Paul C. Stern. "The Short List: The Most Effective Actions U.S. Households Can Take to Curb Climate Change." *Environment* 50 (2008) 12–25.
Ghosh, Pallab. "First human discovered in Ethiopia." London: BBC. *BBC News* (March 4, 2015).
Giddens, Anthony. *The Third Way*. Cambridge, UK: Polity, 1998.
———. *The Politics of Climate Change*. 2nd ed. Malden, MA: Polity, 2011.
Goossaert, Vincent and David A. Palmer. *The Religious Question in Modern China*. Chicago, IL: University of Chicago Press, 2011.
Gottlieb, Roger S. *A Greener Faith: Religious Environmentalism and Our Planet's Future*. New York: Oxford University Press, 2006.
Gutiérrez, Gustavo. A Theology of Liberation. 2nd ed. Maryknoll, NY: Orbis, 1988.
Gustafson, James. *Ethics from a Theocentric Perspectives*. 2 vols. Chicago, IL: University of Chicago Press, 1981–1984.
Haas, Peter M.,et al. *Institutions for the Earth: Sources of Effective International Environmental Protection*. Cambridge, MA: The MIT Press, 1993.
Habermas, Jürgen. *The Theory of Communicative Action, Volume One, Reason and the Rationalization of Society*, trans. Thomas McCarthy, Boston, MA: Beacon, 1981.
Haidt, Jonathan. *The Happiness Hypothesis: Finding Modern Truth in Ancient Wisdom*. New York: Basic, 2006.
Hamilton, Victor P. *Exodus: An Exegetical Commentary*. Grand Rapids, MI: Baker Academic, 2011.

Han, Shihui, and Georg Northoff. "Culture-Sensitive Neural Substrates of Human Cognition: A Transcultural Neuroimaging Approach." *Nature Reviews Neuroscience* 9 (2008 August) 646–654.

Hardin, Russell. *Collective Action*. Baltimore, MD: Johns Hopkins University Press, 1982.

Hardin, Garrett. "The Tragedy of the Commons." *Science* 162 (1968) 1243–1248.

———. "Living on a Lifeboat: A Reprint from BioScience, October 1974." *The Social Contract*, Fall (2001) 36–47.

Hart, John. *What are They Saying about Environmental Theology?* New York: Paulist, 2004.

Haas, Peter H., Robert O. Keohane, and Marc A. Levy. *Institutions for the Earth: Sources of Effective International Environmental Protection*. Cambridge, MA: The MIT Press, 1993.

Hathaway, Mark. *The Tao of Liberation: Exploring the Ecology of Transformation*. Maryknoll, NY: Orbis, 2009.

Haught, John. 2010. "Science, God and Cosmic Purpose." In *The Cambridge Companion to Science and Religion*, edited by Peter Harrison, L6344-555. New York: Cambridge University Press.

Heilbroner, Robert L. *An Inquiry into the Human Prospect*. New York: W.W. Norton & Company, 1974.

———. *An Inquiry into the Human Prospect: Looked at Again for the 1990s*. New York: W.W. Norton & Company, 1991.

Hemer, Colin J. *The Letters to the Seven Churches of Asia in Their Local Setting. Journal for the Study of the New Testament Supplement 11*. Sheffield, AL: JSOT, 1986.

Henning, Daniel H. *Buddhism and Deep Ecology*. Bloomington, IN: AuthorHouse, 2002.

Herculano-Houzel, S. "The Human Brain in Numbers: A Linearly Scaled-up Primate Brain." *Frontiers in Human Neuroscience*, 3 (2009) 1–11.

Herzog, Frederick. *Justice and Church: The New Function of the Church in North America*. Maryknoll, NY: Orbis, 1980.

Hobbes, Thomas. *Leviathan*. Oxford: Basil Blackwell, 1955.

Hoggan, James. Climate Cover-up: The Crusade to Deny Global Warming. Vancouver, Canada: Greystone, 2009.

Holladay, William L. *A Concise Hebrew and Aramaic Lexicon of the Old Testament*. Built in *BibleWorks 9*. Leiden, the Netherlands: E. J. Brill. 1988.

Hopkin, Michael. "Ethiopia is Top Choice." *Nature News*, February 14, 2015. A recent discovery in Morocco dates Homo sapiens to 300,000 years. "World's oldest *Homo sapiens* fossils found in Morocco," *Science*, http://www.sciencemag.org/news/2017/06/world-s-oldest-homo-sapiens-fossils-found-morocco.

Huddy, Leonie, et al, eds. *The Oxford Handbook of Political Psychology*, 2nd ed. New York: Oxford University Press, 2013.

Hume, David. *The Treatise on Human Nature*. New York: Everyman's Library, 1966.

International Institute for Applied Systems Analysis, "Global temperature rise could hit 2°C threshold by 2050." http://www.iiasa.ac.at/web/home/about/news/160929-FEU-climate.html.

Intergovernmental Panel on Climate Change (IPCC), "Working Group II: Impacts, Adaptation and Vulnerability." http://www.ipcc.ch/ipccreports/tar/wg2/index.php?idp=29.

International Union for Conservation of Nature, "Table 1: Numbers of threatened species by major groups of organisms (1996–2017)." http://cmsdocs.s3.amazonaws.com/

summarystats/20171_Summary_Stats_Page_Documents/2017_1_RL_Stats_Table_1. pdf.

Jackson, Tim. *Prosperity without Growth: Economics for a Finite Planet.* Washington, DC: Earthscan LLC, 2009/2011.

Jeeves, Malcolm. *Minds, Souls and Gods: A Conversation on Faith, Psychology and Neuroscience.* Downers Grove, IL: InterVarsity, 2013.

Jeeves, Malcolm, and Warren S. Brown. *Neuroscience, Psychology, and Religion: Illusions, Delusions, and Realities about Human Nature.* West Conshohocken, PA: Templeton Foundation, 2009.

Jefferson, Thomas. "Jefferson's Wall of Separation Letter." (1802) https://www.usconstitution.net/jeffwall.html.

Jenkins, Willis. *Ecologies of Grace: Environmental Ethics and Christian Theology.* New York: Oxford University Press, 2008.

Jervis, Robert. *Perception and Misperception in International Politics.* Princeton, NJ: Princeton University Press, 1978.

Jones, David and Russell Woodbridge. *Health, Wealth & Happiness: Has the Prosperity Gospel Overshadowed the Gospel of Christ?* Grand Rapids, MI: Kregel, 2011.

Joseph, R. "The Limbic System and the Soul: Evolution and the Neuroanatomy of Religious Experience." *Zygon Journal of Religion and Science* 36 (2001) 105-136.

Jung, Carl G., and von Franz M–L. *Man and His Symbols.* Garden City: Doubleday, 1964.

Kahneman, Daniel. *Thinking, Fast and Slow.* New York: Farrar, Strauss, Giroux, 2011.

Kant, Immanuel. *Religion and Rational Theology.* Translated by Allen W. Wood. New York: Cambridge University Press, 1996.

Kaza, Stephanie, and Kenneth Kraft, eds. *Dharma Rain: Sources of Buddhist Environmentalism.* Boston, MA: Shambhala, 2000.

Kearns, Laurel. "Saving the Creation: Christian Environmentalism in the United States." *Sociology of Religion* 1 (1996) 55–70.

Keller, Catherine. "A Democracy of Fellow Creatures: Feminist Theology and Planetary Entanglement." *Studia Theologica,* 1 (2015) 3–18.

Körtner, Ulrich. "Ecological ethics and creation faith." HTS Teologiese Studies/Theological Studies 4 (2016) a3296. http://dx.doi.org/10.4102/hts.v72i4.3296.

Kuo, Cheng–tian. *Global Competitiveness and Industrial Growth in Taiwan and the Philippines.* Pittsburgh, PA: University of Pittsburgh Press, 1995.

———. *Checks and Balances between the Church and the State: A Biblical Perspective of Church–State Relations* (in Chinese). Taipei, TAIWAN: Chinese Theological Seminary, 2001.

———*Religion and Democracy in Taiwan.* Albany, NY: State University of New York Press, 2008.

———. ed. *Religion and Nationalism in Chinese Societies.* Amsterdam, the Netherlands: Amsterdam University Press, 2017.

———. "Sacred, Secular, and Neo–sacred Governments in China and Taiwan." In *The Oxford Handbook of Secularism,* edited by Phil Zuckerman and John R. Shook, 249-67. New York: Oxford University Press, 2017.

Kim, Heup Young. *A Theology of Dao.* Maryknoll, NY: Orbis, 2017.

Lagerwey, John. *China: A Religious State.* Hong Kong: Hong Kong University Press, 2010.

Lathrop, Gordon. Holy Ground: A Liturgical Cosmology. Minneapolis, MN: Fortress, 2003.

Lenin, V.I. *Imperialism the Highest Stage of Capitalism.* New York: International, 1982.

Lee, Fongmao. "Daoist Tribulation Theories and Contemporary Tribulation: A Religious Observation from the twentieth century to the twenty–first century." In *Gender, Deity, and Taiwanese Religions*, edited by Fengmao Lee and Ronggui Zhu, 131-156. Taipei: Institute of Chinese Literature and Philosophy, Academia Sinica. 1997.

Locke, John. *Two Treatises of Government*. Rutland, VT: Charles E. Tuttle, 1993.

———. *A Letter Concerning Toleration*, New York: Routledge, 1991.

Logan, R.K. "The Extended Mind Model of the Origin of Language and Culture." In G. Nathalie, P. Jean, B. Van, and A. Diederik, eds. *Evolutionary Epistemology, Language and Culture*. Dordrecht: Springer, 2006.

Luther, Martin. *The Bondage of the Will*. Translated by J.I. Packer and O.R. Johnston. Grand Rapids, MI: Felming H. Revell, 1957.

Luther, Martin. *The Martin Luther Collection: 15 Classic Works*. New York: Waxkeep, 2012.

Maclear, J.F. ed. *Church and State in the Modern Age: A Documentary History*. New York: Oxford University Press, 1995.

March, James G., and Herbert A. Simon. *Organizations*. New York: John Wiley & Sons, 1958.

Maslow, Abraham H. *Religions, Values, and Peak–Experiences*. Seattle, WA: Stellar Editions, 2014.

McDaniel, Jay B. *With Roots and Wings: Christianity in an Age of Ecology and Dialogue*. Maryknoll, NY: Orbis, 1995.

McMahon, Darrin M. *Happiness: A History*. New York: Grove, 2006.

McManners, John. ed. *The Oxford Illustrated History of Christianity*. New York: Oxford University Press, 1990.

McMinn, Mark R. *Psychology, Theology, and Spirituality in Christian Counseling*. 2nd ed. Carol Strem, IL: Tyndale House, 2011.

Meadows, Donella, et al. *The Limits to Growth*. New York: Universe Books, 1972.

———. *Beyond the Limits*. Post Mills, VT: Chelsea Green, 1992.

———. *Limits to Growth: The 30–Year Update*. White River Junction, VT: Chelsea Green, 2004.

Mealand, David L. "Community of Goods and Utopian Allusions in Acts II–IV." *Journal of Theological Studies* 28 (1977) 96–99.

Mellor, Mary. *Feminism and Ecology*. New York: New York University Press, 1997.

Miller, James. *China's Green Religion: Daoism and the Quest for a Sustainable Future*. New York: Columbia University Press, 2017.

Milton, Kay. Loving Nature: Towards an Ecology of Emotion. New York: Routledge, 2002.

Moltmann, Jürgen . *God in Creation: A New Theology of Creation and the Spirit of God*. San Francisco, CA: Harper & Row, 1985.

———. *The Spirit of Life: A Universal Affirmation*. Translated By Margaret Kohl. Minneapolis: Fortress, 1992.

———. *The Source of Life: The Holy Spirit and the Theology of Life*. Minneapolis, MN: Fortress, 1997.

———. *Sun of Righteousness, Arise! God's Future for Humanity and the Earth*. Minneapolis, MN: Fortress, 2010.

More, Max and Natasha Vita–More, eds. *The Transhumanist Reader: Classical and Contemporary Essays on the Science, Technology, and Philosophy of the Human Future*. West Sussex, UK: John Wiley & Sons, 2013.

Murphy, Charles. *At Home on Earth: Foundations for a Catholic Ethic of the Environment*. NY: Crossroad, 1989.

NASA, "2016 Climate Trends Continue to Break Records'," https://www.nasa.gov/feature/goddard/2016/climate-trends-continue-to-break-records.

———. "Sea Ice Extent Sinks to Record Lows at Both Poles," https://www.nasa.gov/feature/goddard/2017/glacier-shape-influences-susceptibility-to-melting.

Nash, James. *Loving Nature: Ecological Integrity and Christian Responsibility.* Nashville, TN: Abingdon, 1991.

Newberg, Andrew, and Mark Robert Waldman. *How God Changes Your Brain: The New Science of Transformation.* New York: Ballantine, 2009.

———. *How Enlightenment Changes Your Brain: Breakthrough Findings from a Leading Neuroscientist.* New York: Ballantine, 2016.

Niebuhr, Reinhold. *Moral Man and Immoral Society: A Study in Ethics and Politics.* New York: Charles Scribner's, 1932.

Nilsen, Tina Dykesteen. "Expanding Ecological Hermeneutics: The Case for Ecolonialism." *Journal of Biblical Literature* 4 (2016) 665–683.

North, Douglass C. *Institutions, Institutional Change and Economic Performance.* Cambridge: Cambridge University Press, 1990.

Northcott, Michael S. *The Environment and Christian Ethics.* New York: Cambridge University Press, 1996.

O'Donovan, Oliver. *The Desire of the Nations: Recovering the Roots of Political Theology.* Cambridge: Cambridge University Press, 1996.

Oelschlaeger, Max. *Caring for Creation: An Ecumenical Approach to the Environmental Crisis.* New Haven, CT: Yale University Press, 1994.

Olivier, Nay. "Fragile and Failed States: Critical Perspectives on Conceptual Hybrids," *International Political Science Review* 1 (2013) 326–341.

Orwell, George. *Nineteen Eighty Four.* Harlow, Essex: Longman York, 1983.

Osborne, Grant R. *The Hermeneutical Spiral: A Comprehensive Introduction to Biblical Interpretation.* Downers Grove, IL: InterVarsity, 1991.

———. *Revelation: Baker Exegetical Commentary on the New Testament.* Grand Rapids, MI: Baker Academic, 2002.

Ostrom, Elinor. *Governing the Commons: The Evolution of Institutions for Collective Action.* New York: Cambridge University Press, 1990.

Pagels, Elaine. *Revelations: Visions, Prophecy, and Politics in the Book of Revelation.* New York: Penguin, 2012.

Paine, Thomas. *Rights of Man, Common Sense, and Other Political Writings.* Edited with an introduction by Mark Philp. New York: Oxford University Press, 1776/1995.

Payne, Richard, ed. *How Much is Enough?: Buddhism, Consumerism, and the Human Environment.* Somerville, MA: Wisdom, 2010.

Persinger, Michael. *Neuropsychological Bases of Belief.* New York: Praeger, 1987.

Piketty, Thomas. *Capital in the Twenty–First Century.* Cambridge, MA: Harvard University Press, 2014.

PHYS, "Global warming set to pass 2C threshold in 2050." https://phys.org/news/2016-09-global-2c-threshold.html.

Plato. *The Republic.* New York: Penguin, 1987.

Pope Benedict XVI. *The Garden of God: Toward a Human Ecology.* Washington, DC: Catholic University of America Press, 2014.

Pope, Stephen J. *Human Evolution and Christian Ethics.* New York: Cambridge University Press, 2007.

Porter, Gareth, and Janet Welsh Brown. *Global Environmental Politics*. Boulder, CO: Westview, 1991.
Ramachandran, V.S., and Sandra Blakeslee. *Phantoms in the Brain*. New York: HarperCollins, 1998.
Randers, Jorgen. *A Global Forecast for the Next Forty Years: A Report to the Club of Rome Commemorating the 40th Anniversary of the Limits to Growth*. White River Junction, VM: Chelsea Green, 2012.
Rasmussen, Larry L. *Earth Community, Earth Ethics*. Maryknoll, NY: Orbis, 1996.
Ravitzky, Aviezer, and Michael Swirsky. *Messianism, Zionism and Jewish Religious Radicalism*. Chicago, IL: University of Chicago Press, 1996.
Rhodes, R.A.W., et al, eds. *The Oxford handbook of political institutions*. New York: Oxford University Press, 2006.
Richards, Jay W. *Money, Greed, and God: Why Capitalism is the Solution and Not the Problem*. HarperCollins, 2009.
Robert, Malthus Thomas. *An Essay on the Principle of Population*. Oxford: Oxford University Press, 1798.
Rollings, Wayne G. *Soul and Psyche: The Bible in Psychological Perspective*. Minneapolis, MN: Augsburg Fortress, 1999.
Rolston, Holmes III. *Conserving Natural Value*. NY: Columbia University Press, 1994.
Rotberg, Robert I. *When States Fail: Causes and Consequences*. Princeton, NJ: Princeton University Press, 2004.
Santmire, H. Paul. *Brother Earth: Nature, God, and Ecology in Time of Crisis*. NY: T. Nelson, 1970.
Scarre, Chris .ed. The Human Past: World Prehistory and the Development of Human Societies. London: Thames & Hudson, 2005.
Schaefer, Jame. "Environmental Degradation, Social Sin, and the Common Good." In *God, Creation, and Climate Change: A Catholic Response to the Environmental Crisis*, edited by Richard W. Miller, 69-94. Maryknoll, NY: Orbis, 2010.
Schaff, Philip, ed. *Nicene and Post–Nicene Fathers*. First Series. Peabody, MA: Hendrickson, 1994.
———. *History of the Christian Church: The Complete Eight Volumes in One*. Amazon Digital Services, 2016.
Schwartz, Jeffrey H and Ian Tattersall. "Defining the Genus Homo: Early Hominin Species Were as Diverse as Other Mammals." *Science* 349 (2015) 931–932.
Seidel, Asher. *Inhuman Thoughts: Philosophical Explorations of Postumanity*. Lanham, MD: Lextington, 2008.
Seligman, Martin. *Authentic Happiness: Using the New Positive Psychology to Realize Your Potential for Lasting Fulfilment*. New York: Free, 2002.
Sider, Ronald J. *Just Politics: A Guide for Christian Engagement*. Grand Rapids, MI: Brazos, 2012.
Sideris, Lisa. *Environmental Ethics, Ecological Theology, and Natural Selection*. NY: Columbia University Press, 2003.
Simon, William,et al. *Conquering Chronic Pain after Injury*. Garden City, NY: Avery, 2002.
Skinner, B.F. *Beyond Freedom and Dignity*. New York: Knopf, 1971.
Stark, Rodney. *Discovering God: The Origins of the Great Religions and the Evolution of Belief.* New York: HarperCollins, 2007.

Statista. "Largest producers of CO2 emissions worldwide in 2016, based on their share of global CO2 emissions,". https://www.statista.com/statistics/271748/the–largest–emitters–of–co2–in–the–world/.

Stepan, Alfred C. "Religion, Democracy, and the "Twin Tolerations." *Journal of Democracy*, 4 (2000) 37–57.

Struck, Doug. "Carbon Offsets: How a Vatican Forest Failed to Reduce Global Warming," *The Christian Science Monitor* 20 (April 2010).

Spinoza. *Theological–Political Treatise*. 2nd ed. Translated by Samuel Shirley. Indianapolis, IN: Hackett, 1991.

Sternberg, Robert J. *Cognitive Psychology*, 5th ed. Belmont, CA: Wadsworth, 2010.

Sun, Yi–ping. "Inspiration of Taoist Ecological Wisdom of Nature–Human Integration to the Modern World." *Philosophy of Religion* 71 (2015) 103–115. 孫亦平。。「道教『天人合一』的生態智慧對當代世界的啟示」。宗教哲學，71期，103–115頁。

Tattershall, I. and JH Schwartz. "Hominids and Hybrids," *Proceedings of the National Academy of Sciences* 13 (2009) 7117–7119.

Taylor, Bron, ed. *Encyclopedia of Religion and Nature*, 2 Vols, New York: Continuum, 2005.

Taylor, Véronique A. et al. "Impact of Meditation Training on the Default Mode Network During a Restful State." *SCAN* 8 (2013) 4–14.

Trinkaus, E., and P. Shipman. *The Neanderthals: Changing the Image of Mankind*. New York: Alfred A. Knopf, 1993.

Tuan, Yi–fu. "Discrepancies between Environmental Attitude and Behavior." *Canadian Geographer* 12 (1968) 176–191.

Tucker, Mary Evelyn, and Duncan Ryuken Williams. *Buddhism and Ecology: The Interconnection of Dharma and Deeds*. Cambridge, MA: Harvard University Press, 1998.

United Nations, "World population projected to reach 9.8 billion in 2050, and 11.2 billion in 2100 – says UN." http://www.un.org/sustainabledevelopment/blog/2017/06/world-population-projected-to-reach-9-8-billion-in-2050-and-11-2-billion-in-2100-says-un/.

United Nations Convention to Combat Desertification, "Desertification: A Visual Synthesis."12.http://www.unccd.int/Lists/SiteDocumentLibrary/Publications/Desertification-EN.pdf.

Urbaniak, Jakub and Elijah Otu. "How to Expect God's Reign to Come: From Jesus" through the Ecclesial to the Cosmic Body." *HTS Teologiese Studies/Theological Studies* 4 (2016) a3380. http://dx.doi. org/10.4102/hts.v72i4.3380.

Wallace, Daniel B. *Greek Grammar beyond the Basics: An Exegetical Syntax of the New Testament*. Grand Rapids, MI: Zondervan, 1996.

Wang, Jenn–hwan. *Proceedings of the Conference on Water Governance and Sustainable Development across the Taiwan Strait in 2013*. Taipei, TAIWAN: National Chengchi University, 2013.

Watts, Fraser. "Psychology and Theology." In *The Cambridge Companion to Science and Religion*, edited by Peter Harrison. New York: Cambridge University Press, 2010.

Webb, Stephen H. "Eschatology and Politics." In *The Oxford Handbook of Eschatology*, edited by Jerry L. Walls, 500–517. New York: Oxford University Press, 2008.

Weber, Max. 2001. *The Protestant Ethic and the Spirit of Capitalism*. Translated by Talcott Parsons. New York: Routledge.

Wee, Teo Cheng. "China Renews "Green GDP" Initiative." *Environmental Protection*, 13 (April 2015). https://eponline.com/Articles/2015/04/13/China–Renews–Green–GDP– Initiative.aspx?Page=1.

Weigel, George. "The Church's Political Hopes for the World: or, Diognetus Revisited," In *The Two Cities of God: The Church's Responsibility for the Earthly City*, edited by Carl E. Braaten and Robert Jenson. Grand Rapids, MI: Eerdmans, 1997.

Weller, Robert P. *Discovering Nature: Globalization and Environmental Culture in China and Taiwan*. New York: Cambridge University Press, 2006.

White, Lynn Jr. "The Historical Roots of Our Ecological Crisis," *Science*, 155 (1967) 1203–1207.

Whybrow, Peter C. *American Mania: When More is Not Enough*. New York: W.W. Norton, 2005.

Williamson, Oliver E. *The Economic Institutions of Capitalism*. New York: The Free, 1985.

World Wild Life Foundation, "Overview." https://www.worldwildlife.org/threats/deforestation.

Yang, Zilu. 'spirit of the Way and Proper Exploitation: New Interpretations of Daoist Ecological Ethics." *History of Chinese Philosophy* 2 (2016) 83–88. 楊子路。「道性與盜機：道教生態倫理思想新詮」。中國哲學史，2期，83–88頁。

Yang, Zishen. ed. *Research on Water Governance and Sustainable Development of China*. Beijing: Social Sciences Academic, 2012.

Yordy, Laura Ruth. *Green Witness: Ecology, Ethics, and the Kingdom of God*. Cambridge, UK: The Lutterworth, 2008.

Zaleha Bernard Daley and Andrew Szasz. "Why Conservative Christians Don't Believe in Climate Change." *Bulletin of the Atomic Scientists* 5 (2015) 19–30.

Ziegler, J.J. "Catholics, the Environment, and a 'Culture of Waste,'" *The Catholic World Report* 17 September, 2013. http://www.catholicworldreport.com/Item/2575/, accessed November 30, 2017.

Subject Index

Anthropocentric, vii, 5, 6, 45, 99, 101, 105, 107, 110–11.
Apocalypse, 98, 107, 114.
Authoritarianism
   Green, see State, Green
   Red, see State, Green/Red

Brain
   Balanced, 24, 83.
   Emotional, 23, 45, 54, 58, 61, 76, 80, 82–83, 106, 109, 113, 150.
   God, 13–15, 17–18, 20–21, 23, 29, 37, 39–40, 43–46, 54, 81–83, 87, 96–97, 106, 109, 110, 113, 150, 189.
   Rational, 23, 28, 45, 54, 62, 75–76, 78, 83, 96–97, 106, 110, 150.
   Spiritual, see Brain, God
Buddhism
   Tibetan, 11.
   Zen, vii, 5.

Capitalism
   Greed, 39, 141, 149–50.
   Green, 130, 157.
   Class, 39, 31, 132, 151, 154.
   State, 14, 34, 140.
   Values, 131, 136, 139.
   Workers, 132, 152.
Catholicism, 93, 121.
China
   Authoritarianism, 159, 160–61.
   Cultural Revolution, 90.
   Ecological programs, 11, 12, 91–94, 161–62, 194, 196.
   Rising, 91, 159, 161.

Church
   Democratic, 124, 189.
Coase Theorem, 128–29.
Collective Action, 13, 36, 92, 97, 102–3, 106, 108, 117, 123, 125, 160–61, 195–96.
Confucianism, 40, 90, 92–94.
Council of Nicene
   Ante-Nicene, 9, 10, 12, 41, 61, 118, 172, 176, 178, 186, 188.
   Post-Nicene, 186, 188.
Creationism, 8, 46, 54, 87, 121, 123, 181.

Daoism (Taoism)
   Fengshui, 10, 91, 92.
   Qi, 10
Darwinism, 29, 35.
Decoupling, 135.
Democracy
   Deliberative, 157, 163, 165–67, 169, 191–92, 195–96.
Diversity, 35–36, 101, 105, 139, 163.
Domination/dominion, 5, 16, 21, 101, 105, 110–11, 175.

Eastern Orthodox, 7, 45.
Ecojustice, 103–5, 109, 112.
Ecology
   Definition, 2.
   Deep, 38, 45, 99.
   Environmentalism, 12, 38.
   Human, 99–100, 103.
Environmentalism
   Ecology, see Ecology
   Definition, 12.

Subject Index

Evolution, 25, 27–29, 35, 42, 46–52, 87, 108, 121, 123, 172, 190.

Feminist Ecology, 107, 190.

Genes
  Altruist, 27.
  Selfish, 27.
Giddens' Paradox, 145–46, 168–69, 171, 192.
Gore, Al, 89–90, 125.
Great Commission, 74, 182, 189, 193, 195–97.
Green
  Consumption, 56.
  Economy, 11.
Green/Red Authoritarianism, see State, Green/Red
GDP, 161.
  Messiah, 10, 160.
  Pope, 99, 106, 125.
  Religion, 91.
  State, see State, Green
  Tax, 37, 134.
  Technology, 56, 130–31.

Happiness, 26, 28–32, 34–35, 40, 43, 61–62, 81, 112–13, 123, 141, 145, 147–48, 150, 156, 182.
Homo Sapiens, 25–30, 46–48, 50–53, 75.

India, 6, 7, 102, 124.
Institutionalism, 34–36, 39, 42.

Kingdom of God
  Church, 180, 192.
  Earth, 95, 157, 172–82, 185–186, 192, 196.
  Heaven, 95, 177.
Kingdom of Israel, 72–73, 75, 77–78, 81, 85, 185.

Lamentation/Lament, 72–73, 105, 115–17, 124.
Limits to Growth (LTG), 3–5, 137–38, 157.

Malthus, 129–30
Marxism
  Lenin, 146.
  Marx, 132.
  Organic, 145–46.
Meditation/Meditate, vii, 21, 78, 91, 93, 96–97, 100, 102, 105, 107–9, 113, 115–17, 120, 124–25, 195–96.
Moltmann, Jürgen, 44, 90, 95–96, 104–5, 112, 119, 125.

Natural law, 8, 44–45, 49, 55, 103, 109–10.
Nature, vii, 2, 5, 8, 10, 13–15, 17, 24–26, 33, 38, 42, 44, 57, 86, 91, 100, 121, 151, 159, 195.
Neanderthals, 25, 46–48, 51–52.
Neuroscience
  Definition, 7.
Neurotheology
  Definition, 7.
New Heaven and New Earth, 95–96, 98, 103, 110, 113, 115, 119–20, 122, 123, 138, 173, 177, 197.

Paris Agreement, see Paris Climate Accord
Paris Climate Accord, 4, 171, 192.
Parousia, vii, 4, 5, 90, 93, 97, 101, 107, 113, 115, 119, 122, 185, 189, 191
Pope
  Benedict, 90, 95, 99–104, 107, 112, 115, 142, 150.
  Francis, 5–6, 100, 102, 105, 127, 174.
Post-Ecology
  Definition, 1.
Posthumanism, 40, 42.
Prisoners' Dilemma (PD), 36–37.
Public Goods, 13, 36–37, 163.

Renewable, 115–20, 123, 126, 138, 196.

Saint Francis, 5–6, 100, 102, 105.
Second Vatican Council, 101.
Social Gospel, 39, 175, 190.

Social Sin, 106, 124–25.
Solomon's Dilemma, 179–80.
State
    Authoritarian, 161, 188–89, 191.
    Democratic, 161, 166–67, 169, 189, 191–92.
    Failed, 161, 171.
    Green, 136–38, 157, 160, 164, 167, 169, 195–96.
    Green/Red, 158–60, 163, 191.
Separation of state and church, 173–75, 183, 185, 193, 196.
Stewardship, 101, 104–5, 110–11, 118.
Sustainable Development, 4, 90, 131, 162, 166, 168.

Tragedy of the Commons, 58, 163.
Trump, Donald, 4, 121, 171.
Tzu Chi, 11–12.

White, Lynn, 5, 7, 38, 41, 90, 110, 118, 141, 158, 190.
Witness, vii, 59, 71, 79, 100, 117–18, 127, 185–87.

Xi, Jinping, 162.

Zero-Growth, 135.

www.ingramcontent.com/pod-product-compliance
Lightning Source LLC
Chambersburg PA
CBHW062018220426
43662CB00010B/1382